SMEs Perspective in Africa

Gift Mugano • Nirmala Dorasamy

SMEs Perspective in Africa

Creating Sustainable and Resilient Economies

palgrave
macmillan

Gift Mugano
Faculty of Management Sciences
Durban University of Technology
Durban, South Africa

Nirmala Dorasamy
Faculty of Management Sciences
Durban University of Technology
Durban, South Africa

ISBN 978-3-031-69102-7 ISBN 978-3-031-69103-4 (eBook)
https://doi.org/10.1007/978-3-031-69103-4

This Palgrave Macmillan imprint is published by the registered company Springer Nature Switzerland AG.
The registered company address is: Gewerbestrasse 11, 6330 Cham, Switzerland

Acknowledgements

This project was supported by BRICS' Institutes.

About the Book

The SMEs (small and medium enterprises) have a very important part to modern economies and their contribution to economic development is recognised. These social and economic roles led to consideration of the SME sector as a strategic interest for the economy (Avasilicai, 2009). SMEs account for 95% of businesses globally and also contribute more than half of total employment. Around 200 million firms lack financing they need to invest, develop with, and generate emerging jobs (BIAC, 2016). Of the 90% of the world's jobs generated by the businesses globally, 50% are constituted by SMEs. According to the World Trade Organization (WTO, 2016), SMEs represent over 90% of the business population, 60–70% of employment, and 55% of GDP in developed economies. As SMEs contribute strongly to achieve crucial goals to an economy they represent the main motivation of economic development and backbone of socio-economic development (Drucker, 2009). There are two types of SMEs: the small traditional enterprise that makes goods inherited from past generations and the modern enterprise that uses high technology in search of new markets to maximise their efficiency. In developed countries, 20% of new SMEs last no more than a year, 20% last only two years, and 50% last not more than five years (source). As a result only 10% of SMEs have a chance to survive more than five years. The success of an economy depends on the number and dynamics of SMEs and their success on the market. SMEs serve as a source of entrepreneurship skills, innovation, and employment as they stimulate competition for prices, product design, and efficiency. Without SMEs big enterprises become monopolies. SMEs also help big enterprises in areas such as supply of raw materials, parts, and distribution of products made by them. A study from the United States showed that SMEs make four times higher profit for a dollar invested than big companies (Neagu, 2016).

Notwithstanding their contribution to economic development, in Africa SMEs have witnessed several binding constraints which inter alia include drought of finance, poor market access, capacity constraints, and exogenous shocks such as the COVID-19 pandemic.

This book provides in-depth discussions on the nexus between SMEs and economic development with specific focus on Africa. In addition, the book provides a discourse on the contribution of SMEs on job creation, exports, economic growth, poverty alleviation, and equality. The opportunities and challenges which are likely to be faced by SMEs in the internationalisation agenda are discussed.

In terms of layout, this book is organised as follows: Chap. 1 provides introduction and overview of the book; Chap. 2 showcases the contribution of SMEs in the global economy; Chap. 3 discusses the relationship between SMEs and poverty; Chap. 4 provides an in-depth analysis of the contribution of SMEs to job creation; Chap. 5 discusses the nexus between digital Technologies for SMEs and job creation in Africa; Chap. 6 discusses the relationship between SMEs' access to finance, growth, and job creation; Chap. 7 discusses the state-of-information infrastructure in Africa and how it affects their ability to access finance; Chap. 8 discusses the implication of business environment on the performance of SMEs; Chap. 9 discusses internationalisation of SMEs, challenges, and remedies; and Chap. 10 presents summary, concluding remarks, and policy recommendations arising from the previous chapter.

The book will appeal to academics which inter alia include lecturers and students in several fields such as management, economics, finance, entrepreneurship, and development studies. In addition, because this book places emphasis on the role of SMEs in the global economy, challenges, and possible remedies, it will appeal to international development agencies, think tanks, regional economic communities, policymakers, and the private sector.

Contents

About the Authors

Gift Mugano is Full Professor of Economics and director at the Centre for African Governance Development, Durban University of Technology, South Africa. He is a distinguished scholar, a technocrat, and a global authority on international trade, finance, and development with over 19 years of extensive experience including policy advisory, consultancy, and academic work. Mugano is a leading expert and a community of practice researcher for the BRICS nations' research consortium made up of the Durban University of Technology and National Institute of Humanities and Social Sciences (NIHSS) that houses the South African BRICS Think Tank. He has written several articles in international journals and book chapters in the field of international trade, finance, and development. He authored five books with renowned international publishers, that is, Routledge, Palgrave Macmillan, and AOSIS: (1) *Trade Liberalisation and Economic Development in Africa*; (2) *Special Economic Zones: Impact on Economic Development in Africa*; (3) *SMEs and Economic Development in Africa: Challenges & Policy Options*; (4) *SMEs Perspective in Africa: Creating Sustainable and Resilient Economies*; and (5) *Perspectives on Comprehensive Internationalisation of Higher Education*. Mugano has supervised six PhD degrees to successful completion and several other postgraduate students in the field of international trade, finance, and development, and examined ten doctoral theses (PhDs) and several postgraduate theses. He has consulted for the Government of Zimbabwe; the private sector and international institutions including the World Bank; United Nations Economic Commission for Africa; United Nations Office of the High Representative for the Least Developed Countries, Landlocked

Developing Countries and Small Island Developing States; United Nations Development Programme; United States Agency for International Development (USAID); UNICEF; Foreign, Commonwealth and Development Office of the United Kingdom (FCDO); Germany Corporation for International Cooperation (GIZ); International Labour Organisation (ILO); European Union; GFA Consulting Group (Germany); Integration Consulting Group (Germany); National Opinion Research Centre at the University of Chicago (USA); COMESA; British Council; NIR Sweden; Adam Smith International (UK); IMC Worldwide LTD (UK); Cardno Emerging Markets (Belgium); KPMG (UK); the Palladium Group (UK); Ecorys (UK); Transparency.

Nirmala Dorasamy is a National Research Fund-rated full professor in the Department of Public Management and Economics at the Durban University of Technology, South Africa. She has received several awards at the Durban University of Technology, including Top Senior Researcher (2014), Top Woman Researcher (2017), and Top Faculty Researcher (2021). She was nominated for and awarded an international staff exchange opportunity in the Faculty of Regional Development at Mendel University in the Brno, Czech Republic; Federation University in Australia; and the Department of Forestry in Nepal. Her international associations involve collaborative research with the Swinburne University of Technology, Federation University, and Monash University in Australia; the American University in Cairo; MUST University in Kenya; and Mendel University. The focus of this international collaboration is linked to governance, leadership excellence, and ethical practices. She has successfully supervised and graduated several master's and doctoral students while being recognised as a local and international examiner for postgraduate research. She has co-authored textbooks for senior secondary learners and books for higher education purposes, and she has written in local and international journals as well as presented papers at national and international conferences. She has been instrumental in initiating the establishment of the Centre for African Governance and Development at the Durban University of Technology.

List of Boxes

List of Tables

CHAPTER 1

Introduction: Overview of the Book

Gift Mugano and Nirmala Dorasamy

1.1 SMEs Defined

There is no universal definition of small and medium enterprises (SMEs) nor is there a similar set of parameters used to measure the size of SMEs (Mugano, 2024). Across the globe, countries' own legislations are used to inform a country's own definition of SMEs by paying special attention to what constitutes a "small" and "medium" enterprise in relation to the size of the domestic economy (Mugano, 2024). In this regard, in South Africa, SMEs are defined as follows: own-account, that is, enterprises which are owned by entrepreneurs only or sole traders and as these have no employees; micro (1–4 workers); small (5–9 workers); medium (10–49 workers); and large (employing a minimum of 50 workers) (Bhorat et al., 2018).

On the contrary, in the OECD, firms employing up to 249 workers are classified as SMEs broken down as: micro (1–9 people), small (10–49 people), and medium (50–249 people) (OECD, 2017). Based on this illustration, it is clear that in some territories such as advanced economies, what is categorised as a medium enterprise is actually a large enterprise in developing countries as in the South African case.

G. Mugano (✉) • N. Dorasamy
Faculty of Management Sciences, Durban University of Technology,
Durban, South Africa
e-mail: nirmala@dut.ac.za

G. Mugano, N. Dorasamy, *SMEs Perspective in Africa*,
https://doi.org/10.1007/978-3-031-69103-4_1

1.2 SMEs and Economic Development

Evidence shows that there is common consensus that SMEs are the backbone of the global economy. The Organisation for Economic Co-operation and Development (OECD) (2017), for example, observed that SMEs contribute approximately 60% of global gross domestic product (GDP). Similarly, Mugano (2024), Di Bella et al. (2023), and Ayyagari et al. (2011) observed that, on average, in advanced economies, formal SMEs contribute up to 50% of GDP. Likewise, in developing countries like the African continent, Runde et al. (2021) underscored that in terms of employment creation and contribution to economic growth, approximately 80% of jobs across the continent and at least 50% of GDP are contributed by SMEs in Sub-Saharan Africa (SSA).

Of significant interest to the United Nations' Sustainable Development Goals (SDGs), Mugano (2024) argued that SMEs contribute to economic development through various channels which inter alia include economic growth, employment creation, and poverty reduction which are important elements of the SDGs.

Studies by Beck et al. (2005), for example, show that there is a close relationship between SME development and economic growth. Strikingly, Beck et al. (2005) revealed that, after taking into account other growth determinants, there is robust and positive relationship between economic growth and the relative size of the SME sector.

With respect to job creation, Mugano (2024) and Di Bella et al. (2023) observed that SMEs are key drivers of job creation across the globe. For example, in the OECD countries, about 67% of the formal workforce is employed by SMEs with less than 250 employees (Beck et al., 2008; Dietrich, 2010; Mugano, 2024; Di Bella et al., 2023). In line with this observation, in demonstrating the efficacy between SMEs growth and job creation, between 2002 and 2008, a study by the European Commission (EC) (2009) revealed that, on an annual basis, the number of jobs in SMEs increased at a rate of 1.9% while the number of jobs in large enterprises increased by a mere 0.8%. In terms of job creation, between 2002 and 2008, in absolute numbers, 9.4 million jobs were created by SMEs in the European Union (EU) (EC, 2009).

Evidence shows that in the EU, in 2022, SMEs constitute 99.8% of total businesses, that is 22.7 million SMEs against a mere 40,000 active larger enterprises (Di Bella et al., 2023). SMEs are the major driver of the economies' GDP, biggest employer for both the EU and worldwide (Di

Bella et al., 2023). To be specific, in 2022, SMEs employed 85 million people, that is, accounting for 64.4% of total employment while large enterprises contribute 35.6% of total jobs in the EU and, on average, contribute 51.8% of value added (Di Bella et al., 2023).

Evidence shows that Sub-Saharan Africa (SSA) alone is home to 44 million micro, small, and medium enterprises (MSMEs) (Runde et al., 2021). Evidence shows that approximately 90% of businesses in SSA, that is, both in rural and in urban areas, are made up of SMEs (Akugri et al., 2015; Runde et al., 2021). In SSA, in terms of employment creation and contribution to economic growth, approximately 80% of jobs across the continent and at least 50% of GDP are contributed by SMEs (Runde et al., 2021).

1.3 Challenges Affecting Small and Medium Enterprises

Guriria (2020) underscored that although SMEs play a significant role in the economic progress of OECD countries, they face a number of challenges which inter alia include low productivity, poor access to finance, slow pace of digitalisation and access to markets.

With respect to productivity challenges, Guriria (2020) noted that the level of productivity of micro-SMEs is about 50% lower than that of large SMEs while productivity rate of larger SMEs is lower than large companies. Of concern is the fact that productivity gap has widened as a result of the global crisis, that is, the disruptions which were brought about by the COVID-19 pandemic and the Russia–Ukraine war (Di Bella et al., 2023). The impact of these overlapping crises on productivity is more defined in the manufacturing sector which has resulted in worsening income and inequality (Di Bella et al., 2023). Guriria (2020) argued that the challenges associated with low productivity are further exacerbated by regulatory uncertainty, inconsistency, and complexity. To be specific, excessive regulatory requirement and high tax burden result in informality which leads to a low productivity trap as SMEs are excluded from the mainstream businesses (Guriria, 2020).

With respect to access to finance, the 2018 OECD Scoreboard on Financing SMEs and Entrepreneurs reports show that in the Netherlands and the United Kingdom new lending to SMEs, on a year-on-year, dropped by 17.1% and 4.1%, respectively.

Guriria (2020) noted that in the OECD, most SMEs are missing the opportunities which come from globalisation and digitalisation, that is, a priori requirement for raising productivity, sustainable and inclusive growth. Digital technologies are critical as they facilitate SMEs to emerge as "born global" firms which present new opportunities for established SMEs to grow, raise productivity, and establish themselves as global actors (Guriria, 2020).

With respect to access to market, Guriria (2020) underscored that the majority of SMEs in the OECD struggle to convert the potential of digitalisation into better stronger productivity and access to markets. Evidence shows that only 20% of SMEs drives sales through the e-commerce platform while 40% of larger enterprises are engaged on e-commerce.

To make matters worse, the participation of SMEs on global value chains, which is key in creating new market opportunities for SMEs, remains uneven across the SMEs in the OECD countries. To be specific, across the OECD countries, evidence shows that only 15% of micro-firms are engaged in international trade, compared to 60% of small businesses and 80% of medium-sized businesses (Di Bella et al., 2023). Small businesses are harmed more by trade restrictions as compared to large firms. For example, evidence shows that an average level of trade restrictiveness for cross-border export of services is equivalent to an additional 12% tariff for SMEs, relative to large firms (Di Bella et al., 2023).

Abisuga-Oyekunle et al. (2019) and Oyekunle and Sirayi (2018) underscored that although SMEs make significant contribution to economic development in SSA through various channels which include job creation, poverty alleviation, and contribution to GDP, several challenges inhibit SMEs to unleash their potential. Six major binding constraints which affect SMEs in SSA are lack of right technologies, access to markets, lack of innovative culture, ease of doing business, poor access to electricity and finance (Oyekunle & Sirayi, 2018; Abisuga-Oyekunle et al., 2019; UNECE, 2022; Mugano, 2024).

Chapter 2 provides a thorough analysis of the nexus between SMEs, economic development, and associated challenges.

1.4 Audience and Structure of the Book

The book will appeal to academics which inter alia include lecturers and students in several fields such as management, economics, finance, entrepreneurship, and development studies. In addition, because this book places emphasis on the role of SMEs in the global economy, challenges and possible remedies, it will appeal to international development agencies, think tanks, regional economic communities, policymakers, and the private sector. In terms of the layout, the rest of the book is organised as follows:

Chapter 2 provides a detailed analysis of the contribution of SMEs in advanced economies such as the OECD countries, the European Union, the United States, Asian economies, Latin America, and Sub-Saharan Africa. In addition, a thorough examination of challenges affecting SMEs with specific emphasis on Africa is provided.

Critically, in addressing challenges affecting SMEs in Africa and building resilience, this book provides practical solutions which are grounded on experience from other countries and contextualised to Africa's setting.

Chapter 3 provides a detailed analysis of the level of poverty in Africa and how SMEs can be effective vehicles for poverty eradication if existing binding constraints are addressed. In view of this, this chapter presents grounded remedies focused on addressing constraints affecting SMEs which inter alia include poor access to finance, lack of technology, infrastructure deficits, access to markets, and macroeconomic instability.

Chapter 4 provides a comprehensive analysis of the contribution of SMEs on employment creation. In this regards, using a funnel approach, this chapter presents facts on the contribution of SMEs to job creation by providing stylised facts from global and advanced economies, emerging markets, regional and country levels. In the same vein, the book showcases challenges affecting SMEs in realising their full potential on job creation and possible remedies.

Chapter 5 discusses the nexus between digital Technologies for SMEs and job creation in Africa. This chapter presents a puzzle on technological advancement and job creation by showing circumstances under which changes in technology lead to job losses and vice versa.

Chapter 6 discusses the relationship between SMEs' access to finance, growth, and job creation. This chapter shows that empirical underpinning perspective, existing finance, and growth literature show that finance is critical for SMEs' growth and ultimately economic growth. However, in view of the fact that African SMEs have difficulties in accessing finance, this book argues for the use of blended finance, credit guarantee schemes, use of development finance institutions with no interferences from governments, and use of alternative financial instruments such as asset-based lending, factoring, and lease financing.

Chapter 7 discusses the state-of-information infrastructure in Africa and how it affects their ability to access finance. In addition, this chapter presents various strategies aimed at improving access to information which inter alia include training, use of technology, and building a culture of keeping information within SMEs.

Chapter 8 discusses the implication of business environment on the performance of SMEs.

To be specific, the chapter showcases how SMEs are affected by the following factors: starting a business, electricity, regulatory legislations, registration, acquisition of property, credit facilities, security, investment status, taxes and taxation, employment regulations and laws, accessing and acquisition of business locations, and finance routine operational requirements.

Chapter 9 discusses internationalisation of SMEs, challenges and remedies. In this chapter, evidence across the globe will be used to showcase that internationalisation of SMEs is an effective growth strategy as well as a vehicle to build resilience and sustainability which must be adopted by African countries.

Chapter 10 presents a summary, concluding remarks, and policy recommendations arising from the previous chapter. This chapter places emphasis on the fact that SMEs can be used as effective vehicles required to build more resilience and sustainable development in African economies.

References

Abisuga-Oyekunle, O. A., Patra, S. K., & Muchie, M. (2019). SMEs in sustainable development: Their role in poverty reduction and employment generation in sub-Saharan Africa. *African Journal of Science, Technology, Innovation and Development, 12*(4), 405–419. https://doi.org/10.1080/20421338.2019.1656428

Akugri, M. S., Bagah, D. A., & Wulifan, J. K. (2015). The Contributions of Small and Medium Scale Enterprises to Economic Growth: A Cross-Sectional Study of Zebilla in the Bawku West District of Northern Ghana. *European Journal of Business and Management, 7*(9), 262–274.

Ayyagari, M., Demirgüç-Kunt, A., & Maksimovic, V. (2011). Firm Innovation in Emerging Markets: The Role of Finance, Governance, and Competition. *A Journal of Financial and Quantitative Analysis, 46*(6), 1545–1580.

Beck, T., Demirgüç-Kunt, A., & Levine, R. (2005). SMEs, Growth, and Poverty: Cross-Country Evidence. *Journal of Economic Growth, 10*, 199–229.

Beck, T., Demirgüç-Kunt, A., & Peria, M. S. M. (2008). *Bank Financing for SMEs Around the World: Drivers, Obstacles, Business Models, and Lending Practices.* Policy Research Working Paper 4785. World Bank, Washington, DC.

Bhorat, H., Asmal, Z., Lilenstein, K. & van der Zee, K. (2018). *SMMES in South Africa: Understanding the Constraints on Growth and Performance.* Development Policy Research Unit Working Paper 201802. DPRU, University of Cape Town.

Di Bella, L., Katsinis, A., Lagüera-González, J., Odenthal, L., Hell, M., & Lozar, B (2023). *Annual Report on European SMEs 2022/2023.* Publications Office of the European Union, Luxemburg, 2023. https://doi.org/10.2760/028705JRC134336

Dietrich, C. (2010). Decision making: Factors that influence decision making, heuristics used, and decision outcomes. *Inquiries Journal, 2*, 3.

EC (European Commission). (2009). *European SMEs Under Pressure: Annual Report on EU Small and Medium-Sized Enterprises 2009.* European Commission.

Guriria, A. (2020). *SMEs are Key for More Inclusive Growth.* OECD.

Mugano, G. (2024). Role of SMEs on Economic Development in Africa. In G. Mugano & N. Dorasamy (Eds.), *SMEs and Economic Development in Africa: Challenges and Policy Options.* Routledge.

OECD. (2017). *Enhancing the Contributions of SMEs in a Global and Digitalised Economy.* Meeting of the OECD Council at Ministerial Level Paris, 7–8 June 2017, OECD, Paris.

Oyekunle, O. A., & Sirayi, M. (2018). The Role of Creative Industries as a Driver for a Sustainable Economy: A Case of South Africa. *Creative Industries Journal, 11*(3), 225–244.

Runde, D. F., Savoy, C. M., & Staguhn, J. (2021). *Supporting Small and Medium Enterprises in Sub-Saharan Africa through Blended Finance.* Center for Strategic and International Studies.

UNECE. (2022). Conference of European Statisticians, Group of Experts in Measuring Poverty and Inequality. UNECE.

CHAPTER 2

SMEs and Economic Development: Global and African Perspectives

Gift Mugano

2.1 Introduction

SMEs are the bedrock of the global economy. For example, on average, 60% of the global gross domestic product (GDP) is contributed by SMEs (Organisation for Economic Cooperation and Development (OECD), 2017a). Most importantly, SMEs contribute to economic development through a number of channels which inter alia include exports, job creation, reduction in inequality, and poverty eradication, which are key elements of inclusive growth (Mugano, 2024; OECD, 2017a). Studies by Beck et al. (2005), after controlling other determinants of economic growth, revealed a robust positive relationship between economic growth and the relative size of the SME sector and economic growth.

Although it is undeniable that SMEs play a critical role in various aspects of economic development in the global economy, the role of SMEs in economic development in advanced economies, emerging economies, and African economies is heterogeneous. This chapter builds on discussions presented in Chap. 1 and provides a more detailed analysis of the

G. Mugano (✉)
Faculty of Management Sciences, Durban University of Technology, Durban, South Africa

G. Mugano, N. Dorasamy, *SMEs Perspective in Africa*,
https://doi.org/10.1007/978-3-031-69103-4_2

heterogeneity in the contribution of SMEs on economic development across the globe and draw lessons for African economies.

In this regard, this chapter provides a detailed analysis of the contribution of SMEs in advanced economies such as the OECD countries, the European Union, the United States (US); Asian economies, Latin America and Sub-Sahara Africa. In this regard, this chapter is presented as follows: Sect. 2.2 discusses the contribution of SMEs on economic development in the global economy; Sect. 2.3 discusses the role of SMEs on economic development in advanced economies; Sect. 2.4 discusses the role of SMEs on economic development in transition economies; Sect. 2.5 discusses the role of SMEs in African Economies; Sect. 2.6 discusses bottlenecks affecting African SMEs; and Sect. 2.7 presents concluding remarks.

2.2 SMEs and Economic Development in the Global Economy

Evidence shows that the contribution of SMEs to national economies across the world, in terms of job creation, value addition, economic growth, and social well-being, is diverse (Mugano, 2024). To be specific, as reported by OECD (2017b) and OECD (2016b), 99% of businesses in the OECD countries are SMEs. In line with this observation, evidence shows that, in terms of job creation and value creation, on average, SMEs account for approximately 70% of jobs and generates between 50% and 60% of value-added goods (OECD, 2016a).

In emerging economies, studies by the OECD (2017a) shows that the contribution of SMEs to GDP and job creation is 33% and 45%, respectively. When the informal businesses are considered, the contribution of SMEs to employment and economic growth was noted by the World Bank to be more than 50% (International Finance Corporation (ICF), 2010).

SMEs stand out as effective vehicles which can foster inclusive growth (Mugano, 2024; OECD, 2017a). This view is grounded on the fact that SMEs are dotted across the country and as such they create job opportunities across sectors and geographic areas which give them leverage to employ broad segments of workforce which included both skilled and unskilled; improve access to health care and social services for the employed workers; and provide opportunities for skills development.

Studies by Eurostat (2014), OECD (2017a), and OECD (2010) show that SMEs play a significant role in innovation. To be specific, OECD (2017a) argued that the contribution of SMEs to innovation has increased resulting in SMEs building their competitiveness, establishing a niche market demand, reducing structural disadvantages arising from inability to secure economies of scale and resource constraints. In biotechnology-related fields in Europe, for example, Eurostat (2014) noted that SMEs account for approximately 20% of patents. These innovations enabled SMEs to supply new or niche products which is key in responding to ever-changing and diverse customer needs. OECD (2010) observed that since the turn of the new millennium the global economy has moved to a knowledge-based economy which is characterised by increase in non-technological innovation and rising network-based modes of innovation which has enabled SMEs to play a critical role in innovation. This is particularly so because SMEs' innovation is to a greater extent influenced by access to networks, knowledge spillovers, and opportunities to partner with larger businesses. The wave of globalisation which has seen the rise of cross-border collaboration in innovation, that is, in both securing inputs for the innovation from abroad, that is, finance, ideas, skills, and technologies, and utilising its outputs in foreign markets, that is, patents, licences, and products and services (Mugano, 2024).

Outside of these standard economic indicators, SMEs provide an important impetus for the development of economic diversification and resilience especially in resource-rich countries which are exposed to the vagaries of commodity price fluctuations (Mugano, 2024).

In developed countries such as in the European Union, SMEs play important roles in addressing the needs of the society through provision of public goods and services (EU/OECD, 2016). Through provision of innovative solutions to the problems of unemployment, social exclusion, and poverty, social enterprises in particular, they close gaps in public service delivery (EU/OECD, 2016). Evidence shows that the contribution of social and solidarity economy in areas of social enterprises they operate in, as a share of the economy, is significant. For example, in 2014, in France, 10% of GDP was contributed by the social economy. In 2015, the contribution of SMEs to jobs social enterprises in Belgium and United Kingdom stood at 17% and 41% of the total private sector employment, respectively (EU, 2016; SEUK, 2015).

From a definition perspective, as outlined in Chap. 1, European Union (EU) (2021) defines an SME as a business enterprise with at most 250 employees with a total balance sheet of at most EUR 43 million or an annual turnover of at least EUR 50 million. The EU (2021) underscored that the definition of SMEs varies from country to country. For instance, in the United States, SMEs are defined as business enterprises with at most 500 workers (Garcia-Martinez et al., 2023). In the EU, SMEs are further divided into three categories: the smallest category of enterprises, that is, micro-firms (<9 workers), small firms (10–49 workers), and medium-sized enterprises (50–249 workers) (Garcia-Martinez et al., 2023).

In the EU, as in the rest of the world, SMEs are the most dominant type of business (Garcia-Martinez et al., 2023). In the EU, over and above the dominant feature of SMEs, they make a massive contribution in innovation, job creation, and economic growth (European Union, 2021) (see Table 2.1).

Evidence shows that in the EU, in 2022, SMEs constitute 99.8% of the total businesses, that is, 24.2 million SMEs against a mere 40,000 active larger enterprises (Di Bella et al., 2023). SMEs are the major drivers of the economies' GDP, biggest employer for both the EU and worldwide (Di Bella et al., 2023). To be specific, in 2022, SMEs employed 85 million people, that is, accounted for 64.4% of total employment while large enterprises contribute 35.6% of total jobs in the EU and, on average, contribute 51.8% of value added (see Table 2.1) (Di Bella et al., 2023).

Of interest is the fact that most of the SMEs in the EU are micro, that is, 93.5% of total businesses (22.7 million businesses) (Di Bella et al., 2023). However, in terms of contribution to employment and value-added goods, the contribution of micro businesses is a mere 29.4% and 18.6%, respectively. Ironically, large enterprises, which constitute 0.2% of businesses in the EU, generate more jobs (35.6%) and value added (48.2%) than micro businesses (see Table 2.1).

Similarly, in the OECD, SMEs represent 99% of total businesses (Guriria, 2020). In terms of employment creation, in the OECD, SMEs account for 75% of jobs in the services sector and 60% of total employment in the manufacturing sector (Guriria, 2020). Most importantly, on average, SMEs generated between 50% and 60% of value added (Guriria, 2020).

In addition, building on experience from the OECD, Guriria (2020) underscored that SMEs are an effective vehicle which can foster inclusive

Table 2.1 The contribution of SMEs on economic development in the European Union

Class size	*Number of enterprises*		*Number of people employed*		*Value added*	
	Number	*Share (%)*	*Number*	*Share (%)*	*Billion*	*Share (%)*
Micro	22,744,173	93.5	38,790,351	29.4	1419.4	18.6
Small	1,332,200	5.5	25,602,334	19.4	1259.8	16.5
Medium	204,786	0.8	20,493,722	15.5	1266.5	16.6
SMEs	24,281,159	99.8	84,886,407	64.4	3945.8	51.8
Large	43,112	0.2	46,918,978	35.6	3673.8	48.2
Total	**24,324,271**	**100**	**131,805,385**	**100**	**7619.6**	**100**

Source: Eurostat national accounts data

growth through various channels such as employment creation across sectors and regions; provision of health care and social services to their employees; and creation of opportunities for skills development. Most importantly, Guriria (2020) argued that, in the OECD, SMEs are a powerful weapon against the curse of informality.

However, Guriria (2020) underscored that although SMEs play a significant role in the economic progress of the OECD countries, they face a number of challenges which inter alia include low productivity, poor access to finance, slow pace of digitalisation, and access to markets.

With respect to productivity challenges, Guriria (2020) noted that the level of productivity of micro-SMEs is about 50% lower than that of large SMEs while productivity rate of larger SMEs is lower than large companies. Of concern is the fact that productivity gap has widened as a result of the global crisis, that is, COVID-19 pandemic and the Russia–Ukraine war (Di Bella et al., 2023). The impact of these overlapping crises on productivity is more defined in the manufacturing sector which has resulted in worsening income and inequality (Di Bella et al., 2023). Guriria (2020) argued that the challenges associated with low productivity are further exacerbated by regulatory uncertainty, inconsistency, and complexity. To be specific, excessive regulatory requirement and high tax burden results in informality which leads to a low productivity trap as SMEs are excluded from the mainstream businesses (Guriria, 2020).

With respect to access to finance, the 2018 OECD Scoreboard on Financing SMEs and Entrepreneurs reports show that in the Netherlands and the United Kingdom new lending to SMEs on a year-on-year dropped by 17.1% and 4.1%, respectively.

Guriria (2020) noted that in the OECD, most SMEs are missing the opportunities which come with globalisation and digitalisation, that is, a priori requirement for raising productivity, sustainable and inclusive growth. Digital technologies are critical as they facilitate SMEs to emerge as "born global" firms which present new opportunities for established SMEs to grow, raise productivity, and establish themselves as global actors (Guriria, 2020).

With respect to access to markets, Guriria (2020) underscored that the majority of SMEs in the OECD struggle to convert the potential of digitalisation into better stronger productivity and access to markets. Evidence shows that only 20% of SMEs drive sales through the e-commerce platform while 40% of larger enterprises are engaged on e-commerce.

To make matters worse, the participation of SMEs on global value chains, which is key in creating new market opportunities for SMEs, remains uneven across the SMEs in the OECD countries. To be specific, across the OECD countries, evidence shows that only 15% of micro-firms are engaged in international trade, compared to 60% of small businesses and 80% of medium-sized businesses (Di Bella et al., 2023). Small businesses are harmed more by trade restrictions as compared to large firms. For example, evidence shows that an average level of trade restrictiveness for cross-border export of services is equivalent to an additional 12% tariff for SMEs, relative to large firms (Di Bella et al., 2023).

2.3 SMEs and Economic Development in Transition Economies

In transition economies[1] the contribution of SMEs with respect to job creation, GDP, and as a share of total number of businesses is significant (see Table 2.2). To be specific, in Albania, in 2018, the contribution of SMEs to GDP, total number of businesses and employment stood at 70%, 99.8%, and 79.8%, respectively. As shown in Table 2.2, SMEs makes up the economies of transition economies as the majority of countries have close to 100% of businesses being SMEs.

On the contrary, in Russian Federation and to some extent Belarus, SMEs' contribution to the economies was somehow weak. For example, in the Russian Federation, in 2020, the contribution of SMEs to GDP, total number of businesses and job creation stands at 19.8%, 27%, and 18.8%, respectively. In Belarus, in 2020, the contribution of SMEs to GDP, total number of businesses and job creation stands at 28.8%, 78.3%, and 30.7%. In these two countries, it is given that large businesses play a significant role in the economic development as opposed to SMEs.

2.4 SMEs and Economic Development in Emerging Economies

Like in advanced economies, SMEs make significant contribution on economic development in emerging economies (Asian Development Bank, 2022). To be specific, the contribution of SMEs on jobs and GDP in emerging economies stands at 45% and 33%, respectively (Asian

[1] These include Albania, Armenia, Azerbaijan, Belarus, Bosnia & Herzegovina, Georgia, Kazakhstan, Montenegro, North Macedonia, Republic of Moldova, Russian Federation, Serbia, Tajikistan, Turkmenistan, Ukraine, and Uzbekistan.

Table 2.2 The contribution of SMEs in transition economies

Country	*Contribution of SMEs to GDP [%]*	*% of SMEs in the total number of companies (businesses)*	*Share of workers employed in SMEs [% of total workforce]*	*Year*	*Source*
Albania	70.0	99.8	79.8	2018	Albanian statistical report on SMEs, 2018
Armenia	60.0	99.8	68.0	2020	OECD, SME Policy Index: Eastern Partner Countries: Armenia, 2020
Azerbaijan	6.4	95.0	18.5	2020	OECD, SME Policy Index: Eastern Partner Countries: Azerbaijan, 2020
Belarus	28.8	78.3	30.7	2020	OECD, SME Policy Index: Eastern Partner Countries: Belarus, 2020
Bosnia & Herzegovina	60.0	99.1	64.0	2017	OECD, European Training Foundation, European Union, EBRD, SME Policy Index: Western Balkans and Turkey, 2019
Georgia	61.6	99.7	67.0	2020	ABDI, Report on Central Asia Regional Economic Cooperation (CAREC) Program Landlocked Countries, 2021
Kazakhstan	26.0	96.0	33.0	2017	ABDI, Report on CAREC Landlocked Countries, 2021
Montenegro	70.5	99.8	80.1	2018	OECD, European Training Foundation, European Union, EBRD, SME Policy Index: Western Balkans and Turkey, 2019
North Macedonia	63.8	99.7	75.0	2017	OECD, European Training Foundation, European Union, EBRD, SME Policy Index: Western Balkans and Turkey, 2019

(*continued*)

Table 2.2 (continued)

Country	*Contribution of SMEs to GDP [%]*	*% of SMEs in the total number of companies (businesses)*	*Share of workers employed in SMEs [% of total workforce]*	*Year*	*Source*
Republic of Moldova	70.7	98.7	59.8	2018	OECD, SME Policy Index: Eastern Partner Countries: Republic of Moldova, 2020
Russian Federation	19.8	27.0	18.8	2020	Report of the commission for the protection of the rights of entrepreneurs, Russian Federation, 2021
Serbia	57.4	99.0	65.0	2018	OECD, European Training Foundation, European Union, EBRD, SME Policy Index: Western Balkans and Turkey, 2019
Tajikistan	30.0	N/A	35.0	2017	ADBI, Leveraging SME Finance through Value Chains in Tajikistan, 2019
Turkmenistan	N/A	98.9	N/A	2016	EBRD, Turkmenistan Diagnostics, 2019
Ukraine	49.0	99.8	63.0	2018	OECD, SME Policy Index: Eastern Partner Countries: Ukraine, 2020
Uzbekistan	54.9	90.0	78.0	2017	ADBI, Report on CAREC Landlocked Countries, 2021

Source: United Nations Economic Commission for Europe (UNECE) (2022)

Development Bank, 2022). In the Asian region, in particular, SMEs constitute the largest share of businesses (Asian Development Bank, 2022). To be specific, in 2021, SMEs constituted 98.9% of all businesses in Asia, 46.1% of total employment, and 40.7% of the region's GDP regardless of it being gross value added or in gross domestic product (GDP) (Asian Development Bank, 2022).

However, the contribution of SMEs on economic development in emerging economies varies from country to country. In China, for example, in 2020, total number of SMEs topped 140 million and SMEs' contribution to jobs, GDP, tax income, and technological innovation stands at 79%, 60%, 50%, and 70%, respectively (UNECE, 2022).

From a regional perspective, the contribution of SMEs on job creation varies across regions, for example, South Asia (76.6%), Southeast Asia (67.3%), Central and West Asia (40.8%) (Asian Development Bank, 2022). As noted by the Asian Development Bank (2022), most of the SMEs in Asia are concentrated in cities or urban areas. In terms of sectors of the economy, SMEs in Asia are largely involved in manufacturing and services particularly retail, wholesale and transport and logistics (Asian Development Bank, 2022). In terms of exports, evidence shows that about one-third of SMEs in Asia are export oriented (Asian Development Bank, 2022).

Like in the OECD, the use of digital technologies such as e-commerce worrisomely remains a small share of total business transactions in Asia.

In Latin American economies SMEs are the backbone of the economy because they are the major contributors of employment and have significant shares of total businesses in the region (Dini & Stumpo, 2018). To be specific, micro-enterprises only account for more than 90% of total businesses and 67% of total employment (Dini & Stumpo, 2018).

However, in terms of their contribution to GDP, on average, because SMEs' productivity levels lag far behind large enterprises, their contribution to GDP is relatively low (Dini & Stumpo, 2018). When compared with similar SMEs in OECD countries, the differences in productivity levels in the Latin American economies are much larger than those prevailing in the OECD countries (Dini & Stumpo, 2018).

Their output largely caters to domestic markets, and, as a result, a significant share of the region's population and economy depends on their operations. At the same time, unlike their counterparts in more developed countries, Latin American SMEs account for a small share of exports, typically around 10%, because of their lacklustre competitiveness (Ferraro & Stumpo, 2010).

2.5 SMEs and Economic Development in Sub-Saharan Africa

Evidence shows that Sub-Saharan Africa (SSA) alone is home to 44 million micro, small, and medium enterprises (MSMEs) (Runde et al., 2021). Evidence shows that approximately 90% of businesses in SSA, that is, both in rural and in urban areas, are made up of SMEs (Akugri et al., 2015; Runde et al., 2021). In SSA, in terms of employment creation and contribution to economic growth, approximately 80% of jobs across the continent and at least 50% of GDP are contributed by SMEs (Runde et al., 2021) (see Box 2.1). This evidence shows that SMEs are an important vehicle of economic development in Africa.

Box 2.1 The Role of SMEs in Job Creation in Sub-Saharan Africa

In SSA, evidence shows SMEs are effective in fostering job creation which is of paramount importance in improving the quality of life of the poor and promoting inclusive growth, that is, making them an integral part of economic development in SSA (Abisuga-Oyekunle & Fillis, 2016). SMEs have strong record in creating new firm activities, new enterprises, new economic sectors, and innovations in firms. Abisuga-Oyekunle and Fillis (2016) noted that SMEs plays critical roles which are important for economic development such as the development of new technologies which lowers the cost of production, provision of goods and services for the society and employment creation. In this way, SMEs play a critical role in import substitution and expansion of exports which is key in preserving a country's foreign exchange (Mugano, 2024; Carree & Thurik, 2002). Evidence shows that SMEs create more jobs than large enterprises notwithstanding the fact that larger firms are more productive than SMEs (Ayyagari et al., 2011).

This view was corroborated by the findings of Abisuga-Oyekunle et al. (2019) who noted that, in Africa, on average, firms which are about two years old contribute about 9.3% of total employment. Abisuga-Oyekunle et al. (2019) further observed that in Africa, firms with 5–49 employees with at least five years old constituted 23% share of total employment, that is, the highest share of total employment. In direct contrast with trends in advanced economies, of interest to note is the fact that the large enterprises with employees ranging from 250 to 1000 have a small contribution to total employment in the SSA countries yet, (Abisuga-Oyekunle et al., 2019). Abisuga-Oyekunle et al. (2019) underscored that although there is general consensus in literature that SMEs are major contributors to job creation globally, SMEs in SSA are outstanding in their contribution to job creation when compared with SMEs in developed countries.

Source: Abisuga-Oyekunle et al. (2019)

The scope for SMEs to be used as channels for poverty reduction and inclusive growth is massive in developing countries especially in African countries (OECD, 2017b). This is particularly so because SMEs, that is, both formal and informal, can help countries to improve the quality of low-skilled employees and escape from low productivity traps if governments help SMEs to upgrade productivity (OECD, 2009, 2017b).

With respect to the impact of SMEs on economic development in Africa, South Africa provides a classic example of the contribution of SMEs on economic development (see Box 2.2).

At a country level, the South African case study provides a detailed analysis of the contribution of SMEs on economic development.

Box 2.2 SMEs and Economic Development in South Africa

In this section, SMEs' contribution on poverty eradication, job creation, and GDP is used to unpack SMEs' contribution on economic development in South Africa.

Job Creation

Evidence shows that SMEs constitute 91% of total businesses in South Africa (Kalane, 2015). In South Africa, in 2019, in terms of SMEs' contribution to job creation, the SME sector employed 10.8 million people, that is, 66% of the country's total employment (16.5 million) (Small Enterprise Development Agency (SEDA), 2019). In South Africa, unlike large businesses, SMEs have the capacity and high potential to create jobs for the country because they are labour-intensive (Saah, 2021). In line with the observations of Saah (2021), Oduntan (2014) argued that, in comparison with large enterprises, SMEs in South Africa create more jobs per unit of venture capital and per unit of energy consumed which is key in reducing high levels of unemployment in South Africa.

Contribution to GDP

Because SMEs hire both skilled and unskilled workers and provide them with income, SMEs help the country to reduce the unemployment problem, which is key in contributing to economic growth and inclusive development (Saah, 2021). Building on evidence from the Department of Trade and Industry (DTI) and SEDA, Labuschagne (2015) noted that, between 2004 and 2014, the contribution of SMEs to South Africa's GDP remained flat at 40%.

(*continued*)

Box 2.2 (continued)
Based on this observation, it can be argued that SMEs are at the centre of economic development in South Africa. However, Saah (2021) argued that South African SMEs have the potential to contribute more than 40% of the country's GDP if given the right conditions such as decent working space, access to finance, and market access.

Poverty alleviation

In addition, Ndofirepi (2016), Oduntan (2014) and Saah (2021) argued, through job creation and provision of income to poor communities in particular, SMEs play a critical role in reducing poverty and inequality which is rampant among the South Africans. SMEs uplift the poor through SMEs' role in provision of infrastructural development to impoverished societies, creation of access to markets to poor communities, skills transfers in host communities and provision of income which improves the livelihoods of indigenous populations (Saah, 2021 and Agupusi, 2007). These interventions by SMEs, when combined, trigger socio-economic development and economic transformation (Saah, 2021 and Agupusi, 2007).

Source: Saah (2021)

2.6 Challenges Affecting SMEs in Sub-Saharan Africa

Abisuga-Oyekunle et al. (2019) and Oyekunle and Sirayi (2018) underscored that although SMEs make significant contribution to economic development in SSA through various channels which include job creation, poverty alleviation, and contribution to GDP, several challenges inhibit SMEs from unleashing their potential. Six major binding constraints which affect SMEs in SSA are lack of right technologies, access to markets, lack of innovative culture, ease of doing business, poor access to electricity and finance (Oyekunle & Sirayi, 2018; Abisuga-Oyekunle et al., 2019; UNECE, 2022 and Mugano, 2024) (see Box 2.3).

Box 2.3 Challenges Affecting SMEs

(a) Weaknesses in regulatory and institutional framework

Although it is given that a properly functioning institutional and regulatory framework is essential for all businesses, it is more important for SMEs (UNECE, 2022). Although the majority of transition economies such as Armenia, Azerbaijan, Belarus, Georgia, the Republic of Moldova, and Ukraine have made significant progress in improving the institutional framework and regulatory for SMEs, most countries in SSA face serious hurdles. Noticeable progress has been made by Armenia, Azerbaijan, Belarus, Georgia, the Republic of Moldova, and Ukraine. These countries provided a solid institutional framework for SMEs by establishing agencies with support programmes for SMEs, reducing institutional barriers, developing legislation which simplifies businesses, subsidisation of interest rates on commercial bank loans to SMEs and provision of SMEs' infrastructure (business incubators, operating space, and support for microfinancing). To be specific, out of 46 countries in SSA, only 7 countries stand out as best in terms of ease of doing business, that is, Botswana, Ghana, South Africa, Namibia, Ethiopia, Kenya, and Rwanda (Abisuga-Oyekunle et al., 2019).

(b) Challenges with access to domestic and foreign markets

In developing countries, because of size limitations, SMEs find it difficult to enter both domestic and foreign markets (UNECE, 2022). Mugano (2024) observed that access to markets for SMEs in SSA, in particular, is further compounded by challenges such as shortage of skills and know-how, lack of access to finance, and informality.

(c) Lack of an innovation culture

Evidence shows that innovation plays a critical role in the country's economic progress through job creation and value creation (UNECE, 2022). In advanced economies such as the European Union, innovative SMEs are categorised as Innovative High-Growth Enterprises (IHGEs). These SMEs respond to new incentives, experiment with new ideas, create new markets, and integrate the domestic economy into the global economy which is key in fostering economic transformation.

(*continued*)

Box 2.3 (continued)

In developing countries such as those in SSA, the scope for innovation is limited due to lack of supportive infrastructure and institutional frameworks which inter alia include business incubators, unfair competition or absence of anti-trust laws, and absence of agencies with support programmes tailored for SMEs.

(d) Access to finance

Although most transition economies have made significant progress in access to finance especially non-banking financial instruments, SMEs in most of SSA face serious hurdles in accessing finance. In SSA, evidence shows that financial institutions are reluctant to offer working capital facilities and long-term lending to SMEs which are critical for business development due to lack of collateral and informality (World Bank, 2015; Abisuga-Oyekunle et al., 2019; African Development Bank, 2014; and Oyekunle, 2014). Abisuga-Oyekunle et al.'s (2019) study shows that, based on SMEs interviewed, Namibia (52.9%), Ghana (58%), and Mali (48.3%) pointed out access to finance as the major obstacle to growth of SMEs.

(e) Shortcoming in technology

In a new global order with disruptive technology and artificial intelligence, access to technology has been singled out as an instrument for SMEs to improve communication, facilitate quick access to information, improve access to both domestic and foreign markets, and access to finance (UNECE, 2022). Evidence shows that both in advanced economies and transition economies, countries such as Azerbaijan, Armenia, Belarus, Georgia, and the Republic of Moldova provide training platforms for SMEs to acquire digital skills required to integrate into global value chains (UNECE, 2022). In contrast, in Africa, this kind of support to SMEs is elusive. This situation is further compounded by the absence of software and hardware which include erratic supply of electricity, internet, and absence of gadgets such as computers and smart phones.

(f) Lack of access to electricity

Abisuga-Oyekunle et al. (2019) cited reliable and regular supply of electricity is one of the major hindrances faced by SMEs in Africa. A study by Abisuga-Oyekunle et al. (2019) showed that 23.3% of

(*continued*)

Box 2.3 (continued)
small firms interviewed highlighted that their biggest challenge is access to reliable electricity. In the same vein, the World Bank (2018) showed that 49% of SMEs in SSA considers electricity as the major impediment. In fact, Abisuga-Oyekunle et al. (2019) went further to argue that Africa is the only continent in the world where SMEs' capacity to innovate and develop is constrained by lack of reliable supply of electricity.

Source: Mugano (2024) and UNECE (2022)

2.7 Conclusion

In this chapter, various scholars which inter alia include Mugano (2024), Runde et al. (2021), Beck et al. (2005), OECD (2017a), OECD (2017b), Abisuga-Oyekunle et al. (2019), and Oyekunle and Sirayi (2018) underscored that SMEs are the bedrock of the global economy. These scholars argued that SMEs contribute to economic development through a number of channels which inter alia include exports, job creation, reduction in inequality and poverty eradication which are key elements of inclusive growth.

In line with this view, this chapter showed that SMEs contribute to about 60% of the global gross domestic product (GDP) (Organisation for Economic Cooperation and Development (OECD), 2017a; Mugano, 2024).

Of specific concern, as exhibited in this chapter, is the fact that the contribution of SMEs to national economies across the world, in terms of job creation, value addition, economic growth, and social well-being, is diverse (Mugano, 2024).

In advanced economies like OECD countries which have 99% of businesses as SMEs, these entities account for approximately 70% of jobs and generate between 50% and 60% of value-added goods (OECD, 2016a). In direct contrast, in Africa, evidence shows the contribution of SMEs to value addition is elusive notwithstanding the fact that 90% of businesses both in rural and urban areas are made up of SMEs (Akugri et al., 2015; Runde et al., 2021). However, notwithstanding this observation, in terms of employment creation and contribution to economic growth, approximately 80% of jobs across the continent and at least 50% of GDP are contributed by SMEs (Runde et al., 2021).

In developing countries, especially in the African continent, SMEs' potential to job creation, poverty eradication, and economic growth is largely constrained by a number of binding constraints which inter alia include lack of right technologies, access to markets, lack of innovative culture, ease of doing business, poor access to electricity and finance (Oyekunle & Sirayi, 2018; Abisuga-Oyekunle et al., 2019; UNECE, 2022 and Mugano, 2024).

In order to strengthen the capacity of SMEs, build resilience for African economies, and foster a deeper role of SMEs in economic development, policies such as improving access to finance, access to global markets and knowledge networks, improving the business environment, improving access to information communication technologies and training should be considered by African governments.

References

Abisuga-Oyekunle, O. A., & Fillis, I. R. (2016). The Role of Handicraft Micro-enterprises as a Catalyst for Youth Employment. *Creative Industries Journal, 10*(1), 59–74.

Abisuga-Oyekunle, O. A., Patra, S. K., & Muchie, M. (2019). SMEs in Sustainable Development: Their Role in Poverty Reduction and Employment Generation in Sub-Saharan Africa. *African Journal of Science, Technology, Innovation and Development*. https://doi.org/10.1080/20421338.2019.1656428

African Development Bank. (2014). *Trade Finance in Africa*. The African Development Bank.

Agupusi, P. (2007, July). Small Business Development and Poverty Alleviation in Alexandra, South Africa.

Akugri, M. S., Bagah, D. A., & Wulifan, J. K. (2015). The Contributions of Small and Medium Scale Enterprises to Economic Growth: A Cross-Sectional Study of Zebilla in the Bawku West District of Northern Ghana. *European Journal of Business and Management, 7*(9), 262–274.

Asian Development Bank. (2022). Small and Medium Enterprises Monitor 2022, Volume 1, Country and Regional Reviews, Mandaluyong City, 1550 Metro Manila, Philippines.

Ayyagari, M., Demirgüç-Kunt, A., & Maksimovic, V. (2011). Firm Innovation in Emerging Markets: The Role of Finance, Governance, and Competition. *A Journal of Financial and Quantitative Analysis, 46*(6), 1545–1580.

Beck, T., Demirgüç-Kunt, A., & Levine, R. (2005). SMEs, Growth, and Poverty: Cross-Country Evidence. *Journal of Economic Growth, 10*, 199–229.

Carree, M., & A. Thurik. 2002. The Impact of Entrepreneurship on Economic Growth. In Z. Acs & D. Audretsch (Eds.), International Handbook of Entrepreneurship Research. http://people.few.eur.nl/thurik/Research/Books/Thurikf.pdf

Di Bella, L., Katsinis, A., Lagüera-González, J., Odenthal, L., Hell, M., & Lozar, B (2023). Annual Report on European SMEs 2022/2023, Publications Office of the European Union, Luxemburg, 2023. https://doi.org/10.2760/028705JRC134336.

Dini, M., & Stumpo, G. (2018). *Mipymes en América Latina. Un frágil desempeño y nuevos desafíos para las políticas de fomento.* CEPAL.

EU. (2016). *Social Enterprises and their Eco-systems: Developments in Europe.* European Commission, Luxembourg: Publications Office of the European Union.

EU. (2021). *Annual Report on European SMEs 2020/2021.* European Innovation Council and SMEs Executive Agency (EISMEA), Brussels, Belgium.

EU/OECD. (2016). Policy Brief on Scaling the Impact of Social Enterprises, European Union and OECD. Retrieved December 15, 2023, from http://www.oecd.org/cfe/leed/Policy-brief-Scaling-up-social-enterprises-EN.pdf.

Eurostat. (2014). Patent Statistics at Eurostat. Mapping the Contribution of SMEs in EU Patenting. Eurostat Manuals and Guidelines, Luxembourg. Retrieved January 20, 2024, from http://ec.europa.eu/eurostat/documents/3859598/6064260/KS-GQ-14-009-EN-N.pdf/caa6f467-11f8-43f9-ba76-eb3ccb6fab6d

Ferraro, C., & Stumpo, G. (Comps). 2010. *Políticas de apoyo a las pymes en América Latina Entre avances innovadores y desafíos institucionales.* Santiago de Chile: Comisión Económica para América Latina y el Caribe (Economic Commission for Latin America and the Caribbean, CEPAL).

Garcia-Martinez, J.L., Kraus, S., Breier, M., & Kallmuenzer, A. (2023). Untangling the Relationship Between Small and Medium-Sized Enterprises and Growth: A Review of Extant Literature. International Entrepreneurship and Management Journal 19: 455–479. https://doi.org/10.1007/s11365-023-00830-z

Guriria, A. (2020). *SMEs are Key for More Inclusive Growth.* OECD.

IFC. (2010). *Scaling-Up SME Access to Financial Services in the Developing World, International Finance Corporation.* World Bank Group, Washington, DC. Retrieved January 10, 2024, from http://www.enterprise-development.org/wpcontent/uploads/ScalingUp_SME_Access_to_Financial_Services.pdf

Kalane, L. (2015). *Reasons for Failure of SMEs in the Free State.* Master's dissertation, University of The Free State—Bloemfontein.

Labuschagne, R. C. (2015). *Assessing selected success factors of SMEs in the North West Province* (Master's dissertation, North-West University).

Mugano, G. (2024). Role of SMEs on Economic Development in Africa. In G. Mugano & N. Dorasamy (Eds.), *SMEs and Economic Development in Africa: Challenges and Policy Options.* Routledge.

Ndofirepi, T. M. (2016). *The Impact of Technological Creativity and Entrepreneurship Education on the Entrepreneurship Intentions of Students at Particular Tertiary Institutions in Zimbabwe and South Africa*. Doctoral dissertation, Central University of Technology—Free State.

Oduntan, K. O. (2014). The Role of Small and Medium Enterprises in Economic Development: The Nigerian Experience. In *International Conference on Arts, Economics and Management (ICAEM'14)* (pp. 75–78). ICAEM.

OECD. (2009). *Doing better for the children*. OECD.

OECD. (2010). *SMEs*. OECD Publishing.

OECD. (2016a). The Productivity-Inclusiveness Nexus, Meeting of the OECD Council at Ministerial Level, Paris, 1–2 June 2016 [C/MIN(2016)3].

OECD. (2016b). *Entrepreneurship at a Glance 2016*. OECD Publishing.

OECD. (2017a). *Enhancing the Contributions of SMEs in a Global and Digitalised Economy*. Meeting of the OECD Council at Ministerial Level Paris, 7–8 June 2017, OECD, Paris.

OECD. (2017b). *Increasing Productivity in Small Traditional Enterprises: Programmes for Upgrading Management Skills and Practices*. OECD Working Party on SMEs and Entrepreneurship, CFE/SME(2016).

Oyekunle, O. A. (2014). Building the Creative Industries for Sustainable Economic Development in South Africa. *International Journal of Sustainable Development, 7*(12), 47–72.

Oyekunle, O. A., & Sirayi, M. (2018). The Role of Creative Industries as a Driver for a Sustainable Economy: A Case of South Africa. *Creative Industries Journal, 11*(3), 225–244.

Runde, D. F., Savoy, C. M., & Staguhn, J. (2021). *Supporting Small and Medium Enterprises in Sub-Saharan Africa through Blended Finance*. Center for Strategic and International Studies.

Saah, P. (2021). The Impact of Small and Medium-Sized Enterprises on the Economic Development of South Africa. *Technium Social Sciences Journal, 24*, 549–561.

SEUK. (2015). *Leading the World in Social Enterprises, State of Social Enterprise Survey 2015*. Social Enterprise UK Publishing.

Small Enterprises Development Agency (SEDA). (2019). *Annual Report*. SEDA.

UNECE. (2022). *Small and Medium Enterprises in Economies in Transition: Challenges and Opportunities and UNECE Tools*. Informal Paper, UNECE, Geneva.

World Bank. (2015). *Small beginnings for great opportunities: Lessons learned from 20 years of microfinance projects in IFC. IFC Smart Lessons Book*. World Bank Group.

World Bank. (2018). *Doing business 2018: Reforming to create jobs*. World Bank.

CHAPTER 3

SMEs and Poverty Reduction in Africa

Nirmala Dorasamy

3.1 Introduction

There is no doubt that Africa is in a crisis of a different magnitude. With the COVID-19 national lockdown, many citizens lost their jobs without alternative means of livelihood. While unemployment continues to rise, the poverty level has also increased, with many small business enterprises being forced to close their businesses. As of May 2021, more than 50% of the global population were living in extreme poverty (people living on US $1.90 per day) and are domiciled in Africa (Saleh, 2021). By implication, Africa produces the largest number of poor people globally. Nigeria has the highest with 12.6%. One of the factors responsible for this is unemployment among the population. This is partly a manifestation of the weak industrial base that could provide job opportunities for citizens.

In developed countries, private business outlets and organisations provide employment opportunities to citizens, thereby creating a sustainable source of income for daily needs. Indeed, private business ventures and large corporations are the tools of economic growth and development in developed countries (Doran et al., 2018). Doran et al. (2018), in their

N. Dorasamy (✉)
Faculty of Management Sciences, Durban University of Technology, Durban, South Africa
e-mail: nirmala@dut.ac.za

G. Mugano, N. Dorasamy, *SMEs Perspective in Africa*,
https://doi.org/10.1007/978-3-031-69103-4_3

study of 55 countries, discovered that business enterprises contributed more to the gross domestic product (GDP) of developed countries than those of developing countries. Thus, the financial well-being of citizens depends mostly on the health of the economy.

One of the aims of establishing Small and Medium Enterprises (SMEs) in Africa is to combat the rising tide of poverty, caused largely by unemployment (Abisuga-Oyekunle et al., 2020). Indeed, scholars have acknowledged the role of SMEs in poverty reduction (Rotar et al., 2019; Kowo et al., 2019; Manzoor et al., 2019; Nursini, 2020). As such, addressing poverty through Small and Medium-sized Enterprises (SMEs) in Africa requires a multifaceted approach that involves various stakeholders, including governments, NGOs, and the private sector. In South Asia, for instance, the governments of the regional body, the South Asian Association of Regional Cooperation (SAARC) developed their poverty eradication strategies through the SMEs (Manzoor et al., 2019). The development of SMEs in the region explored the rich natural potentials of the countries to create employment opportunities for citizens through the production of commodities that meet the demands of each locality. This contributed immensely to the export earnings of the countries, thereby strengthening their national economics (Manzoor et al., 2019). According to Manzoor et al. (2019, 10), "entrepreneurial attitudes are significant and positive for high-income economies but insignificant in explaining economic growth in middle/low-income economies. Entrepreneurs in high-income economies may be more innovative, internationalised and growth focused than entrepreneurs in middle/low-income economies."

While Africa has recorded a measure of improvement in the establishment of SMEs, with encouraging results indicating resilient growth for sustainability, they cannot withstand the economic stress created by emergencies and developments such as the global economic meltdown and the recent COVID-19 pandemic (Fatoki, 2014; Kowo et al., 2019). While some have shown a measure of excellent results with demonstrable growth signs and innovation for sustainable productivity, they operate in unfavourable competitive environments besieged by challenges that stifle their future. As Fatoki (2014, p. 922) noted that the "high failure rate of new SME creation paints a bleak picture of the SME sector's potential to contribute meaningfully to job creation, economic growth and poverty reduction." The consequences of these failures, as related to poverty, include loss of productivity, inability to pay wages and debt obligations, loss of jobs, soaring income inequality, and loss of revenue for the government (Fatoki, 2014). The social consequences of this development, which also increase the crisis of governance in society, include the proliferation of criminal activities such as robberies, theft, as well as other debasing and degrading social means and methods of livelihood.

3.2 Conceptualising Poverty

A precise universally acceptable definition of poverty is a rarity. Scholars and development agencies have sought to craft a definition of the concept, but it has been characterised by divergent views and perspectives occasioned by the general lack of unanimity of a definitional description of social issues. Different authors view poverty from different dimensions (Cario, 2019). Early sociological theorists such as Karl Marx, Emile Durkheim, Max Weber, and Friedrich Engels, among others, situate poverty within the context of the economic order of society, which generates socio-economic and political inequality (Shildrick & Rucell, 2015). While Marx and Engels identified inequality created by class struggles, Weber harped on the perpetual dominant relationships generated by "the influence of power, status and prestige" within the political and economic environments (Shildrick & Rucell, 2015, p. 3). This generic sociological ascription divides society into two distinct groupings in the context of inequality: the haves and the have nots. This construct has laid the foundation for the interrogation of the nature of socio-economic and political relationships among citizens in society.

Central to this relationship is the access to resources, tangible or intangible, within the socio-economic and political enclave. The quantum of access to these resources determines one's state of possession. Thus, poverty occurs when individuals have the least resources which places them in a disadvantaged position compared to others (Alkire & Foster, 2011; Ridge & Wright, 2008; Dorling, 2019). In other words, the consciousness of poverty revolves around the gap that exists between those who have access to resources and those who do not, thereby dividing society into two unequal sets of people. The concentration of resources with an individual or groups of individuals, by whatever means, is the foundation of poverty. In this regard, Ridge and Wright (2008) identified those who have fewer resources as people who have experienced or are experiencing disadvantaged positions in the socio-economic ladder of society. Such people "have inadequate resources to secure what is deemed a reasonable or expected standard of living within a given country" (Shildrick & Rucell, 2015, p. 4). The consequence of this is social stratification in society with an entrenched culture of dependency and exclusion.

Subsequent definitions and descriptions of poverty revolved around this sociological perspective of access to socio-economic and political resources. This chapter looks at the economic resource aspect of poverty. The World Bank measured poverty in terms of available resources in US dollars, to an individual for a living per day. Thus, extreme poverty is measured as people living on less than US $1.90 per day (Prydz & Jolliffe, 2019). This is the international poverty line (IPL) valued in 2011 based on the purchasing power parity (PPP). The inference is that if "$1.90 defines the cost of basic needs in some of the poorest countries of the world, then certainly someone living on less than this must be viewed as poor regardless of where they live" (Prydz & Jolliffe, 2019).

Thus, the World Bank's definition of poverty in the economics sense identified variables such as hunger, lack of access to medical facilities, lack of access to education, and lack of shelter as poverty indicators. Other indicators are unemployment, fear of a sustainable future, being powerless, and a bondage or dependence on others for sources of livelihood.

3.3 Factors That Engender Poverty

There have been different perspectives on the causes of poverty in society. Myers (2018) identified nine factors that are responsible for poverty across the globe: Insufficiency of and lack of access to healthy food and clean water; unemployment/underemployment; conflict and political crisis; lack of access to good education; socio-economic inequality; infrastructural deficit; climatic/weather change; weak government capacity; and drought and famine. These factors manifest in different forms to provide the environment for citizens to live below the threshold of US $1.9 per day. These factors have no racial or regional boundaries, but they are present in all countries, depending on their severity.

In developing countries, these factors manifest in varying degrees. Weak government capacity, for instance, is a manifestation of corruption and mismanagement of public resources by political leaders *(Panchal,* 2020*). Most African countries, especially the oil-rich economies, are suffering from the resource curse syndrome (Mulwa & Mariara,* 2016*). The resource curse, also known as the Dutch disease, connotes the institutional deficit in the management of abundant resources for the promotion of the economic wellness of the nation and by extension, citizens' welfare (Mulwa & Mariara,* 2016*; Henri,* 2019*). In other words, the positive effects of abundant resources are a function of the institutional context of the country's governance structure. Where defiance characterises the management of the public sector, as is the case in most of the African countries, the consequence is the paradox of poverty amid abundant resources.*

The point here is that poverty is prevalent in Africa not necessarily because of the lack of resources, but the inability of governments to transform the abundant resources into wealth, in a manner that would promote equitable distribution to the welfare needs of citizens. Institutional failure that promotes corruption and unethical leadership in the public sector negatively affects the access of citizens to the necessary resources that could boost welfare and living conditions. Henri (2019) noted that this institutional deficiency is exacerbated by the abuse of the rule of law, injustice, ineffective public service, incoherent public policies, and the general lack of accountability.

This limited capacity of the African government has weakened the environment for the promotion of inclusive public policy capable of assuaging the poverty level. This is a critical challenge in the poverty eradication initiatives, as the political leadership exploits such lofty programmes as a network of corruption. At the heart of poverty in Africa are three principal factors: corruption, unemployment, and inequality (Panchal, 2020). These factors are interconnected and constitute a strain on the structures of governance and weaken the capacity of governments.

There is no doubt that corruption is a global phenomenon (Imiera, 2020). However, its severity and consequence on governance in African countries are monumental (Fagbadebo, 2019; Fagbadebo & Dorasamy, 2021). Corruption is a cancer that eats the fabrics of growth and development, thereby engendering poverty. The consequence is the disruption of the national economy. According to Imiera (2020, 87), officials of African governments often "divert public funds meant for the promotion of the wellbeing of people for their individual purposes." Consequently, corruption constitutes a severe strain and confronts society with acute and stunted "growth in income and wealth inequality" (Imiera, 2020, 87). In the 2020 Corruption perception Index (CPI) of Transparency International (TI), Sub-Saharan Africa (SSA) was the lowest scoring region of 32% (TI, 2021). The bulk of countries with abysmal corruption perception were in Africa. This has been the pattern of the corruption performance of the continent since 2018.

In the global poverty index, SSA has the highest number of citizens living in poverty. The World Bank (2021) reported that out of the ten countries with the highest poverty rates in the world, nine are from Africa. These countries are South Sudan (82%), Equatorial Guinea (76.80%), Madagascar (70%), Guinea-Bissau (69.30%), and Eritrea (69%). Others are Sao Tome and Principe (66.70%), Burundi (64.90%), Democratic

Republic of Congo (63.90%), and Central African Republic (62%). These countries are also the bastion of corruption, according to the CPI report.

In 2019, Transparency International (TI) described Africa as the world's second-fastest growing region with more than 100 million citizens living in extreme poverty (TI, 2019). Comparing the situation with the 1990s, the global anti-corruption watchdog noted that the largest share of poor people across the globe domiciled in Africa. To the TI, corruption was the greatest obstacle to the various poverty eradication initiatives in Africa. Public institutional structures designed to fight corruption are weak and easily compromised to become promoters of defiance and impunity. Citizens' access to public service is usually conditioned on the payment of bribes and gratifications. This corruption phenomenon in the continent is complex, as international actors whose countries prioritised anti-corruption campaigns in developing countries are culprits in "perpetuating corruption in Africa, chipping away at the region's sustainable development" (TI, 2019).

The resource curse in Africa is real. While the continent usually realises billions of dollars in resources, the impact is less feasible in infrastructural development and the well-being of citizens. Rather, the bulk of the stolen money is repatriated to the West through illicit financial flows (TI, 2019). It has been estimated that Africa loses US $50 billion to illicit financial flows every year (TI, 2019). According to TI (2019, p. 15), the "money could have been used to fund initiatives and public services that improve the lives of African citizens." Unfortunately, the political elite acquired the money through illegal means and thus, stashed "abroad using offshore financial structures and often with the help of complicit or negligent banks, lawyers, accountants and real estate agents" (TI, 2019).

One of the consequences of corruption is the stifling of the national economy and depletion of the governance structures that support employment. Thus, unemployment is a derivative of corruption and is a very strong factor that generates poverty. The more people lose their jobs, the more their resources are depleted and the less they can meet their basic needs of life. The priority of most African governments is inimical to inclusive growth capable of generating sufficient manpower demands because of the mono-economy syndrome that services the corruption appetite of the political leaders. In Nigeria, for instance, concentration on oil resources has led to the neglect of other productive and employment-generating sectors of the economy. The strains of unemployment, therefore, have degenerated to a level whereby citizens are involved in criminal self-help activities such as banditry, kidnapping, trade in illicit drugs, and nefarious activities that have posed a greater security threat to society.

While the political elites and their acolytes are gainfully employed in government, a majority of the population are beheld roaming the street with no decent employment, thereby increasing daily the number of poor people on the street. This inequality in the social and economic strata of most countries in Africa has remained a potent source of poverty. African leaders are fond of using jobless citizens as their foot soldiers in their titanic battle for political dominance. Inadequate education and most importantly, lack of a decent source of income would attract such agile young people to be instruments of political violence and disruptions. Resources are poorly allocated; productive sectors of the economy are unable to function properly because of corruption and the lack of government support. The inequality gap in Africa is a major attraction that has driven many into the poverty lines, as their inability to meet up with the means of livelihood has made them dependents of the wealthy political and economic elites, whose access to public resources had made them tower above their peers.

3.4 Africa and the Burden of Poverty

Africa leads the poverty in the world with an estimated 490 million (36% of the total population) citizens living in extreme poverty, as against 481 in 2019 (Human, 2021). Even though it is estimated that the poverty rate was declining, the number of poor people has been increasing. While the economy of North Africa has been favourable to the reduction in poverty, Sub-Saharan Africa (SSA) has the worst poverty phenomenon (Human, 2021). Nigeria, the largest economy in the continent, described as the global poverty headquarters in 2020 (Panchal, 2020), has an estimated 90 million people, representing 46% of the country's over 200 million population, living in extreme poverty (Human, 2021). South Africa has 16 million people, representing 26% of its estimated 58 million population, living in extreme poverty.

In 2021, the poverty rate in Burundi, Central African Republic, Madagascar, Republic of the Congo and Democratic Republic of Congo (DRC) were 80%, 79%, 75%, and 74%, respectively (Human, 2021). In the World Poverty Clock, Egypt, Gabon, and Mauritania are the three African countries that are meeting the target of poverty eradication while the other African countries are experiencing daily rise in poverty (World

Data Lab, 2021). In 2020, the South African Department of Statistics (DOS) (2020) disclosed that more than 6 out of 10 children, representing 62.1% of the total children population, "are identified as multidimensionally poor, according to a report on Child Poverty in South Africa released by Statistics South Africa today." Relatedly the report gives an in-depth analysis of the Living Conditions Survey that was conducted in 2015. Child poverty in South Africa is multi-sectoral, with the majority of children (0–17 years) suffering from multiple deprivations simultaneously. Black African children (68.3%) show the highest percentage of multidimensional poverty as compared to their peers from other population groups. Multidimensional poverty is highly prevalent amongst double orphans (77.3%) and paternal orphans (75.0%) as opposed to non-orphans and maternal orphans (DOS, 2020). The reports bear testimony to the high levels of poverty, which is negatively impacting the overall well-being of societies.

With a fragile economy and weak infrastructural facilities, Africa is a victim of the poverty consequences of the COVID-19 pandemic. The World Bank (2021) estimated that an additional 40 million Africans could be pushed into extreme poverty as a result of the COVID-19 pandemic, thereby complicating the crisis of governance associated with poverty in the continent. This estimation was in tandem with UNECA's projection that the total African population living in extreme poverty would be 514 million (UNECA, 2021b). UNECA had warned that should the economic impact of the lockdown associated with the COVID-19 pandemic continue in 2021, between 29 and 59 million Africans would be living below the US $1.90 per person per day (UNECA, 2021b). With the advent of the COVID-19 pandemic and its associated measures to curtail its spread, Africa has been identified as one of the emerging hot spots "where multiple threats to poor people's lives and livelihoods converge" (World Bank Group, 2020). The World Bank thus estimated that because of this report, Sub-Saharan Africa was expected to be a region where one-third of the newly impoverished people as a result of the COVID-19 pandemic reside.

In Africa, aside from the COVID-19 pandemic, some factors make poverty to be increasingly concentrated in societies. These factors include intermittent armed conflicts; climate change risk such as flooding that displaced people from the locations of the sources of their livelihood such as farms; and locust swarms and other insects' invasions that destroyed farmlands and crops (World Bank Group, 2020). The World Bank Group

(2020, p. 1) reported that "armed conflict is also driving increases in poverty in some countries and regions. In the Middle East and North Africa, for example, extreme poverty rates nearly doubled between 2015 and 2018, from 3.8% to 7.2%, spurred by the conflicts in the Syrian Arab Republic and the Republic of Yemen." Thus, climate-related factors, as well as humanity-induced circumstances, are threatening the welfare of citizens, while the anti-poverty drive by governments and public institutions is relapsing. As the World Bank noted, "poverty is already intertwined with vulnerability to climate-related threats such as flooding and vector-borne diseases" (World Bank Group, 2020, p. 1). Relatedly, analysts have presented a series of analytical studies that have established "the convergence of poverty and flood risks, especially in Sub-Saharan Africa" (World Bank Group, 2020, p. 1).

Unfortunately, Sub-Sahara Africa (SSA) has been spotted as a region with a high concentration of poverty. According to the World Bank, the increasing level of concentration of poor people in SSA has become a setback to the global poverty reduction drive, because the region "is experiencing a slower reduction in poverty than are other regions" (World Bank Group, 2020, p. 3). The World Bank Group (2020, p. 6) claimed that "Sub-Saharan Africa would be the next most affected region, with between 26 million and 40 million additional people predicted to be pushed into extreme poverty. Overall, some 72 million of the projected new poor in the baseline scenario will be in middle-income countries, more than four fifths of the total new poor." More so, when applying the higher regional poverty thresholds appropriate for upper-middle-income countries (US $5.50 a day) and lower-middle-income countries (US $3.20 a day), the poverty impact of the COVID-19 pandemic will be much greater.

This grim analysis of the poverty situation in the African continent is a cause for worry and concern, given the rate of population increase in the continent. Africa is a blessed continent, but lives in a paradox of poverty amid abundant resources. The World Bank (2021) described Africa as a diverse continent with abundant "human and natural resources that have the potential to yield inclusive growth and eradicate poverty in the region, enabling Africans across the continent to live healthier and more prosperous lives." Africa has the largest free trade area globally, with a vast market of 1.2 billion traders. This asset could be harnessed further with sustainable SMEs leveraging on the abundant human and material resources.

3.5 SMEs as a Poverty Alleviation Mechanism

SMEs as small-scale investments have been proven as potential sources of employment. Aside from contributing to the national economy, SMEs are also a source of income to the owners and the staff employed in the running of the business ventures. Going by the various conceptualisation of SMEs, it is apt to state that they have gained global recognition as a vital sector that generates employment opportunities for citizens, thereby contributing immensely to the livelihood of the poor (Ali et al., 2014).

With active participation in economic activities, SMEs are vehicles for increased economic productivity and growth, invariably accelerating the welfare of citizens. In Asia, for instance, SMEs contribute over 90% of total enterprises in each country, thereby generating more employment than the public sector (Yoshino & Taghizadeh-Hesary, 2016). Invariably, SMEs in Asian countries are avenues for wealth creation and depletion of poverty among citizens. When an economy witnesses increased productivity, public welfare will be enhanced thereby reducing the level of poverty among the people. SMEs, therefore, complement the role of industrialisation in the promotion of a strong and stable economy that has its impact on the welfare of citizens. A stable and prosperous national economy is an antidote to poverty (Manzoor et al., 2019).

Globally, SMEs have been supporting the government's effort at boosting employment and eradicating poverty. In 2006, the International Labour Organisation (ILO) commissioned a study on poverty reduction, noting that SMEs were in the minds of people living in poverty as veritable means of lifting them out of poverty (Vandenberg, 2006). As such for many poor people, work means being the owner of or an employee in a micro- or small enterprise. The poor often work alone as the owner, manager and sole employee of their enterprise, or they involve their family members; and permanent or casual labourers. In many cases, poor people opt for such work because they have little choice, either because of inadequate paid employment or the work they do on the family farm is inadequate to satisfy domestic needs (Vandenberg, 2006, p. 1).

In other words, people prefer working for themselves in small-scale business ventures where they could be self-employed and employers of labour providing essential services to citizens within their localities. This consensus position is a manifestation of the common awareness of poverty as well as the need to reduce its severity through ownership of and association with small-scale enterprises. Indeed, the findings of the study by

Vandenberg (2006, p. 1) boosted the focus on small business development initiatives as a mechanism to combat the rising poverty in the global system. The study discovered that this "emerging consensus" at the time "is reassuring and generally helpful in developing pro-poor small business strategies" (Vandenberg, 2006, p. 1). Because of this, subsequent developments that focused on the development of SMEs and anti-poverty strategies evolved to the level of acceptability among nations of the world, thereby constituting an instrument with international recognition. SMEs thus became a universal phenomenon, "playing an essential and vital role in a nation's economic and social configuration" (Manzoor et al., 2021, p. 1).

With the global perception of SMEs as a noteworthy structure of economic growth and prosperity, wider attention has been drawn to its poverty alleviation components. In developing countries, in particular, the SME sector of the economy has assumed a prominent source of employment and income generation in the face of the failing government infrastructure to support the yearnings of the majority of citizens. For example, about 85% of the manufacturing employment in Ghana is provided by the SME sector. This sector consists of 92% of businesses and contributes 70% of the GDP in Ghana whereas in South Africa this sector contributes to 52–57% of the GDP and provides 61% of employment (Abor & Quartey, 2010). SMEs constitute 91% of the formal business in South Africa. Thus, it can be argued that with concerted strategies to improve the sustainability of SMEs as an avenue for poverty alleviation, SMEs can play a prominent role in national socio-economic growth and development.

SMEs cannot fulfil their poverty alleviation role if they are continually faced with challenges that restrict their capability and operational strengths. Thus, sustainable SMEs are drivers for poverty eradication. In Asian countries, SMEs have proven their mettle as generators of employment and poverty alleviation (OECD, 2017; Yoshino & Taghizadeh-Hesary, 2016). Compared to Africa, SMEs in Asia are more productive and active in terms of employment and poverty alleviation, with more than 50% contributing to the GDP (Omozusi, 2020). While African and Asian countries adopt similar strategies for the growth of their SMEs through soft loans, the management of the policies towards the attainment of the desired goal differs (Omozusi, 2020).

In Africa, SMEs are faced with a myriad of challenges that stifle their operational capacities for sustainability. Aside from the challenges of increased competition with multinational organisations and retail outlets, they do not have access to sufficient funds like their competitors (Yoshino & Taghizadeh-Hesary, 2016; Quartey et al., 2017; Omozusi, 2020). While SMEs continue to expand in the continent, the commitment of governments in terms of effective management of the finance sector of the national economy has remained a challenge that has continuously retarded the ability to adapt to rapidly changing market demands and technological change in the global market (Quartey et al., 2017).

Yoshino and Taghizadeh-Hesary (2016) have identified some factors that challenge SMEs in the realisation of their job creation and poverty eradication pursuit. Central to this are inadequate resources, which are not limited to finance but also include technical skills and mastery; access to market information and research; and innovative creativity. Other challenging factors include "lack of economies of scale and scope; higher transaction costs relative to large enterprises; and the lack of networks that can contribute to a lack of information, know-how, and experience of domestic and international markets (Yoshino & Taghizadeh-Hesary, 2016, p. 5)." Also included are the increased nature of market competition and concentration from large multinational enterprises caused by globalisation and economic integration; and the inability of SMEs to compete against larger firms with greater resources and outlets, and low entrepreneurial zeal. Most of these factors are related to the financial capacity of SMEs.

Additionally, as Quartey et al. (2017) have noted, the inability of SMEs in Africa to access the necessary funds for their expansion and operational activities have remained a challenge. Despite the availability of comprehensive finance programmes, SMEs in the continent still depend on unconventional sources of funds to activate their operations. According to Quartey et al. (2017), the various schemes by the governments of SSA and the international donor agencies and other informal sources to finance SMEs are mere alternatives, as the various in-country financial institutions remain the best mode of funding the operations of SMEs. As posited by Quartey et al. (2017, p. 22), "official schemes are often set up with the primary motive of increasing the flow of finance and credit to SMEs to enable them to increase their operational capacities, productivity and competitiveness in the local and international markets." While this is understandable, public financial sources in Africa are networks of corruption.

Informal and most unconventional sources of the funds have remained the options for SMEs owners to secure adequate funds for their businesses. These sources include personal savings of the individual owners of businesses; borrowing from moneylenders at exorbitant interest rates and stringent repayment conditions; financial assistance from friends and relatives; credit loans from cooperative savings associations; and other traditional lending outlets. The implication of the aforementioned is the reality that SMEs in Africa are not advantaged in terms of adequate access to official sources of finance and resources. The economic environments presented in Africa, especially with the presence of multinational corporations, with unlimited access to resources, in competition with local business outlets, have weakened the capacity of African SMEs to harness robust markets as key players in wealth creation, employment opportunities, and poverty alleviation (OECD, 2017).

The OECD (2017) has identified the business environment as being critical to the success of SMEs. For SMEs to compete effectively in the global economy, a "sound business environment and a well-functioning entrepreneurial 'eco-system' for businesses is needed at the national and local levels, as this is critical for inclusive participation and success (OECD, 2017, p. 14). This is even more crucial in the current context, as increased competitive pressures and the fast pace of technological change demand good public governance; agility; innovative behavior; and ease of access to strategic resources" (OECD, 2017, p. 14). This business ecosystem includes the features of the institutional and regulatory framework that dictates the pace and format of the operation of the SMEs. Since these features are legalistic, most SMEs in Africa do not have the necessary and requisites capacity to fulfil these rules that are not even stable. Mostly, they are susceptible to manipulation to satisfy the pecuniary interest of the regulators (OECD, 2017). Thus, in a system besieged by graft and impunity, official rules are compromised to promote the individualistic interests of the political and economic elites, who are in control of the institutions of government.

Most of these regulatory rules and statutes are characterised by "uncertainty, complexity and inconsistency," which disproportionately affect the operations of the SMEs (OECD, 2017). This malaise has a direct impact on the capacity of SMEs to operate effectively, because of the lack of expertise and skills necessary to comply with the regulatory features and norms. For example, when SMEs lack information or in-house expertise, they often incur other indirect costs such as paying for external advisors' expertise or investing in specific training of staff to comply with new obligations. Thus, the complexity of regulatory procedures and conditions for regulatory compliance are especially important for SMEs to deal with for purposes of effective operations (OECD, 2017, p. 14). Given this and the need to survive within the available pace, most SMEs in African countries operate in the informal sector to circumvent the stringent conditions imposed by the SMEs' ecosystem, thereby limiting their capacity to generate more employment and creating wealth opportunities for the poor. Most of them struggle to break even in terms of profitability. This environmental misfit has lowered the expectations of the capacity of African SMEs to serve as mechanisms and outposts for the promotion of an indigenous business culture that could stimulate growth in employability and poverty eradication.

Ultimately, SMEs play a crucial role in alleviating poverty in Africa by contributing to economic growth, job creation, and increased access to essential goods and services. Below are some examples of how SMEs are making a positive impact in Africa:

- Job Creation: SMEs are significant contributors to employment in Africa. According to the African Development Bank, SMEs are estimated to create 80% of the continent's employment opportunities. This is particularly important in a region with a high youth unemployment rate, as SMEs often provide entry-level job opportunities (ILO, 2015; United Nations Economic Commission for Africa, 2021a).
- Income Generation: SMEs provide opportunities for individuals to generate income and improve their livelihoods. A study by the International Labour Organization (ILO) found that SMEs in Africa contribute to poverty reduction by offering income-generating activities for people with limited formal job prospects.
- Access to Finance: SMEs often struggle to access financing from traditional banks. Microfinance institutions and fintech startups in Africa have emerged to fill this gap, providing loans and financial services tailored to the needs of SMEs. This enhances their ability to grow and contribute to poverty alleviation. For instance, organisations like M-Pesa in Kenya have facilitated access to financial services for SMEs and individuals alike (ILO, 2015; United Nations Economic Commission for Africa, 2021a).
- Promotion of Local Industries: SMEs are instrumental in promoting local industries, manufacturing, and agricultural sectors. For instance, in Nigeria, SMEs are contributing to the growth of the agribusiness

sector, which has the potential to significantly reduce poverty by boosting agricultural productivity and creating value-added products.

- Innovation and Technology: SMEs in Africa often drive innovation and technology adoption. They develop cost-effective solutions to local challenges, such as solar-powered devices, healthcare technologies, and e-commerce platforms. These innovations can improve access to basic services and create new economic opportunities (ILO, 2015; African Development Bank Group, 2020).
- Women and Youth Empowerment: SMEs play a critical role in empowering women and young entrepreneurs in Africa. Initiatives like the African Development Bank's Affirmative Finance Action for Women in Africa (AFAWA) are specifically designed to support women-led SMEs, helping to reduce gender inequality and poverty (African Development Bank Group, 2021; United Nations Economic Commission for Africa, 2021a).
- Rural Development: SMEs are essential for rural development in Africa. They encourage economic activity in rural areas, reducing the urban–rural income gap. For example, small-scale agriculture and agribusinesses create jobs and enhance food security in rural communities (African Development Bank Group, 2021; United Nations Economic Commission for Africa, 2021a).
- Export Growth: SMEs are increasingly participating in export activities, contributing to foreign exchange earnings for African countries. Organisations like the African Export-Import Bank (Afreximbank) provide support and financing to SMEs looking to expand their export capabilities (African Development Bank Group, 2021; United Nations Economic Commission for Africa, 2021a).
- Community Development: Many SMEs in Africa have a strong sense of social responsibility and engage in community development initiatives. They invest in education, health care, and infrastructure, which indirectly contribute to poverty alleviation (ILO, 2015; African Development Bank Group, 2020).

3.6 Routing Poverty Through SMEs in Africa

Globally, every government is concerned about poverty because of its adverse consequence on social cohesion. Inequality has remained a potent source of conflict and crisis in society. Ancient theorists of state such as Thomas Hobbes, Thomas Aquinas, John Locke, among others, did spot inequality as a characteristic feature of society that often drives an individual to engage in conflicts. Thus, poverty reduction has remained a cornerstone of the public policy of modern governments (Maziriri & Chivandi, 2020). "Unfortunately, most African countries are characterised by poverty indices, including acute economic inequality; inadequate wages and incomes to guarantee the acquisition of assets; lack of vocational skills; poor health care; poor quality of life; limited access to training and other fundamental services; increased mortality because of disease; vagrancy; risky social conditions; as well as social segregation and rejection" (Maziriri & Chivandi, 2020). The central factor in these indices is inadequate funds.

Entrepreneurial education is a critical path for the development of SMEs in a manner that would cure the poverty syndrome in Africa. Since unemployment is a source of poverty, entrepreneurial education would prepare school leavers with business skills that could make them self-employed upon the completion of their education. Education is critical for skills acquisition and the application of such skills. With entrepreneurial skills, young school leavers are potential SMEs owners scattered along with the informal sector of the economy. Thus, entrepreneurial education is a pro-SME strategy and anti-poverty mechanism in developing African countries. Educated and entrepreneurially skilled Africans are potential sources of employment and advocates of prosperity.

Indeed, Africa has the highest share of the informal sector of the national economy, with 43% of African countries deriving their GDP from this important sector (CISLAC 2019). Central and Southern American countries only generate 4% of their GDP from the informal sector, while the informal sector in the East and Central Europe contribute 39% to their countries' GDP; and Asian countries and OECD countries derive 30% of their GDP from the informal sector (Etim & Daramola, 2020). At the global scale, the informal sector of national economies, which also includes SMEs, is optimistic about creating two billion jobs and driving away from a substantial number of citizens living in poverty (Etim & Daramola, 2020).

In Africa, the informal sector constitutes 20% of the GDP of South Africa, Lesotho, and Namibia, while Tanzania and the Benin Republic realise 60% of their GDP from the informal sector (Medina et al., 2017). In South Africa, the common SMEs in the informal sector include micro-enterprises such as spazas, shebeens liquor shops, and other petty trading located in townships and informal settlements (Etim & Daramola, 2020). Others include restaurants, haircare saloons, street vendors, automobile repair workshops, small farmers, and retails shops. In some aspects, there are also manufacturing; financial services; construction; social and community services; wholesale and retail trading; transport and haulage; storage and warehousing; communication; and information technology SMEs.

In Nigeria, for instance, the drivers of the informal sector of the economy in villages and cities are the young school leavers who have acquired relevant skills in small businesses and established their enterprises to boost their incomes. They are found mostly in the informal sector, which constitutes 65% of the economy which is central to the growth of the Nigerian economy (Etim & Daramola, 2020; CISLAC, 2019). These petty businesses being run by the younger generation are found mostly in agriculture; mining; quarrying; fashion design; entertainment; local machine fabrication; and construction. On a larger scale, Nigeria's informal sector SMEs include business setups with formal and informal documentation, including sole proprietorships and partnerships. The agriculture and allied industries are found mostly in semi-urban cities and scattered among the different regions in the West and Eastern parts of the country. In differentiating between SDMEs in rural and urban centres, Etim and Daramola (2020, p. 16) noted that in rural centres, agriculture and allied industries, blacksmithing, weaving, and pottery are prevalent, while in urban centres of Lagos, Abuja, Kaduna, Port Harcourt, and Enugu, informal businesses such as trading, small-scale manufacturing and repairs, including upholstery, furniture making, woodworks, metal works, bakery, masonry, and printing are prevalent, These drives indicate the potential of SMEs as anti-poverty strategies in Africa. Despite these promising outcomes of SMEs in Africa, poverty is still a prevailing phenomenon.

Given these prospects and the challenges facing the growth and development of SMEs in Africa, governments and private entities must prioritise the entrepreneurial empowerment of citizens as an intensified strategy to reduce poverty levels. In this direction, training and skill acquisition drive would serve the purpose of empowering university undergraduates and graduates to expand employment opportunities. Entrepreneurial education should be mandatory in all tertiary institutions. This will complement the efforts of the various vocational centres and institutions (Zafar et al., 2018).

Training and skill acquisition opportunities would build the culture of investment and entrepreneurial culture in young school leavers who would be desirous of becoming self-employed upon the completion of their qualifications, rather than waiting for the scarce white-collar jobs. This will serve multiple purposes. One, training empowerment would guarantee a depletion in the unemployment market, and the search for the establishment of business enterprises that could cater for growth and development. Subsequent growth would impact the economy of society, thereby implicating positive national economy (Zafar et al., 2018). With the seemingly little contribution to the growth of the economy, poverty among the people would decrease, as the owners of the business are employers of labour, no matter how little. This humble beginning of SMEs is appropriate for Africa because of the communal nature of most African societies and the ready market in terms of meeting the needs of the people for the immediate environment. This informal sector of the economy of townships, locations, and semi-urban centres would provide the necessary relief for citizens and the government in coping with the exigencies of the provision of basic needs. Most transnational wholesale and retail SMEs, including those involved in services, are concentrated in big cities and urban centres. Thus, the grassroots development of SMEs through training and skill acquisition would go a long way in stimulating local economic growth in rural areas as well.

Given the aforementioned strategies, private sector involvement in this empowerment drive would boost the growth and sustainability of SMEs in Africa. For instance, in Nigeria, a humanitarian foundation has instituted a fund for the empowerment of women entrepreneurs (Adenubi, 2021). "The Flourish Africa Foundation with an endowment of N 1 billion funds (i.e., US $652,473.19) and promotes female-owned businesses in Africa" (Adenubi, 2021). The initiative was designed to support the "entrepreneurial activities of at least 2,500 female-owned businesses through funding and structured training over a period of five years" (Adenubi, 2021). The training component of this initiative is an appropriate approach for sustainable SMEs poised to contribute to poverty eradication through employment and product services. The OECD has noted the importance of training resources for the success of SMEs, especially in the area of management practices. SMEs in Africa are hampered by higher skills deficiencies because of weak training programmes for their employees (John-Akamelu & Muogbo, 2018; Kowo et al., 2019). This has created the problem of attracting and retaining staff with skills that are relevant to their operations.

Similarly, another private initiative, Africa House, has instituted another US $1 million startup to fund ten African enterprises in technical and business assistance (Soriyan, 2021). This startup funding links investors and provides a support ecosystem for entrepreneurs and innovators of African descent (Soriyan, 2021). The essence of the initiative is to empower the African continent to unlock the SME potential and transform the vast entrepreneurial opportunities into wealth for the benefit of citizens. The initiators of such schemes seek to unlock the prosperity potential of the rich African continent to solve the humanitarian crisis created by poverty by boosting the GDP (Soriyan, 2021). In the absence of firm commitment from the government, African countries need more of these initiatives from the private sector and philanthropists, individuals and organisations, as a new strategy of poverty eradication through SMEs.

The success of these private initiatives is predicated on an institutional commitment by the various government structures, especially in the area of statutory regulatory frameworks. In Nigeria, for instance, SMEs have become important avenues for employment and poverty alleviation for the majority of hitherto unemployed youth, even though with minimal income (Kowo et al., 2019). This is a common phenomenon in Africa. In South Africa, the Broad-Based Black Economic Empowerment (BEE) policy was designed to lift a majority of black citizens who were historically denied access to economic empowerment to develop their entrepreneurs' establishments through government funding (Rheede, 2020; Dreyer et al., 2021). In as much as these public initiatives are well designed, their implementation and success in the attainment of their desired objectives have been hampered by various factors.

For SMEs to be drivers of wealth creation, African governments need to address the scourge of infrastructural inadequacies and decay (Kowo et al., 2019). The survival of SMEs depends on the quality of infrastructural facilities such as electricity, water, roads, among others. Thus, African governments should address the pervasive infrastructural deficits to allow SMEs to operate successfully. As Kowo et al. (2019) have noted, a deplorable state and inadequate infrastructure would hamper the growth of SMEs and deny society of the benefits associated with thriving small businesses in African society.

Another friendly ecosystem that would stimulate the growth of SMEs is the tax regime. Taxation is a veritable source of income to the government (Tee et al., 2016; Zhang & Matiashviu, 2020). High taxes and in other places double or multiple taxations often scare away SMEs' business owners. Where the tax regime creates an unfriendly business ecosystem, SMEs would not thrive. If they operate, it would be within the limit of their financial obligations and capacity, thereby stifling their potential to create employment opportunities and wealth creation. While government should not shy away from its financial obligations to society, it would be more appropriate if concessions are given to SMEs, especially the local small-scale business as incentives for their growth and development.

The tax regime is a composite of the country's fiscal policy. Thus, in addressing the issues of the national economy, the government should factor the prospects of SMEs as part of the growth mechanisms with adequate priority (Kowo et al., 2019; Zhang & Matiashviu, 2020). In other words, government fiscal policies and programmes should ensure a consistent focus on the measures to stimulate the growth of SMEs within the ambit of the national economy. Government should be consistent and transparent in the implementation of the various policies and programmes designed to boost the growth of SMEs. African governments are not a deficit in terms of laudable policies and programmes designed for the growth of SMEs. Nevertheless, consistency in terms of implementation has remained a challenge. Such policies have become the conduit pipe for corruption.

Given the various challenges within the prospects of thriving SMEs in Africa as poverty eradication mechanisms, governments must prioritise policies and programmes that would ensure a sustainable approach to promote the development and growth of local businesses. As such the promotion of an entrepreneurial culture among the youth population, together with adequate skills and knowledge necessary to establish and run small businesses, would go a long way in addressing the scourge of poverty that has plagued the African continent. Africa has the requisite resources in terms of raw materials and human capital to create a hub of SMEs amidst its blossoming market advantage created by its vast population. Thus, government commitment is imperative for birthing this giant potential lying wasted.

Some of the mechanisms and strategies to address poverty through SMEs in Africa include:

- Access to finance:
  - Establishing and strengthening microfinance institutions and SME-focused banks to provide affordable credit and financial services to SMEs (Beck, 2007).
  - Promoting innovative financing models such as peer-to-peer lending and mobile banking (Morduch, 2018).

- Microfinance and microcredit: Providing access to small loans and financial services to SMEs and entrepreneurs in impoverished areas. Organisations like the Grameen Bank in Bangladesh have successfully implemented this model, and similar initiatives exist in Africa, such as Equity Bank in Kenya (Morduch, 2018).
- Venture capital and angel investors: Encouraging private investment in startups and SMEs. The African Fintech ecosystem has attracted significant venture capital, with companies like Flutterwave and Andela securing substantial funding (African Union, 2014).

• Capacity building and skills development:

- Providing training and technical assistance to SMEs to improve their management, marketing, and production skills (ILO, 2019).
- Supporting entrepreneurship education and vocational training programmes (UNDP, 2017).
- Entrepreneurship training: Offering training programmes and workshops to help entrepreneurs develop business skills. For instance, the Tony Elumelu Foundation Entrepreneurship Program in Nigeria provides training, mentorship, and funding to young entrepreneurs.
- Business incubators and accelerators: Supporting SMEs through mentorship and resources. The African Fintech Accelerator ecosystem, including MEST Africa and Y Combinator, is an example of successful accelerator programmes.

• Market access and export promotion:

- Trade facilitation: Promoting exports by simplifying customs procedures and reducing trade barriers. The East African Community (EAC) and the African Continental Free Trade Area (AfCFTA) are initiatives that aim to enhance intra-African trade and market access.
- Agritech platforms: Platforms like Twiga Foods in Kenya connect smallholder farmers to markets, helping them access a wider customer base.

- Strengthening regional economic communities and promoting cross-border cooperation to create larger markets and foster SME growth (African Union, 2019).
- Harmonising trade and investment policies among African countries to reduce barriers to SME expansion (AfDB, 2018).

• Infrastructure development:

- Energy and connectivity: Improving access to reliable electricity and internet connectivity, which is crucial for business operations. The Rural Electrification Agency (REA) in Nigeria is working to expand rural electrification.
- Transportation: Investing in infrastructure to reduce transportation costs and improve the movement of goods. The Northern Corridor Transit and Transport Coordination Authority (NCTTCA) in East Africa is an example of such efforts.
- Investing in physical infrastructure, such as transportation and energy, to reduce production costs and improve supply chain efficiency (African Development Bank, 2020).
- Expanding access to reliable internet and electricity in rural areas to support online businesses (World Bank, 2020).

• Supporting innovation and technology adoption:

- Technology hubs: Establishing technology hubs and innovation centres to foster entrepreneurship and innovation. The iHub in Kenya and the CcHub in Nigeria are renowned examples.
- Digital payment systems: Promoting the adoption of mobile money services like M-Pesa in Kenya, which have facilitated financial transactions and access to financial services for SMEs.
- Access to technology: Promoting technological innovation and providing SMEs with access to modern technology and research (Adeoti, 2020).
- Supporting technology hubs and incubators for startups and tech-focused SMEs (African Union, 2014).

• Regulatory reforms:

  - Streamlined business registration: Simplifying the process of registering and licencing SMEs. Rwanda is often cited as a success story for its efficient business registration system.
  - Tax incentives: Offering tax incentives to SMEs, such as reduced tax rates or tax holidays, to encourage growth and investment.
  - Implementing business-friendly policies and reducing bureaucratic hurdles for SMEs (Kayanula & Quartey, 2000).
  - Strengthening property rights and legal frameworks to protect SMEs and encourage investment (ECA, 2016).

- Access to markets and value chains:

  - Facilitating SMEs' access to regional and international markets through trade agreements and market linkages (UNCTAD, 2020), and encouraging e-commerce and digital platforms for SMEs to reach a wider customer base (World Bank, 2019).
  - Supplier development programmes: Encouraging SMEs to become part of larger value chains. For example, Unilever's Shakti programme in India involves rural women entrepreneurs in its distribution network.
  - Local sourcing initiatives: Encouraging larger companies to source goods and services from local SMEs, as seen in South Africa's Broad-Based Black Economic Empowerment (B-BBEE) policies.

- Social entrepreneurship and impact investing:

  - Impact investors: Attracting impact investors who focus on creating social and environmental benefits alongside financial returns. Examples include the Acumen Fund and Investisseurs & Partenaires (I&P).

- Gender-inclusive approaches:

  - Women entrepreneurship programs: Promoting women's entrepreneurship through targeted initiatives, like the African Women in Agribusiness Network (AWAN) and the She Leads Africa accelerator program (UNESCO, 2019)
  - Promoting women's participation in SMEs through targeted support programmes and gender-sensitive policies (UN Women, 2020)

- Ensuring that marginalised groups, including persons with disabilities, have equal access to resources and opportunities (ILO, 2020)

- Government policies and support:

  - SME-friendly policies: Enacting policies that promote SME growth, such as tax incentives, access to credit, and infrastructure development. The Kenyan government's "Big Four" agenda is one such example (AfDB, 2018).
  - Implementing business-friendly policies and reducing bureaucratic hurdles for SMEs (Kayanula & Quartey, 2000).
  - Strengthening property rights and legal frameworks to protect SMEs and encourage investment (ECA, 2016).

- Monitoring and evaluation:

  - Establishing robust data collection and evaluation systems to assess the impact of SME development programmes on poverty reduction (World Bank, 2021a).
  - Regularly reviewing and adjusting policies and interventions based on evidence and feedback (UNDP, 2021).

- Social protection programmes:

  - Introducing social safety nets, such as conditional cash transfers, to protect vulnerable populations and promote entrepreneurship (IFAD, 2018)
  - Implementing health care and education programmes to improve the well-being and productivity of SME owners and employees (UNESCO, 2019)

These mechanisms should be adapted to the specific context of each African country, as challenges and opportunities vary widely across the continent. Collaboration among governments, NGOs, and the private sector is essential to drive sustainable economic development and poverty reduction through SMEs in Africa.

3.7 Conclusion

This chapter discussed the connection between SMEs and poverty eradication, with specific reference to Africa. It also noted the need for a conducive business ecosystem, bolstered by friendly fiscal policies that would stimulate the birth and growth of small businesses. Central to this environmental imperative is the need to avert the incessant violent crises that have engulfed the continent. Poor public service delivery, mismanagement of national resources, and the pervasive culture of impunity have plunged African countries into the abyss of the crisis of governance. This sort of volatile political environment is not conducive for sustainable SMEs in a continent characterised by the fancy for foreign goods and services.

At every turn of political violence, local SMEs suffer greatly, thereby creating more avenues for poverty. For instance, the recent violence in some parts of South Africa has led to the loss of jobs among the African population, thereby pushing the already bloated job market into a crisis. Aside from this, small African businesses, especially in the informal sectors, have suffered irreparable losses that would take years to recover. For instance, over 50,000 informal sector traders lost their businesses, as they were vandalised and destroyed in the carnage (Nxumalo, 2021). Reports had it that "the damage to property and equipment amounted to R15 billion and more than 50 000 informal traders had been affected" (Nxumalo, 2021). In addition, no less than 40,000 other businesses were adversely affected, while others have lost the prospect of recovery. In this situation, no less than 150,000 people from these damaged businesses have to contend with the loss of their jobs, while more than 1.5 million people are not able to earn an income due to the unrest (Nxumalo, 2021). Aside from the loss to individuals and businesses, the national economy has its share of the loss. In the eThekwini area alone, an estimated R20 billion has been lost in terms of its GDP. The implication of this is that a dwindled government economy is a catalyst for poverty.

References

Abisuga-Oyekunle, O. A., Patra, S. K., & Muchie, M. (2020). SMEs in Sustainable Development: Their Role in Poverty Reduction and Employment Generation in Sub-Saharan Africa. *African Journal of Science, Technology, Innovation and Development, 12*(4), 405–419. https://doi.org/10.1080/20421338.2019.1656428

Abor, J., & Quartey, P. (2010). Issues in SME Development in Ghana and South Africa. *International Research Journal of Finance and Economics, 39*, 218–228.

Adenubi, D. (2021). Alakija Launches N1bn Fund to Promote Female Entrepreneurship. *The Punch*, July 16. https://punchng.com/alakija-launches-n1bn-fund-to-promote-female-entrepreneurship/

Adeoti, J. O. (2020). Small and Medium-Sized Enterprises (SMEs) and Innovation in Developing Countries: Evidence from Nigeria. *Sustainability, 12*(4), 1572.

AfDB. (2018). African Economic Outlook 2018.

African Development Bank. (2020). African Economic Outlook 2020.

African Development Bank Group. (2020). African Economic Outlook 2020.

African Development Bank Group. (2021). Affirmative Finance Action for Women in Africa (AFAWA).

African Union. (2014). Agenda 2063: The Africa We Want.

African Union. (2019). African Continental Free Trade Area Agreement.

Ali, S., Rashid, H., & Khan, M. A. (2014). The Role of Small and Medium Enterprises and Poverty in Pakistan: An Empirical Analysis. Theoretical and Applied. *Economics, 21*(4), 67–80.

Alkire, S., & Foster, J. (2011). Understandings and Misunderstandings of Multidimensional Poverty Measurement. *Journal of Economic Inequality, 9*, 289–314. https://data.worldbank.org/indicator/SI.POV.NAHC?view=map&year_high_desc=true. https://doi.org/10.1007/s10888-011-9181-4

Beck, T. (2007). *Financing Constraints of SMEs in Developing Countries: Evidence, Determinants, and Solutions.* World Bank Policy Research Working Paper, 4373.

Cario, C. T. (2019). Revisiting the Sociological Theories of Poverty: Conceptualizing a Framework for Rural Poverty in the Philippines. *Transatlantic Journal of Rural Research, 1*(1), 34–52.

Civil Society Legislative Advocacy (CISLAC). (2019). Expanding the Tax Base in the Informal Sector in Nigeria. https://maketaxfair.net/policy-brief-on-expanding-the-tax-base-in-the-nigerian-informal-sector/

Department of Statistics, Republic of South Africa. (2020, July 7). More than 60% of South African Children are Poor. http://www.statssa.gov.za/?p=13438

Doran, J., McCarthy, N., & O'Connor, M. (2018). The Role of Entrepreneurship in Stimulating Economic Growth in Developed and Developing Countries. *Cogent Economics & Finance, 6*(1). https://doi.org/10.1080/23322039.2018.1442093

Dorling, D. (2019). *Inequality and the 1%* (Paperback Edition). Verso Books

Dreyer, J. A., Viviers, S., & Mans-Kemp, N. (2021). Reflecting on Compliance with Broad-Based Black Economic Empowerment Codes of Good Practice: Trends and Suggestions. *South African Journal of Business Management, 52*(1), 1945–1963.

ECA. (2016). Economic Report on Africa 2016: Greening Africa's Industrialization.

Etim, E., & Daramola, O. (2020). The Informal Sector and Economic Growth of South Africa and Nigeria: A Comparative Systematic Review. *Journal of Open Innovation, Technology and Market Complexity, 6*(4), 134.

Fagbadebo, O. (2019). Corruption, and the Challenge of Accountability in the Post-Colonial African States: A Discourse. *Journal of African Union Studies, 8*(1), 9–32. https://doi.org/10.31920/2050-4306/2019/v8n1a1

Fagbadebo, O. M., & Dorasamy, N. (2021). Political Leadership, Corruption, and the Crisis of Governance in Africa: A Discourse. *African Renaissance, 18*(1), 27–52.

Fatoki, O. (2014). The Causes of the Failure of New Small and Medium Enterprises in South Africa. *Mediterranean Journal of Social Sciences, 5*(20), 922–927.

Henri, P. O. A. (2019). Natural Resources Curse: A Reality in Africa. *Resources Policy, 63.* https://doi.org/10.1016/j.resourpol.2019.101406; https://datatopics.worldbank.org/world-development-indicators/stories/societal-poverty-a-global-measure-of-relative-poverty.html; https://guardian.ng/business-services/africa-house-empowers-10-startups-with-1m-entrepreneurial-support/; https://www.borgenmagazine.com/the-poverty-capital-of-the-world-nigeria/; https://www.developmentaid.org/#!/news-stream/post/84943/highest-poverty-rates-in-africa; https://www.iol.co.za/mercury/news/kzn-on-high-alert-amid-new-threat-to-shut-down-province; https://www.statista.com/statistics/1228553/extreme-poverty-as-share-of-global-population-in-africa-by-country/

Human, J. H. (2021). *African Countries Continue to Have the Highest Poverty Rates in the World.* Development Aid News Stream, February 25.

IFAD. (2018). Rural Development Report 2019: Creating Opportunities for Rural Youth.

Imiera, P. P. (2020). The Corruption Race in Africa: Nigeria versus South Africa, Who Cleans the Mess First? *De Jure, 53*, 70–89.

International Labour Organization (ILO). (2015). SMEs and Poverty Reduction: An Overview of Current Evidence.

International Labour Organization (ILO). (2019). Small and Medium-Sized Enterprises for Decent and Productive Employment Creation.

International Labour Organization (ILO). (2020). Disability-Inclusive Development in Africa.

John-Akamelu, C. R., & Muogbo, U. S. (2018). Role of Small & Medium Enterprises in Poverty Eradication in Nigeria. *European Journal of Research and Reflection in Management Sciences, 6*(2), 33–49.

Kayanula, D., & Quartey, P. (2000). *The Structure of the SME Sector in Ghana: An Empirical Analysis.* African Economic Research Consortium.

Kowo, S. A., Adenuga, O. A. O., & Sabitu, O. (2019). The Role of SMEs Development on Poverty Alleviation in Nigeria. *Insights into Regional Development, 1*(3), 214–226.

Manzoor, F., Wei, L., Nurunnabi, M., & Abdul Subhan, Q. (2019). Role of SME in Poverty Alleviation in SAARC Region via Panel Data Analysis. *Sustainability, 11*(22), 6480. MDPI AG. https://doi.org/10.3390/su11226480

Manzoor, F., Wei, L., & Sahito, N. (2021). The Role of SMEs in Rural Development: Access of SMEs to Finance as a Mediator. *PLoS ONE, 16*(3), e0247598. https://doi.org/10.1371/journal.pone.0247598

Maziriri, E. T., & Chivandi, A. (2020). Modelling Key Predictors That Stimulate the Entrepreneurial Performance of Small and Medium-Sized Enterprises (SMEs) and Poverty Reduction: Perspectives from SME Managers in an Emerging Economy. *Acta Commercii, 20*(1), 763–773.

Medina, L., Jonelis, A., & Cangul, M. (2017). *The Informal Economy in Sub-Saharan Africa: Size and Determinants.* IMF Working Paper, WP/17/156; Washington, DC: International Monetary Fund (IMF).

Morduch, J. (2018). The Microfinance Schism: Theories and Evidence. *Annual Review of Economics, 10*, 173–196.

Mulwa, R., & Mariara, J. (2016). *Natural Resource Curse in Africa: Dutch Disease and Institutional Explanations.* AGRODEP Working Paper 0029. African Growth and Development Policy.

Myers, K. (2018). *The Top 9 Causes of Global Poverty.* Relief Web, May 3. https://reliefweb.int/report/world/top-9-causes-global-poverty

Nursini, N. (2020). Micro, Small, and Medium Enterprises (MSMEs) and Poverty Reduction: Empirical Evidence from Indonesia. *Development Studies Research, 7*(1), 153–166. https://doi.org/10.1080/21665095.2020.1823238

Nxumalo, S. (2021). KZN on High Alert amid New Threat to Shut Down Province. *IOL*, July 19.

OECD. (2017). *Enhancing the Contributions of SMEs in a Global and Digitalised Economy.* Meeting of the OECD Council at Ministerial Level Paris, 7–8 June 2017. https://www.oecd.org/industry/C-MIN-2017-8-EN.pdf

Omozusi, S. (2020). Trust on the Use of Trade Credit: A Major Hindrance to the Growth of MSMEs. *Journal of Finance, Accounting and Management, 11*(1), 1–11.

Panchal, K. (2020). The Poverty Capital of the World: NIGERIA. *Burgen Magazine*, August 28.

Prydz, E. B., & Jolliffe, D. (2019). Societal Poverty: A Global Measure of Relative Poverty. *The World Bank*, Sep 11.

Quartey, P., Turkson, E., Abor, J. Y., & Iddrisu, A. M. (2017). Financing the Growth of SMEs in Africa: What are the Constraints to SME Financing within ECOWAS? *Review of Development Finance, 7*(1), 18–28.

Rheede, J. V. (2020). The Broad-Based Black Economic Empowerment Act 53 of 2003 and the Ways in Which the Commission of Fronting Practices Affects the Achievement of Its Objective. *African Journal of Democracy and Governance, 7*(1), 101–118.

Ridge, T., & Wright, S. (2008). Introduction. In T. Ridge & S. Wright (Eds.), *Understanding Inequality, Poverty and Wealth: Policies and Prospects.* Policy Press.

Rotar, L. J., Pamić, R. K., & Bojnec, S. (2019). Contributions of Small and Medium Enterprises to Employment in the European Union Countries. *Economic Research, 32*(1), 3302–3314. https://doi.org/10.1080/1331677X.2019.1658532

Saleh, M. (2021). Extreme Poverty as Share of Global Population in Africa 2021, by Country.

Shildrick, T., & Rucell, J. (2015). *Sociological Perspectives on Poverty.* Joseph Rowntree Foundation Report. www.jrf.org

Soriyan, O. (2021). Africa House Empowers 10 Startups with $1M Entrepreneurial Support. *The Guardian*, July 18.

Tee, E., Boadi, L., & Opoku, R. (2016). The Effect of Tax Payment on the Performance of SMEs: The Case of Selected SMEs in Ga West Municipal Assembly. *European Journal of Business and Management, 8*(20), 119–125.

The World Bank. (2021). The World Bank in Africa. https://www.worldbank.org/en/region/afr/overview

Transparency International. (2019). Where are the Africa's Billions? *Transparency International*, July 11. https://www.transparency.org/en/news/where-are-africas-billions?utm_source=newsletter&utm_medium=email&utm_campaign=weekly-16-07-2021

Transparency International. (2021). Corruption Perceptions Index 2020. https://www.transparency.org/en/cpi/2020/index/nzl

UN Women. (2020). Progress of the World's Women 2019-2020: Families in a Changing World.

UNCTAD. (2020). Economic Development in Africa Report 2020: Tackling Illicit Financial Flows for Sustainable Development in Africa.

UNDP. (2017). Entrepreneurship and Innovation for African Development.

UNDP. (2021). Human Development Report 2020: The Next Frontier, Human Development and the Anthropocene.

UNESCO. (2019). Education for Sustainable Development Goals: Learning Objectives.

United Nations Economic Commission for Africa (UNECA). (2021a). Promoting Agribusiness SMEs for Inclusive and Sustainable Development in Africa

United Nations Economic Commission for Africa (UNECA). (2021b, March 2). 514 Million Africans Risk Falling Below the Extreme Poverty Line in 2021 Due to COVID-19. https://www.uneca.org/stories/514-million-africans-risk-falling-below-extreme-poverty-line-in-2021-due-to-covid-19

Vandenberg, P. (2006). *Poverty Reduction through Small Enterprises Emerging Consensus, Unresolved Issues and ILO Activities.* SEED Working Paper No. 75. Geneva: International Labour Organisation.

World Bank. (2019). Digital Entrepreneurship in Africa.
World Bank. (2020). World Development Report 2020: Trading for Development in the Age of Global Value Chains.
World Bank. (2021a). Poverty Headcount Ratio at National Poverty Lines (% of Population).
World Bank Group. (2020). *Poverty and Shared Prosperity 2020: Reversals of Fortune*. International Bank for Reconstruction and Development / The World Bank.
World Data Lab. (2021). World Poverty Clock. https://worldpoverty.io/map
Yoshino, N., & Taghizadeh-Hesary, F. (2016). *Major Challenges Facing Small and Medium-sized Enterprises in Asia and Solutions for Mitigating Them*. ADBI.
Zafar, M., Waqas, M., & Butt, M. N. (2018). The Role of Small and Medium Enterprises on Poverty Reduction in Developing Country: A Case of Pakistan. *Pakistan Business Review, 20*(3), 703–713.
Zhang, M., & Matiashviu, T. (2020). Tax Authorities Have a Role to Play in Helping SMEs Weather the COVID-19 Crisis. *The World Bank*, October 26. https://blogs.worldbank.org/psd/tax-authorities-have-role-play-helping-smes-weather-covid-19-crisis

CHAPTER 4

SMEs and Job Creation

Nirmala Dorasamy and Eustache Tanzala Kikasu

4.1 Introduction

Small and Medium-sized Enterprises (SMEs) play a crucial role in job creation and economic development in Africa. They are considered the backbone of many African economies due to their ability to generate employment opportunities and promote inclusive growth. SMEs are substantial job creators in Africa. They offer employment opportunities for a large segment of the population, particularly in sectors like agriculture, manufacturing, and services (African Development Bank, 2018). SMEs contribute significantly to GDP and employment. For example, in Sub-Saharan Africa, SMEs make up about 90% of all businesses (African Development Bank, 2018).

The original version of the chapter has been revised. A correction to this chapter can be found at https://doi.org/10.1007/978-3-031-69103-4_11

N. Dorasamy (✉)
Faculty of Management Sciences, Durban University of Technology, Durban, South Africa
e-mail: nirmala@dut.ac.za

E. T. Kikasu
Dept of Public Management and Economics, Durban University of Technology, Durban, South Africa

G. Mugano, N. Dorasamy, *SMEs Perspective in Africa*,
https://doi.org/10.1007/978-3-031-69103-4_4

One of the challenges facing most African countries is unemployment. In 2019, there were 34 million unemployed people in Africa (ILO, 2020). The continent's economic environment, according to the International Labour Organization (ILO) (2020), did not present a favourable outlook capable of stimulating the labour market. With an envisaged increase in growth rate, African economies' "reliance on low value-added sectors characterized by poor pay and a dependence on domestic demand" does not provide the necessary incentives for the labour market (ILO, 2020: 1). The continent's per capita incomes have remained low over the years, and its growth rates volatile. The future forecast of improved growth rate and a clement environment for accelerated job creation is very gloomy as well.

The ILO has identified several factors which impacted Africa's labour market over the years. Africa has high rates of labour force participation, which stood at 63.1% in 2019. This was higher than the global average of 60.1% (ILO, 2020). With more jobless graduates, formal employment opportunities in the public and private sectors continues to shrink while people are forced to take up employment in the informal sector. Aside from this, there is a decline in employment share among the core sectors. The agriculture sector declined from 53.5% in 2011 to 50.5% in 2020, while the share of the service sector increased from 34% in 2011 to 36.1% in 2019 (ILO, 2020). The employment share of the industrial sector has been on a steady decline over the years.

The disparity in sectorial employment in Africa is another factor. In East, Central, and West Africa, agriculture has remained the main source of most employment opportunities, while Southern African countries depend more on service-sector employment; the industry sector is the source of employment in North Africa (ILO, 2020). The informal sector employment has remained high with 40.2% in Southern Africa, while Central, Eastern, and Western Africa had more than 90% informal sector employment (ILO 2020).

More so, there are more women in the informal sector employment, representing 80%. Most of the informal employment opportunities are in the agriculture sector. This development implies that most African citizens would continue to roam the streets, by populating the unemployment market. Instructively, African governments, especially in the Sub-Saharan region, where the industry sector is lagging in employment opportunities, should, as a matter of urgency, follow the path of effective promotion of the Small and Medium Enterprises (SMEs) to reduce dependency on the larger goods and services employment sectors.

This chapter discusses various mechanisms that could accelerate the development of SMEs to make the sector a hub of employment opportunities. The first section provides a conceptual analysis of SMEs. This is followed by a discussion on the various types of SMEs. The third section discusses the nexus between SMEs and job creation, while the fourth section interrogates how SMEs could boost employment opportunities in Africa. Section five concludes with recommendations.

4.2 SMEs in a National Economy

As far back as 1975, Auciello (1975) noted that there were more than 75 countries with different definitions of SMEs. Thus, the absence of a common definition of SMEs is a manifestation of the diverse socio-economic environment that characterises modern society. Modern societies have demonstrated different industrial capabilities, which have defined the size of their business, the nature of their assets, and the varieties of their products. This variety dictates the description of the various economic outlets that shape economic growth and development. Businesses with 250 employees are regarded as SMEs in Germany, while Belgium defines its SME as any business outfit that employs less than 100 people (Muriithi, 2017). In Canada and the United States, any business venture with less than 500 employees is an SME, while small businesses are enterprises with less than 100 employees (USITC, 2010).

The Organisation of Economic Cooperation and Development (OECD) provided a statistical description of SMEs as firms with a maximum of 249 employees (OECD, 2017). In this regard, SMEs are categorised as micro, small, and medium businesses. An SME is micro when it comprises 1 to 9 persons as employees, a small SME employs 10 to 49, and a medium SME employs between 50 and 249 persons (OECD, 2017). This stratification is a general benchmark, even though countries across the globe have different conventions to describe the scope and limits of SMEs.

Other countries do have their categories of SMEs. South Africa, for instance, acknowledges SMEs "as productive drivers of inclusive economic growth and development" globally, and as such, is committed to harnessing the benefits, especially in the area of employment opportunities (The Banking Association of South Africa, n.d.). The National Small Business Amendment Act 2003, Act No. 26, 2003 defines SMEs in South Africa in categories, within specific industry sectors (South Africa, 2003). Business enterprises with employees' turnover of 100 are regarded as a medium SME, while those with 50, 10, and 5 employees' turnover are categorised as small, very small, and micro-SMEs, respectively. Each of these categories has corresponding total financial and asset value, respectively. The defining features and criteria of SMEs run through the various sectors of the country's economy, as shown for South Africa in Table 4.1. The

Table 4.1 Categories of SMEs in South Africa

Sector or subsector in accordance with the Standard Industrial Classification	*Size of class*	*The total turnover of the equivalent of paid employees*	*Total turnover*	*Total gross asset value (fixed property excluded)*
Agriculture	Medium	100	R5 million	R5 million
	Small	50	R3 million	R3 million
	Very small	10	R0.50 million	R0.50 million
	Micro	5	R0.20 million	R0.10 million
Mining and quarrying	Medium	200	R39 million	R23 million
	Small	50	R10 million	R6 million
	Very small	20	R4 million	R2 million
	Micro	5	R0.20 million	R0.10 million
Manufacturing	Medium	200	R51 million	R19 million
	Small	50	R13 million	R5 million
	Very small	20	R5 million	R2 million
	Micro	5	R0.20 million	R0.10 million
Electricity, gas, and water	Medium	200	R51 million	R19 million
	Small	50	R13 million	R5 million
	Very small	20	R5 million	R1.90 million
	Micro	5	R0.20 million	R0.10 million
Construction	Medium	200	R26 million	R5 million
	Small	50	R6 million	R1 million
	Very small	20	R3 million	R0.50 million
	Micro	5	R0.20 million	R0.10 million
Retail and motor trade and repair services	Medium	200	R39 million	R6 million
	Small	50	R19 million	R3 million
	Very small	20	R4 million	R0.60 million
	Micro	5	R0.20 million	R0.10 million
Wholesale trade, commercial agents, and allied services	Medium	200	R64 million	R10 million
	Small	50	R32 million	R5 million
	Very small	20	R6 million	R0.60 million
	Micro	5	R0.20 million	R0.10 million
Catering, accommodation, and other trade	Medium	200	R13 million	R3 million
	Small	50	R6 million	R1 million

(*continued*)

Table 4.1 (continued)

Sector or subsector in accordance with the Standard Industrial Classification	*Size of class*	*The total turnover of the equivalent of paid employees*	*Total turnover*	*Total gross asset value (fixed property excluded)*
	Very small	20	R5.10 million	R1.90 million
	Micro	5	R0.20 million	R0.10 million
Transport, storage, and communications	Medium	200	R26 million	R6 million
	Small	50	R13 million	R3 million
	Very small	20	R3 million	R0.60 million
	Micro	5	R0.20 million	R0.10 million
Finance and business services	Medium	200	R26 million	R5 million
	Small	50	R3 million	R3 million
	Very small	20	R3 million	R0.50 million
	Micro	5	R0.20 million	R0.10 million
Community, social, and personal services	Medium	200	R13 million	R6 million
	Small	50	R6 million	R3 million
	Very small	20	R1 million	R0.60 million
	Micro	5	R0.20 million	R0.10 million

Source: National Small Business Amendment Act. 2003, Act No. 26, 2003

categorisation provides the opportunity for different people to undertake business ventures within the limit of their financial means.

This implies that South Africa categorises SMEs in terms of their forms, inclusive of the formally registered business enterprises and the informal wholesale and retail business outlets. According to Dhanah (2016), the various categories of SMEs can play an important role as key drivers of economic growth, innovation, job creation and contribute significantly to national GDP. Therefore, governments in their different structures (national or local) will have to create an enabling environment for SMEs' sustainable development by putting in place attractive policies, strategies, and programmes that stimulate small business development. For example, in South Africa, the principal legislative framework, National Small Business Act. No 102 of 1996, made provisions for the establishment of structures for the control of SMEs in South Africa. It established the National Small Business Council and the Ntsika Enterprise Promotion Agency as pillars of support for small business enterprises in the country. This comprehensive definition of SMEs in South Africa indicates the commitment of the government to harness the potential of SMEs as major drivers of economic growth and job creation. More so, SMEs in South Africa constitute 91% of its over 3 million formal and informal business outfits, with a 7.3 million workforce, which is 60% of the country's employment pool, and has remained a formidable source of employment (OECD, 2020).

Hence, the South African government like other African governments considers SMEs as important contributors to the country's economic growth and as drivers of employment. The recognition of the informal business outlets has boosted the development of small shops in locations and townships, including street vendors. These outlets have created enormous employment opportunities for citizens.

Thus, SMEs are substantial job creators in Africa. They offer employment opportunities for a large segment of the population, particularly in sectors like agriculture, manufacturing, and services (African Development Bank, 2018).

4.3 Employment Creation Opportunities Through Various Types of SMEs

There are different types and categories of SMEs. Juergensen et al. (2020) identified three types of SMEs. These are stand-alone, specialist-supplier, and knowledge-based, which are mostly found in the manufacturing industry. The stand-alone SMEs are producers of final goods, with a distinct brand, for consumers and industrial markets. Although they often "struggle to achieve economies of scale, and many of them seek to differentiate themselves, by operating in (global) niches," they lack the capacity to compete with their counterparts with larger manufacturing outlets (Juergensen et al., 2020, 501). They have restricted supply capacity, especially during an unprecedented change in the economic environment. They operate often in industries with elastic demand. Thus, when consumers of their products are faced with certain constraints like uncertainties in employment and financial predicaments, their demand also declines (Juergensen et al., 2020). In other words, stand-alone SMEs that focused on consumers are vulnerable to the consequences of operational environments occasioned by socio-economic forces.

Nevertheless, those servicing the industrial markets have an edge as they are susceptible to benefiting "from their niche position, as they face few substitutes and, therefore, customers may be reliant on them," depending on the severity of the shock in the economic environment (Juergensen et al., 2020, 502). The implication here is that any disruption in the production process in the industry would limit their operational capacity. The specialist-supplier SMEs are entities common in oligopolistic economies, serving as the providers of intermediate goods and services for larger manufacturing firms (Juergensen et al., 2020). They are characterised by the production of service goods such as automobile spare parts, as well as other composite products necessary or the complete functioning of larger manufacturing firms. They operate either as the sole supplier of goods or through a network of inter-dependent entities operating in cooperation for a complete production process of larger manufacturing firms. This category of SMEs is faced with supply and demand factors. Those operating as sole suppliers for a specific entity are faced with the problem of declining productivity when the larger manufacturing firms face operational challenges. In other words, if the larger operation ceases production, the SMEs also will stop production because their continuity is dependent on the sustainability of the larger firms. If the larger firm goes under, the specialist-supplier SME will cease operation (Narula, 2019; Speldekamp et al., 2020 and Shih, 2020). They are vulnerable to external shocks with little or no capacity to survive major national economic failures.

The knowledge-based SMEs "generally develop emerging, pre-paradigmatic technologies, supplying specialized knowledge-based assets to other firms or consumer Markets" (Juergensen et al., 2020: 501). This category of SMEs provides technical services as subject matter experts (ITU, 2016). The SMEs are found mostly in the telecommunication industry, biotechnology, and medical research, among others, collaborating with multinational organisations, providing technical assistance in their setup. These SMEs provide the major impetus for job creation across the globe, given the rapid expansion and deployment of information and communication technology into all facets of societal development. They constitute more than 95% of all businesses and provide two-thirds of formal employment across the globe (ITU, 2016). They also account for about 70% of the gross domestic product (GDP) in the global economy. These three categories of SMEs characterise the global economy, operating at different levels and creating different impacts on society in terms of employment. They are also susceptible to the strains of the global environment as well as the developments in national economies.

Thus, the success and impacts of these SMEs in national economies depend largely on the nature and structure of each society, especially infrastructural development. In Africa, the structural and economic foundations necessary for sustainable growth and development of SMEs are very weak (Quartey et al., 2017; Tsatsenko, 2020). In terms of sound economic policies and the political will to accomplish their implementation, bureaucratic inertia often stifles the propensity towards the proper functioning of small business enterprises. Hence, prospective entrepreneurs often resort to informal structural platforms to accomplish their objectives in the absence of effective official responses in a national economy characterised by policy instability. Thus, fluctuating national economic growth, with its effects on the GDP, has its effects on the sustainability of SMEs in Africa (Tsatsenko, 2020). A thriving SME would serve the national economy more in terms of contributing to the national GDP as well as providing employment opportunities in society.

4.4 SMEs and Job Creation

Many countries including South Africa have seen SMEs emerging as a tool to fight unemployment and poverty. Accordingly, the expansion of this sector can boost employment and reduce poverty. Dhanah (2016) indicated that SMEs are more labour-intensive than large firms and thus the growth of the SMEs could result in higher levels of employment, with considerable implications for economic policies and the nation's ability to create jobs. Al-Haddad (2019) and Dhanah (2016) emphasised that the promotion and development of SMEs was considered by the World Bank and other multilateral agencies as a key policy in the process of poverty reduction, social growth, and economic development. In other words, the ability of the state to provide policies that promote infrastructural development is one of the significant factors contributing to the development of SMEs and creation of jobs.

One pivotal infrastructural development that could accelerate job creation prospects is the ICT environment. The explosion of ICT in the digital economy in the last years has bolstered the mode of operation of organisations across the globe. Indeed, ICT and its revolution in the digital economy have promoted globalisation and encouraged global interconnectedness in business activities (ITU, 2016). This has rendered SMEs to occupy the position as drivers of national economic growth. While knowledge-based SMEs have thrived in this venture, it has further increased the skills of youth who have explored ICT, thereby creating employment opportunities in different forms. Globally, SMEs have proven to be a source of employment. Developed economies have leveraged the opportunities of job creation provided by SMEs and the consequential impact on their economic growth (Schreyer, 1996; OECD, 2017). SMEs are a critical stakeholder component and pivotal to national economic growth. They are avenues for income generation, increase in economic outputs, and providing avenues for individuals in society to access employment opportunities. In Europe, SMEs are the backbone of the economy and employment drive (European Commission, 2017, 2019).

The annual SMEs' employment growth in Europe stood at 20% (European Commission, 2019). Constant innovative strategies and commitment to the implementation of policies designed for the stability of SMEs contributed immensely to this feat. Innovative strategies that characterise SMEs in Europe represent the causal driver for the leap growth in employment. While this applies to the growth of SMEs, it has been noted that SMEs with declining employment were less likely to innovate (European Commission, 2019). However, there have been enough evidence from several developed and developing countries including China and Pakistan that support the theory that investing in SMEs development could stimulate economic growth and thus reduce the unemployment rate. Unfortunately, South Africa's scenario looks quite different, as in recent years, while the number of SMEs has been on the rise, unemployment has also been on the rise simultaneously (Dhanah, 2016).

But, in general, there is commitment that SMEs are innovative and a generator/locomotive of jobs creation. Thus, the more innovative the SMEs, the more likely they will experience employment growth. For example, the innovative strategies and gains in Europe were occasioned by the robust competitiveness and innovation in the manufacturing SMEs (Juergensen et al., 2020). Each SME can develop the capacity to innovate, to expand, and to grow. Consequently, expansion drives would generate more opportunities for new skills, thereby providing a network of employment portfolios for citizens. Even though they struggle for more profits in a competitive business environment, the size, nature, and structure often adapt to external challenges. Manufacturing SMEs are more likely to generate more employment opportunities because of their operational structures.

Globally, SMEs are the major avenues for job creation. Studies have shown that more than 80% of the global workforce is employed by SMEs (Kamunge et al., 2014; ITU, 2016; ILO, 2019a). The International

Labour Organisation (ILO, 2015, 2019a) described SMEs as engines of global development, with a 70% contribution to the global GDP. SMEs in the service industry, which is more prevalent in Southern African countries, account for over 60% of the GDP of the world's developed economies (ILO, 2019a). In the Middle East and North African (MENA) regions, SMEs are the backbones of employment opportunities. SMEs in the MENA region constitute over 62% of the total workforce in the formal sector (Baduel et al., 2019). They also account for larger sales, thereby constituting a major source of economic growth.

Nevertheless, the Arab Spring, as well as other structural factors, impacted negatively on operations of the SMEs, thereby reducing their capacity for rapid employment growth. SMEs as a potential source of employment are incapacitated by their level of operation and profitability. Thus, "the capacity of SMMEs to amass profits, grow, employ and retain employees is inextricably linked to their ability to resist a variety of formidable challenges they encounter in the internal and external environment such as finance, training and skills, regulations and 'unsustainable' competition" (Mutyenyoka & Madzivhandila, 2014: 72). SMEs in most African states operate under financial and structural pressure, which constrains their employment generation potentials.

SMEs are a significant source of employment in Africa. Governments across Africa are recognising the importance of SMEs and implementing policies and programmes to support their growth and job creation efforts.

They are often labour-intensive and can quickly adapt to market demands, leading to the creation of jobs at a faster rate than larger corporations. Some of the contributions to support job creation include:

- Source for entrepreneurial opportunities for young people and addressing the youth unemployment challenge in Africa (African Development Bank, 2018).
- The growth of SMEs contributes to overall economic development by increasing income levels, improving living standards, and reducing poverty (Masurel et al., 2018).
- Supportive policies and financial inclusion initiatives to help SMEs to thrive (World Bank, 2019).
  - Special projects to support women entrepreneurs, through opportunities for them to participate in the workforce, promoting gender equality and economic empowerment (International Finance Corporation, 2019).

- Various international organisations' initiatives to support SME development and job creation, such as the African Union's Agenda 2063 which emphasises the role of SMEs in driving economic transformation and job creation (African Union, 2015).
- Trade policies, regional integration efforts, and infrastructure development to facilitate market access for SMEs (African Union, 2015)
- Initiatives such as microfinance institutions and fintech innovations are helping SMEs secure funding to expand their businesses and create more jobs (International Finance Corporation, 2019).

4.5 Challenges Confronting SMEs in Africa

Generally, Al-Haddad (2019), Dhanah (2016) and the Dalberg Report (2011) ascribed various factors limiting small business growth and development. Table 4.2 illustrates some of these factors/challenges, which are confronting the growth and development of SMEs in Africa, ultimately affecting them as a potential source of employment creation.

In line with Table 4.2, many other studies have shown that SMEs are vulnerable to the shocks arising from inclement socio-economic and political environments (Cant, 2012; Yoshino & Taghizadeh-Hesary, 2016; Baduel et al., 2019; Gamage & Kumara, 2019). Baduel et al. (2019) have pointed out how the 2010/2011 political instability in the MENA region adversely affected and redefined the operations of the SMEs in terms of employment. According to them, the Arab Spring was a reaction to the challenge of regulatory and administrative laxities associated with the operation of SMEs in Tunisia. The region's economic model, which was "inward-looking and state-centric," had created "high unemployment in the region" (Baduel et al., 2019: 4). This model affected the growth of private enterprises, especially the informal sector, thereby stifling their growth rate and capacity. Thus, the business and political environment affected the operations of the SMEs adversely.

SMEs are also faced with innovative and competitive challenges in a globalised world. To compete with other enterprises on the world stage with similar products would require more capital resources, skills, and innovative capabilities (Gamage & Kumara, 2019). The globalisation strategies of SMEs bolstered by the deployment of ICT are challenging, especially in developing countries, where basic supporting infrastructural facilities are yet to be developed fully or lacking in some states. Given this,

Table 4.2 Challenges confronting SMEs development in Africa

- **Cash management**: Proper management of cash flows has been considered as one of the critical reasons why small businesses fail.
- **Financial resources:** More financial resources need to get invested for a while, before any benefits can be realised by the business owner.
- **The dominance by the owner over employees**: The dominance by the owner over employees instead of taking a more leadership role, lack of management depth, and also poor governance structures have shown to be detrimental to their survival. Additionally, increased gearing, overtrading, and employing poor financial information by owners also have debilitating effects.
- **Poor budgeting and controls**: Poor budgeting, lack of staff training, weak personnel relations, poor stock control, and bad customer relations contribute to why SMEs are failing.
- **Crime:** Crime is amongst the reasons why small businesses fail. This serious problem of theft can befall a business from any source, be it from a professional criminal, a customer, a supplier, or an employee. Internal crime within a small business is attributed to the following:

Hiring personnel without a careful background check or employment references

- Failure to enforce strict, uniform rules for even minor infractions
- Failure to establish a climate of trust, confidence, and respect for employees, as well as incentives for outstanding and honest performance
- Failure to apply techniques that will thwart opportunities for an employee to steal and,
- Cost-cutting measures

- **Lack of training:** Lack of training and lack of acquired foreign capital to purchase machinery and small parts. Skills and funding are an impediment to growth in small businesses. Training alone cannot be adequate for success, as the lack of financial resources, lack of access to markets, lack of support services, and low literacy levels are impediments to small business growth.
- **Government officials' harassment:** Government officials' harassment in order to extort money from businesses is another challenge faced by small businesses in Africa.
- **Poor infrastructure**: In most African countries, poor infrastructure such as roads, water supply, electricity supply, and telecommunication systems result in increased overheads for businesses as they now have to spend more to obtain such facilities on their own.
- **Implementation of existing policy:** Policy implementation can cause challenges to small businesses because of the constant changes that come along with governmental administration changes and inter-governmental conflicts.
- **Poor management of skills**: Poor management skills such as poor record keeping, financial management, too little effort to market the business, poor planning, poor pricing practices, poor human resource management, and the business owner's inability to adapt to the changing demands of a business are also amongst barriers that fail small businesses.
- **Shortage of skilled labour** is an impediment to SMEs' sustainable development. This situation occurs when the demand for specific skills (mostly technical skills) exceeds supply. This situation results in skills shortages and usually such technically skilled individuals claim high salaries which become a challenge for small businesses to afford. In other words, acquiring technically skilled or the right skilled individuals in the appropriate position (job) can create a competitive advantage, which is something that may have a direct bearing to the productivity of the SMEs. This implies that employees' skills level could have a direct bearing on the efficiency and effectiveness of SMEs, given that this could create multiplier effects as it will affect parameters such as turnaround time, sales, profit margins, and ultimately the viability of doing business. To the contrary, the lack or shortage of skilled labour may have a negative impact on business performance. For example, in the past six years, in South Africa, the demand for engineers and skilled trade workers has been at its highest. But in general, the most difficult positions to fill this year, in order of difficulty, were skilled trades, engineers, management/executive staff, accounting and finance staff, sales representatives, secretaries, personal assistants, receptionists, administrative assistants and office support staff, drivers, technicians, teachers, and IT personnel. Many of such skills are needed among SMEs.
- **Startup operational costs:** Startup operational costs result in some businesses failing before they even start the business because of failure to forecast some cash flow constraints. Startup costs refer to capital costs used for producing goods or services. It can include physical assets, such as production plants or financial assets, an investment portfolio, knowledge, skills, and abilities that employees contribute to the generation of income as human capital. In the most common aspect, capital can also refer to money invested in a business to purchase assets. Entrepreneurs, owners, or managers of SMEs are therefore seeing capital costs as a barrier to starting or expanding a business because they may have an unrealistic expectation of incoming revenues from sales.

- **Operating costs:** Operating costs are basic types of costs or the routine costs of running a business that must be considered when budgeting. Some of these operating costs include fixed costs, variable costs, and semi-variable costs which impact the sustainability of SMEs.
- **Business location:** There is a distinction between a business located in the townships and a business located in cities. Businesses located in cities have more clients, higher demand for their goods, better infrastructure, and better access to facilities like financial houses and suppliers.
- **Poor planning:** Poor planning could also be the cause for the poor performance of small businesses. Managers in these small businesses do not have clearly outlined job descriptions and thus their key roles of organising, leading, and controlling at times are neglected. Most small businesses fail because their plans are sales-oriented and they need a transition outlook in order to meet customer needs.
- **Lack of employee satisfaction**: The lack of employee satisfaction is one of the major limiting factors for small businesses that hire family members. If employees' objectives are not met, then their commitment to their work can be compromised, which is a scenario that can flow into negative effects on productivity. Research has indicated that family-run businesses have no clearly defined job descriptions which usually result in conflicts. In addition, research noted that if small business owners do not create an environment that encourages personal interaction, employees will never do their best in helping the business prosper.
- **Access to bank credit or insufficient operating funds:** Small businesses lack capitalisation. This is one of the debilitating problems of an entrepreneur. Most entrepreneurs (small businesses) suffer from a shortage of capital that mainly reflects on the supply of finance available to them through the market and in the methods of financing used. Some of the reasons why financial markets do not work perfectly as far as small firms are concerned include the lack of development of finance and credit services in some African countries, which are reflected on poorly developed financial markets and a lack of knowledge on the part of small business managers of some of the contemporary methods of financing. In Africa, SMEs face an underdeveloped commercial market for loan finance, combined with a lack of effective participation by government in supplying finance to SMEs, either directly or indirectly by offering guarantees.
- **Access to markets**: Access to financial capital is not a guarantee for SMEs to successfully enter or access markets. Minimal market penetration or no access to markets can constitute an imminent failure to businesses, considering that SMEs' success comes through sale of products or services. In addition, the inability for SMEs to access competitive markets can be noted as one of the major factors threatening their longevity. Competitiveness factors for SMEs to enter markets are among the fundamental requirements (by credit providers) to access funding. This implies that small businesses located in rural areas can be potentially disadvantaged in terms of accessing markets compared to their urban counterparts.
- **Insufficient demand:** Insufficient demand appears to be one of the limiting factors for SME growth and development in the African continent. Insufficient demand can have critical impact or ramifications on SMEs, since small businesses that are still growing will need increased demand for their sustainability. Demand that is not sustained at the level that supports the current level of quantity supplied into that market because of insufficient demand will result in the price of that commodity falling, leading to some suppliers to exit the market. Eventually prices will fall to the level that satisfies market demand for that commodity, and thus achieve equilibrium.SMEs are usually worst affected by falling prices, because they are just penetrating the market and do not enjoy client loyalty to the extent that they can afford to reduce their prices. Consequently, in the early stages of penetrating the market, new/starting businesses, which are facing the challenge of low/reduced price in the market or even price cuts, cannot survive, and there is imminent risk of closing such businesses.
- **Employees' costs:** Most SMEs are vulnerable to employment costs. In some conditions, employment costs fall into several types. These include recruiting expenses, total remuneration, office space, leave, equipment cost, ongoing administration costs, and training.
- **Exchange rates:** One of the critical economic factors that is confronting the development of SMEs in Africa is the exchange rate. The fluctuation of exchange rates is an important factor limiting the development and growth of SMEs involved in imports and exports. The exchange rate affects the cost of cross-border transfers in the way that a depreciating currency will be profitable to exporters at the expense of importers, as well as strengthening local currency will affect exporters and promote importers. This implies that if the exchange rate of a currency is volatile, it will affect local businesses from a planning perspective as it becomes increasingly difficult to financially forecast. Therefore, currency volatility makes it difficult for businesses to plan ahead and can result in them closing down due to unforeseen currency circumstances.
- **Other factors**: There are many other factors that are confronting SMEs' development and growth in the African continent, including South Africa. These include factors such as the costs of borrowing; poor record keeping and information management; inability to distinguish business capital from personal money; poor planning; lack of employee satisfaction; lack of customer relations; procurement and supplier corruption; HIV/AIDS; absenteeism; loss of skills; inadequate training; replacement of employees; productivity; fluctuating profits; crime; and competition from imports (positive impact of imports and negative impact of imports).

Source: Adapted from Al-Haddad (2019), Dhanah (2016), and the Dalberg Report (2011)

increasing competitive challenges weakens the ability of African SMEs "to adapt to rapidly changing market demand, technological change, and capacity constraints relating to knowledge, innovation, and creativity" (Gamage & Kumara, 2019: 4). There are different ways to address these challenges with a view to harnessing the job creation potentials of SMEs in the African continent. Evidently, most African countries have good SME policies and plans. For instance, the categorisation of SMEs in South Africa has helped in ensuring the establishment of different formalised business enterprises at different scales across the major sectorial components of the nation's economy. With the requisite legislative frameworks to monitor the growth of these businesses, SMEs in South Africa have contributed immensely to the growth of employment, even though the unemployment rate is still high, especially in the COVID-19 era. Approximately 68% of the population of South Africa were employed by SMEs' business outlets in 2012 (Rabie et al., 2016). However, while in 2019, only 47% of the workforce was employed by SMEs in South Africa, it is envisaged that employment opportunities through SMEs would be 90% of the workforce by 2030 (Liedtke, 2019).

In South Africa, the National Development Plan (NDP) 2030 had proposed the feasibility of creating 11 million jobs by 2030 (National Planning Commission, 2012). To accomplish this, the NDP indicated the readiness of the government to improve on the economic policy coordination and implementation through sustainable partnerships with "business and labour to facilitate, direct and promote investment in labour-intensive areas" (National Planning Commission, 2012). The National Planning Commission stated that other measures include "raising competitiveness and export earnings through better infrastructure and public services, lowering the costs of doing business, improving skills and innovation, and targeting state support to specific sectors" (National Planning Commission, 2012: 39). The Commission also planned to strengthen "the functioning of the labour market to improve skills acquisition; match job seekers and job opening; and reduce conflict" (National Planning Commission, 2012: 39). These are lofty achievements and projections. Nevertheless, the realisation of the job creation prospects depends on some factors that have remained obstacles to the flourishing of SMEs in the country.

The Banking Association of South Africa (ND) noted some of the challenges militating against effective operations of SMEs. The factors are also applicable to other SMEs in developing African countries. These factors include crime and corruption, inappropriate technological skills, vital infrastructural deficits leading to low production capacity, low-level management skills, and deficits in skilled labour. Aside from this, the capital requirements in a society characterised by high-level corruption make credit facilities a herculean task. Thus, SMEs are finding it difficult to access markets to develop robust relationships with customers, especially during the COVID-19 era, where restricted movements hampered the operations of SMEs (Bartika et al., 2020; Catalyst for Growth, 2020). Beyond these, SMEs in Africa are confronted with the challenge of gaining wider recognition and patronage by the local larger industrial companies and the government bureaucratic agents. Where there are adequate legislative frameworks, public servants often explore SMEs for the perpetuation of malfeasances, using them as fonts for contracts and tenders (Alert, 2014; Igwe et al., 2018).

Financial constraint is a major challenge to the growth of SMEs in Africa (Quartey et al., 2017). Indeed, policy analysts and policymakers have often expressed their concerns about the paucity of finance for the development and growth of SMEs in Africa (Muriithi, 2017). The small enterprises sector requires sufficient capital for stability to compete favourably with the influx of foreign investments occasioned by globalisation. This financial requirement is important for the SMEs to grow and nurture effective productivity. Modern technologies necessary for facilitating rapid production requires financial outlays that are out of reach for small enterprises. Financing through banks is an option, with major obstacles arising from the conditions for credit facilities.

Most SMEs do not have the requisite collateral to secure sufficient loans from banks and other financial institutions. Aside from the financial bottlenecks, SMEs in Africa are faced with the challenge of effective management. Most of the owners and managers of the SMEs are lacking in the required skills and expertise necessary for innovative operations in production and operational activities (Muriithi, 2017).

Operating any business enterprise requires the basic managerial skills necessary for effective mobilisation and prudent management of human, material, and financial resources. To acquire this sort of skills calls for adequate training on the rudiments of business administration. As noted by Muriithi (2017: 41), "many business owners lack appropriate training and experience to operate their businesses, their management style is basically on trial and error and driven by performance and short-term gains with little attention paid to strategic planning." Even though they might possess certain business ideas and exhibit a level of competence in their various choices of careers and professions, they still need to acquire managerial skills and knowledge necessary for running a successful business enterprise.

Thus, training is crucial for SMEs to acquire personnel with the requisite skills (Rabie et al., 2016). Arising from the aforementioned is poor management. The paucity of training and expertise can potentially jeopardise effective management of any business outfit. Inadequate managerial skills and expertise would render the management of SMEs ineffective in terms of operations and productivity (Bushe, 2019). The success of SMEs requires pragmatic and strategic decision-making (Gopaul & Rampersad, 2020). Strategic planning helps in achieving business goals rather than management by trial and error. Business experience and entrepreneurial mindset are crucial for the success of small business enterprises. For example, the inability of SMEs to properly manage their finances is a manifestation of poor accounting knowledge and skills (Muriithi, 2017). Poor management would lead to poor performance, waste of resources and further opportunities for employment. Thus, the management of SMEs requires sufficient skills and expertise in marketing, human resources, cash flow management, stock inventory, and finance (Bushe, 2019).

In Africa, the lack of governmental support for the growth of SMEs continues to hinder their operations, with its consequential impact on society and as a source for job creation. Multinational companies (MNCs) and organisations enjoy more patronage from the government and society. The implication of this is that public preference and support for the MNCs weakens the strength of small businesses to grow and enable their operational ability and capacity (BusinessTech, 2020). Consequently, there is a threat of the local economy continuing to dwindle, and the expected contributions of SMEs to national economic growth diminishing. Further, the threat of globalisation has contributed to the unemployment market being more saturated. On the one hand, non-functioning SMEs would disengage their workforce because of their inability to pay wages. Similarly, whenever the MNCs decide to rationalise their workforce in order to increase their profits, mass unemployment occurs. Thus, government and public support for SMEs is crucial for the local and national economy as well as creating employment opportunities and job stability. This is succinctly articulated by Muriithi (2017: 42): "A government that does not support SMEs does not only hurt the sector but experiences negative growth in its economic development. The environment created by the government in terms of wages framework, taxation, licensing, opportunities, technological support and infrastructure pave the road to success or failure for the SMEs."

It is the responsibility of governments to provide a desirably conducive environment for SMEs to thrive amidst a competitive globalised economy. The right domestic infrastructural environment and rules and regulations to protect small business enterprises would facilitate the growth and survival of the SMEs sector in the national economy. Adaptable legislative frameworks with particular attention to local economic peculiarities would attract local investors to be innovatively involved in productive small business enterprises.

4.6 Employment Generation and Employment Intensity Trends Among SMEs in Africa

SMEs are considered a crucial driver of employment in Africa. According to the African Development Bank, SMEs account for approximately 80% of the region's employment (African Development Bank, 2021). The employment generation trends in Africa are reflected in the following:

- Growth in SMEs: SMEs have been a significant source of employment in Africa, with a trend towards their growth. According to a report by the African Development Bank (2020a), SMEs contribute to more than 50% of employment opportunities across the continent.
- Many African governments have implemented policies and initiatives to support SME growth and employment generation. These can include financial support, training programmes, and reducing regulatory barriers. Examples include the "African Union's Agenda 2063" and national-level policies in various African countries (The Economist, 2021).
- Informal sector employment: A substantial portion of employment generated by SMEs in Africa is in the informal sector. This trend is particularly prevalent in countries with a large informal economy, where many micro-enterprises operate outside the formal regulatory framework. This sector is characterised by a lack of formal contracts, social security, and government regulation (World Bank, 2021).

- Agriculture and agribusiness: In many African countries, agriculture is a vital sector for employment. Agriculture is a significant sector for SMEs in Africa. Many small-scale farmers and agribusinesses are labour-intensive and provide employment to a large portion of the population. For example, in Kenya, small-scale horticulture farms and dairy enterprises employ a substantial number of people in rural areas, contributing to poverty reduction and rural development. (World Bank, 2021).
- SMEs involved in agribusiness, including smallholder farming and food processing, play a crucial role in providing jobs to the rural population. The International Finance Corporation (IFC) has conducted studies on the role of SMEs in agriculture-related employment in Africa (World Economic Forum, 2022).
- Technology and innovation: The adoption of technology and innovation by SMEs can have a significant impact on their employment generation capabilities. Innovative startups and tech-focused SMEs have been growing in Africa, contributing to employment. There is a growing trend of tech startups and SMEs in Africa, especially in countries like Kenya, Nigeria, and South Africa. These tech-driven SMEs are not only creating high-skilled jobs but also contributing to the development of the digital ecosystem in Africa. Reports from organisations like GSMA and the World Bank provide insights into this trend (World Economic Forum, 2022).
- Youth and women entrepreneurship is a significant focus in Africa, with various programmes aimed at empowering these groups through SME development. Organisations like the African Development Bank have initiatives in this regard (African Development Bank, 2021). African governments and international organisations have been actively promoting youth and women entrepreneurship. Various initiatives and programmes have been launched to support young and female entrepreneurs in starting and growing SMEs, thus contributing to employment opportunities. UNDP and UNIDO have been involved in such initiatives (ILO, 2019a).
- Regional disparities: Employment generation by SMEs can vary significantly from one region to another in Africa. Urban areas tend to have more SMEs and job opportunities compared to rural areas. This disparity is addressed through regional development programmes and initiatives (World Bank, 2021).

- Access to finance: Access to finance remains a challenge for many SMEs in Africa. However, there have been efforts to improve access through microfinance institutions, fintech innovations, and partnerships with financial institutions. Research by the World Bank and the African Union focuses on financial inclusion and SME financing (World Economic Forum, 2022).
- Manufacturing: Some manufacturing SMEs in Africa, such as textile and garment companies, are labour-intensive. Ethiopia has emerged as a hub for such industries. The Hawassa Industrial Park, for instance, hosts several textile and apparel manufacturers and has created thousands of jobs for local workers (The Economist, 2021).
- Tourism and hospitality: Tourism-related SMEs, including hotels, restaurants, and tour operators, are labour-intensive and play a significant role in providing employment opportunities. Tanzania's tourism sector, particularly in places like Zanzibar, has a high employment intensity due to the influx of tourists (UNWTO, 2019).
- Informal sector: The informal sector in Africa includes a wide range of small businesses, from street vendors to micro-enterprises. While often unregistered and unregulated, these businesses collectively provide a substantial number of jobs. Nigeria's informal economy, for example, employs a large portion of the population, especially in urban areas (ILO, 2019a).
- Technology and startups: The technology and startup ecosystem in Africa has been growing, and many tech startups have been successful in creating jobs. For example, companies like Jumia, a Nigerian e-commerce platform, and Andela, a tech talent accelerator, have contributed to job creation in the tech sector across multiple African countries (World Economic Forum, 2022).
- Construction and real estate: Construction projects, including real estate development, infrastructure, and housing, are often labour-intensive. In countries like Rwanda, the construction sector has grown rapidly, leading to increased employment opportunities (African Development Bank, 2021).

While there is evidence of trends supporting SMEs towards job creation, some of the barriers including access to finance, infrastructure deficits, and lack of market access can affect SMEs' ability to generate employment. Understanding these challenges is essential when analysing employment trends. Additionally, the COVID-19 pandemic had a profound effect on employment in Africa, including SMEs. Many SMEs faced disruptions, but some adapted to new opportunities, especially in digital and e-commerce sectors (United Nations, 2021).

Further, the employment intensity of SMEs in Africa can vary significantly depending on the country, sector, and the specific characteristics of each SME. However, SMEs are generally considered a significant source of employment in many African countries. Some key points to consider regarding the employment intensity of SMEs in Africa include (World Economic Forum, 2022; African Development Bank, 2021):

- Variation across countries: Africa is a diverse continent with varying levels of economic development and industrialisation. Some countries have a higher concentration of SMEs, while others may have a larger share of their workforce employed by larger enterprises.
- Importance of the informal sector: In many African countries, a substantial portion of SMEs operates in the informal sector, which means they are not officially registered or regulated. These informal SMEs often play a crucial role in providing employment opportunities, especially in rural and urban slum areas.
- Rural versus urban: SMEs in Africa are found in both rural and urban areas. In rural areas, SMEs often include agricultural activities and small-scale enterprises, contributing to rural employment. In urban areas, SMEs can be involved in a wide range of industries, including retail, services, and manufacturing.
- Job creation: SMEs are often seen as engines of job creation. They are more labour-intensive compared to large corporations and can provide employment opportunities for people with various skill levels. However, the quality of jobs, including wages, benefits, and job security, can vary widely within the SME sector.
- Challenges: SMEs in Africa face various challenges, including limited access to financing, inadequate infrastructure, regulatory barriers, and a lack of skills and training. These challenges can affect their ability to grow and create more jobs.
- Government policies: Some African governments have recognised the importance of SMEs in job creation and economic development. They may implement policies and programmes to support SME growth, such as providing access to credit, offering training and capacity-building initiatives, and simplifying regulatory processes.

- Data limitations: It is essential to note that obtaining accurate and up-to-date data on SMEs and their employment intensity in Africa can be challenging due to the prevalence of the informal sector and limited resources for data collection and analysis.

The employment intensity of Small and Medium-sized Enterprises (SMEs) in Africa can vary significantly depending on various factors, including the sector, location, and economic conditions. The examples provided above highlight the diversity of sectors and activities where SMEs play a significant role in job creation across the continent. Additionally, the impact of external factors such as government policies, access to finance, and global economic conditions also influence SME employment intensity in Africa. However, SMEs are often considered crucial for job creation and economic development in the region. Below, I'll provide some insights and examples of employment intensity in African SMEs, along with references to reputable sources.

4.7 Boosting Employment in Africa Through SMEs

The aforementioned challenges, no doubt, hamper the operational activities of SMEs in Africa. This means that SMEs would not be able to perform beyond the limit of their capacity, even though there is growth potential. This section discusses the various ways SMEs could boost employment opportunities in Africa.

Globally, it is agreed that Small and Medium Enterprises and entrepreneurs have an important role in the development of industries in any country, given that SMEs are inter-dependent on other industries for their raw materials, products, and services (Al-Haddad, 2019). This interdependence has direct, indirect, and induced impacts (supply chain or distribution channel) on jobs creation and economic growth. Therefore, it has been estimated that SMEs are expected to create at least four out of every five jobs with an expectation of creating 600 million jobs by 2030 (Michael, 2019). This projection is comforting. Indeed, available data have shown that Africa has the potential of transforming its SMEs sector into a job-spinning structure. In the continent, SMEs provide two-thirds of the formal employment workforce, while in the informal sector SMEs absorb a majority of petty traders and artisans (BusinessTech, 2020). Most of these SMEs are found in the industrial and manufacturing sectors, competing with multinational organisations for operational spaces and infrastructures. While they strive to break even amid stiff competition, their production capacity dwindles, especially during an emergency like the COVID-19 pandemic. Relatedly, Africa is a destination of multinational corporations because the market is not promoting indigenous African SMEs. In terms of job creation, multinational companies are fond of increasing unemployment whenever they decide to downsize their workforce. The consequence of this is the saturation of the already crowded employment markets. This creates more problems for SMEs as they struggle to absorb a new workforce with limited resources. This calls for the need to strengthen the infrastructural base of African countries, necessary to support the growth of SMEs in the technology, agriculture, enterprises, customer experience, and automation sectors (Michael, 2019; BusinessTech, 2020). These require adequate funding in an environment characterised by a need for adequate infrastructural support such as electricity, good roads, water supply, security, conducive public policies, and legislative frameworks that encourage SMEs' startup and operations.

A support base is crucial to tap into the hidden talents among young and vibrant African youth with imbued innovative perceptions, especially in digital technology. At the centre of technological-based SMEs is an effective internet connectivity structure. Most African youths have been exploring the technological arena to create self-employment opportunities for themselves and becoming employers of labour within the limits of their operational activities and involvements. For instance, cloud infrastructure has become a trend among African citizens and business organisations. In its Cloud in Africa 2020 report, World Wide Worx discovered that a majority of African individuals and corporate organisations "deemed cloud computing to be 'important' in helping with business' response to the crisis" (Goldstuck, 2020). The presence of SMEs in the use of cloud storage and activities has increased, with 69% of business enterprises having entered into operational agreements with multiple cloud providers (Goldstuck, 2020). This is captured by Goldstuck (2020), who posited that "*cloud computing has emerged as a powerful platform for intangible elements of organisations' internal strategy. Almost two-thirds (67%) reported an improvement in cross organisation innovation due to the cloud. Over half (55%) also experienced noticeable brand perception improvements.*" This was more profound during the COVID-19 pandemic, where cloud platforms provided opportunities for SMEs to be operational.

Thus, SMEs' reliance on cloud platforms calls for a reinforcement of the internet infrastructure in the continent. Effective internet connectivity would accelerate innovation in SMEs across the continent with the consequence of creating new services. This would allow Africans to display their creative talents using modern technologies in varying degrees. As Michael (2019) has noted, that "*a new generation of African entrepreneurs that are constantly looking to leverage new tech for product and service improvements will start building businesses on cloud services from day one. In part, this will be driven by cost efficiencies: by doing away with the need for expensive on-premises infrastructure and the technical teams needed to maintain it, cloud lowers the cost of doing business considerably without impeding innovation or competitiveness.*" Thus, the cloud has provided Africans with an opportunity to explore the world of business transactions and management with fewer expenses.

Another notable development that has the potential of increasing the volume of job creation by SMEs in Africa is the agribusiness sector. Investments in agriculture infrastructure are another avenue to boost SMEs activities in Africa. Indeed, *agripreneurship* is fast becoming a rallying point among Africans to explore the rich agricultural potential that is capable of generating substantial income and employment opportunities. The African Development Bank (AfDB) has been at the forefront of promoting a deepening interest in agribusiness with financial supports for African farmers. The Bank decided in 2017 to inject $2.4 billion annually "for 10 years, to build roads, irrigation infrastructure, and storage facilities within Africa to attract high-value investors" (AfDB, 2017).

The financial incentive was designed to provide necessary infrastructural facilities that would accelerate maximum participation in agribusinesses across the continent. Most African farmlands need rural feeder roads for easy transportation of their products to the city centres, while a modern irrigation system would facilitate continuous farming activities irrespective of the season. The Bank's president, Dr Akinwumi Adesina noted that "agriculture is a money-making business. Agriculture is like gold dust because you do not know what it is until you process it into a finished product" (AfDB, 2020b). The agribusiness sector has the potential of generating more SMEs in the services, enterprises, technical assistance and services, among others. For instance, in Kenya, Subculture Company provides farmers with solar-powered irrigation services and a "pay-as-you-grow" service fee programme (AfDB, 2020a). Similarly, in Cote d'Ivoire, an SME, Canaan Land, has been providing training services to women in rural areas to develop sustainable and inclusive agriculture. Apart from generating employment opportunities, booming agribusiness SMEs are an antidote to hunger and poverty in Africa. As Dr Adesina noted that "agriculture is the thing that feeds the world," with a projection that by 2030, agricultural food imports in Africa would increase to $1 trillion (AfDB, 2017). Thus, investments in this sector would witness the establishment of SMEs in food processing, thereby expanding the scope of employment (AfDB, 2020a). Kenya, Ethiopia, and Uganda have been witnessing economic growth through investments in agricultural production activities (AfDB, 2017).

These countries are Africa's major producers and exporters of coffee, tea, and cut-flowers. This sort of growth is capable of stimulating domestic economic stability through industrialisation of food processing with the attendant benefits of strengthening local currencies, while generating foreign reserves. This would provide the opportunity for SMEs to thrive, a development that would necessarily demand an additional workforce. Apart from this, government infrastructural and resources incentives would attract the youth population to farming. With this occupational engagement, excess labour markets would deplete, and the agriculture sector of the national economy in most African states would rebound. This initiative could form part of the school curriculum where students are equipped with practical farming knowledge. Provision of modern farming equipment and infrastructure with easy access to finance would discourage dependence on white-collar jobs upon graduation.

A conducive environment for SMEs to thrive would increase the emergence of networks of enterprises in retail and wholesale trading. The informal sector of the economy would thrive, while every jobless individual would have the opportunity of engaging with the trade of their choices upon completion of their education. Strong entrepreneurship is the backbone of thriving SMEs as argued by Michael (2019) that "*entrepreneurship is not the reserve of start-ups and SMEs. Large enterprises are learning from their smaller counterparts by prioritising entrepreneurship to improve their own innovation capabilities and stave off the challenge posed by smaller, more nimble upstarts.*"

SMEs culture in Africa is growing faster and providing opportunities for citizens to explore the various possibilities offered by human and material resources. Transformation of these resources to substantial SMEs structures through innovative enterprises using modern technology is a weapon against the burgeoning rise in unemployment in the continent.

Adequate interventionist policies and directives by the government would provide the roadmap for the exploration of these vast opportunities and possibilities.

Job creation and supporting small and medium-sized enterprises (SMEs) are critical for economic development in Africa. Some of the challenges facing SMEs and job creation in Africa include:

- Many African SMEs struggle to access affordable loans and credit facilities. High interest rates and collateral requirements make it difficult for them to secure funding for expansion. Many SMEs in Africa struggle to access the necessary capital to start or expand their businesses. This includes difficulties in obtaining loans and credit from financial institutions .Even when loans are available, high interest rates make borrowing expensive for SMEs, limiting their ability to invest in growth and job creation (Beck et al., 2011).
- Limited access to quality education and vocational training programmes can leave potential entrepreneurs without the necessary skills to start and manage businesses (African Development Bank, 2016).
- Inadequate transportation and energy infrastructure can increase production costs and limit market access for SMEs. For instance, unreliable electricity supply hampers manufacturing operations and increases operational costs Also, poor transportation infrastructure can hinder the movement of goods and services, limiting market access and growth opportunities (World Bank, 2017).
- Weak entrepreneurial ecosystems and support systems, such as business incubators and mentorship programmes, can hinder the growth of startups and SMEs (Mthanti & Ojah, 2016).
- Many African SMEs lack access to modern technology and struggle to adopt innovative practices, thus limiting their competitiveness. Many SMEs in Africa may not have access to the latest technology and innovation, which can limit their competitiveness. Also, SMEs often face stiff competition, making it difficult to establish a foothold in the market (UNCTAD, 2019).
- African SMEs often face difficulties in reaching broader markets due to trade barriers, logistics challenges, and lack of information on export opportunities. SMEs may not have access to market information and networks, limiting their ability to find customers and expand (Mattoo & Payton, 2007).

- Ongoing conflicts, political instability, and regulatory uncertainty in some African countries create an unfavourable environment for SMEs to thrive. Political instability and conflicts in some African countries can disrupt business operations and deter investment. Fluctuations in exchange rates and economic instability can impact SMEs' financial stability (UNCTAD, 2019).
- Cumbersome regulations, bureaucratic red tape, and corruption can stifle SME growth. SMEs often struggle with cumbersome and unclear regulations that can be time-consuming and costly to navigate. For instance, lengthy registration processes can discourage entrepreneurs (Kaufmann et al., 2010).
- Many African countries face a shortage of skilled labour, particularly in specialised fields like technology and engineering. This limits the SMEs' ability to innovate. Finding qualified employees can be a challenge, as the education and training systems may not produce a workforce with the necessary skills. Even, some SME owners may lack business management skills and knowledge (World Economic Forum, 2018).

Addressing these challenges requires a multifaceted approach involving government policies, private sector initiatives, and international cooperation to support job creation and SME development in Africa.

4.8 Conclusion

SMEs in Africa are a vital force in job creation, especially for youth and women, and in promoting inclusive and sustainable economic growth. These businesses contribute significantly to reducing unemployment and poverty levels. Supporting and investing in SMEs through policy measures and access to finance is essential for the continued growth and development of African economies.

Future work depends largely on SMEs in Africa, with active government support and encouragement. SMEs are crucial to the campaign against mass unemployment that characterises the African continent. SMEs are not only offering the platforms for employment creation alone; they are the drivers of national economic growth. Creativity, associated with SMEs, is a driver for innovation and competition in markets, thereby increasing skills and knowledge of current trends in society. This often drives the urge to meet the needs of society in terms of productivities in a variety of goods and services. With the development and growth of an enterprise culture, investments in human capital would increase through training and acquisition of modern equipment and technology. A skilled labour force would advance rapid and quality products, but it would also attract more pleasing working conditions. This is capable of stemming the scourge of labour migration in Africa. In other words, the existing productivity gap that has constituted a major challenge to the growth and development of SMEs would have been eliminated or minimised. This is reinforced in the statement by the ILO (2019a) that "*in developing countries, the productivity gap leads to low-income generation, informality, and poor growth performance. To close the gap, we must first understand the problems faced by SMEs, both from the perspective of employers and employees, and in the context of broader challenges facing the world of work.*"

African countries, as part of their trade relations, should foster effective networks to establish effective continental economic relationships on the platforms of SMEs cooperation and exchange. This will significantly accelerate growth through innovative strategies using the comparative advantage as a springboard for productivity. Complementary relationships would activate the productive exchange of ideas and skills that would boost knowledge transfer. The various countries should leverage the advantage of the diverse resources such as human capital and natural endowments to advance employment opportunities for the teeming youth who are eager to risk migration to the West. The government in African countries can assist SMEs in realising their business objectives in different ways, depending on their local economic peculiarities. Institutions and departments of government could facilitate knowledge acquisition and business skills structures to enable small enterprises to access the necessary training opportunities. This would provide them with the necessary skills they needed to grow their businesses. This sort of facilitation can include the knowledge of modern trends in business techniques such as e-marketing, among other innovative information.

Skills development is necessary for SMEs to grow employment opportunities. Aside from this, informal training initiatives should be developed, especially in rural areas to explore various avenues for engagement in small business activities within the context of available markets. This would address the rural–urban drift that has compounded the high rate of unemployment in urban centres. African states should encourage the establishment of skills training centres in different rural locations with a view to encouraging the growth of SMEs in rural areas. Rural areas in Africa are yearning for development. There are abundant resources that could be transformed to local production rather than depending on exportation in exchange for imported finished goods that are usually exorbitantly priced. Industrialised rural areas would boost the local economy and provide massive employment opportunities in the continent. Investment in rural areas would encourage the establishment of agriculture-based SMEs which are a veritable means of increasing food production and processing.

Africa has the potential to lead in industrial transformation through SMEs. What is lacking is the political will to incorporate rural development as a major socio-economic goal of many governments. With abundant natural resources in agriculture, Africa is a potential destination for the establishment of rural and urban SMEs.

References

African Development Bank (AfDB). (2016). *African Development Report 2016: Sustainable Cities and Structural Transformation.* African Development Bank. https://www.afdb.org/en/news-and-events/press-releases/small-and-medium-enterprises-lynchpin-african-agriculture-african-development-bank-37790

African Development Bank (AfDB). (2017). AfDB Agri-Business Funding Lays Strong Foundation for Transforming African Agriculture. https://www.engineeringnews.co.za/article/sme-sector-critical-to-growing-south-africas-economy-pityana-2019-04-11

African Development Bank (AfDB). (2018). African Economic Outlook 2018. https://hbr.org/2020/04/bringing-manufacturing-back-to-the-us-is-easier-said-thandone

African Development Bank (AfDB). (2020a). *Small and Medium Enterprises Lynchpin of African Agriculture*—African Development Bank. https://www.news24.com/fin24/opinion/4-key-sme-trends-that-will-drive-job-creation-20190327-2

African Development Bank (AfDB). (2020b). African Economic Outlook 2021.

African Development Bank (AfDB). (2021). Housing and Construction in Africa: A Promising Future.

African Union. (2015). *Agenda 2063: The Africa We Want. African Union.*

Alert. (2014). Examining the Challenges Facing Small Businesses in South Africa.2014. *Alert: An Occasional Paper of Business Environment Specialists (sbp),* Issue Paper 1. www.sbp.org.za

Al-Haddad, L., Sial, S. M., Imdad Ali, I., Alam, R., Khuong, N. V., & Khanh, H. T. (2019). The Role of Small and Medium Enterprises (SMEs) in Employment Generation and Economic Growth: A Study of Marble Industry in Emerging Economy. *International Journal of Financial Research*, 10 (6): 174–187. https://businesstech.co.za/news/industry-news/371724/how-smes-will-make-africa-great-again/; https://www.afdb.org/en/news-and-events/afdb-agri-business-funding-lays-strong-foundation-for-transforming-african-agriculture-17014; www.worldwideworx.com

Auciello, K. E. (1975). *Employment generation through stimulation of small industries, an international compilation of small-scale industry definitions.* Georgia Institute of Technology.

Baduel, B., Geginat, C., & Pierre, G. (2019). *Private Sector Job Creation in MENA: Prioritizing the Reform Agenda Prepared.* IMF Working Paper WP/19/206. September 2019.

Bartika, A. W., Bertrandb, M., Cullenc, Z., Glaeserd, E. L., Lucac, M., & Stanton, C. (2020). The Impact of COVID-19 on Small Business Outcomes and Expectations. *Proceedings of the National Academy of Sciences of the United States of America (PNAS), 117*(30), 17656–17666.

Beck, T., Demirgüç-Kunt, A. & Pería, M. S. M. (2011). *Banking Services for Everyone? Barriers to Bank Access and Use Around the World.* The World Bank.

Bushe, B. (2019). The Causes and Impact of Business Failure among Small to Micro and Medium Enterprises in South Africa. *Africa's Public Service Delivery and Performance Review, 7*(1), a210.

BusinessTech. (2020). *How SMEs Will Make Africa Great Again.* Business Tech.

Cant, M. (2012). Challenges Faced by SME's in South Africa: Are Marketing Skills Needed? *International Business and Economics Research Journal, 11*(10), 1107–1116.

Catalyst for Growth. (2020). The Impact of Covid-19 on African SMMES Operations: Insights from Entrepreneurs and Business Development Service (BDS Providers. https://www.goethe.de/resources/files/pdf208/c4g-the-impact-of-covid-19-on-african-smmes-operations-online.pdf

Dalberg Report. (2011). Report on Support to SMEs in Developing Countries Through Financial Intermediaries. https://www.eib.org/attachments/dalberg_sme-briefing-paper.pdf

Dhanah, D. (2016). Small Businesses and Job Creation in South Africa. https://open.uct.ac.za/bitstream/handle/11427441/thesis_com_2017_dhanah_darlington.pdf?sequence=1

European Commission. (2017). *Annual Report on European SMEs 2016/2017 Focus on Self-employment.* European Union.

European Commission. (2019). *Annual Report on European SMEs 2018/2019 Research and Development and Innovation by SMEs.* European Union.

Gamage, N., & Kumara, S. (2019). *Global Challenges and Survival Strategies of the SMEs in the Era of Economic Globalization: A Systematic Review.* Munich Personal RePEc ArchiveE (*MPRA) Paper No. 98419.*

Goldstuck, A. (2020). *Cloud in Africa 2020.* World Wide Worx.

Gopaul, R., & Rampersad, R. (2020). An Assessment of Strategic Decision-Making Processes Among Small and Micro Enterprises in South Africa. *Acta Commercii, 20*(1), a819. https://www.oecd-ilibrary.org/science-and-technology/smes-and-employment-creation_374052760815. https://doi.org/10.4102/ac.v20i1.819

Igwe, P. A., Onjewu, A. E., & Nwibo, S. U. (2018). Entrepreneurship and SMEs' Productivity Challenges in Sub-Saharan Africa. In L. P. Dana, V. Ratten, & B. Honyenuga (Eds.), *African Entrepreneurship. Palgrave Studies of Entrepreneurship in Africa*. Palgrave Macmillan. https://doi.org/10.1007/978-3-319-73700-3_9

International Finance Corporation (IFC). (2019). She Trades: A World of Opportunities for Women-Owned Businesses. https://www.itu.int/dms_pub/itu-s/opb/gen/S-GEN-MSMES-2016-PDF-E.pdf

International Labour Organisation (ILO). (2015). Report on International Labour Conference, 104th Session, 2015: Small and Medium-Sized Enterprises and Decent and Productive Employment Creation. https://ilo.org/wcmsp5/groups/public/ed_norm/relconf/documents/meetingdocument/wcms_358294.pdf.

International Labour Organisation (ILO). (2019a). Women and Men in the Informal Economy: A Statistical Picture.

International Labour Organization (ILO). (2020). *Report on Employment in Africa (Re-Africa): Tackling the Youth Employment Challenge*. International Labour Organization.

International Telecommunication Union (ITU). (2016). Trends in Tech MSMEs and Startup Support. https://mpra.ub.uni-muenchen.de/98419/

Juergensen, J., Guimón, J., & Narula, R. (2020). European SMEs amidst the COVID-19 Crisis: Assessing Impact and Policy Responses. *Journal of Industrial and Business Economics, 47*, 499–510. https://doi.org/10.1007/s40812-020-00169-4

Kamunge, M. S., Njeru, A., & Tirimba, O. I. (2014). Factors Affecting the Performance of Small and Macro Enterprises in Limuru Town Market of Kiambu County. *International Journal of Scientific and Research Publications, 4*(12), 1–20.

Kaufmann, D., Kraay, A., & Mastruzzi, M. (2010). The Worldwide Governance Indicators: Methodology and Analytical Issues. *Hague Journal on the Rule of Law, 2*(02), 220–246.

Liedtke, S. (2019). SME Sector 'Critical' to Growing South Africa's Economy—Pityana. *Engineering News*, April 11.

Masurel, E., Naudé, W., & Visser, K. (2018). The Missing Middle and the Dynamics of SMEs in Africa. *World Development, 110*, 87–101.

Mattoo, A., & Payton, L. (2007). *Services Trade and Development: The Experience of Zambia*. The World Bank.

Michael, J. (2019). 4 Key SME Trends that Will Drive Job Creation. *fin24*, March 27.

Mthanti, T., & Ojah, K. (2016). The Role of Business Incubators in Fostering Growth-Oriented Women Entrepreneurs in South Africa. *The Southern African Journal of Entrepreneurship and Small Business Management, 8*(1), 1–10.

Muriithi, S. M. (2017). African Small and Medium Enterprises (SMES) Contributions, Challenges and Solutions. *European Journal of Research and Reflection in Management Sciences, 5*(1), 36–48.

Mutyenyoka, E. M., & Madzivhandila, T. S. (2014). Employment Creation Through Small, Medium and Micro Enterprises (SMMEs) in South Africa: Challenges, Progress and Sustainability. *Mediterranean Journal of Social Sciences, 5*(25), 66–72.

Narula, R. (2019). Enforcing Higher Labor Standards within Developing Country Value Chains: Consequences for MNEs and Informal Actors in a Dual Economy. *Journal of International Business Studies, 50*, 1622–1635.

National Planning Commission. (2012). National Development Plan 2030: Our Future—Make It Work. https://www.gov.za/issues/national-development-plan-2030

Organisation of Economic Cooperation and Development (OECD). (2017). Enhancing the Contributions of SMEs in a Global and Digitalised Economy. https://www.oecd.org/industry/C-MIN-2017-8-EN.pdf

Organisation of Economic Cooperation and Development (OECD). (2020). Financing SMEs and Entrepreneurs 2020: An OECD Scoreboard.

Quartey, P., Turkson, E., Abor, J. Y., & Iddrisu, A. M. (2017). Financing the Growth of SMEs in Africa: What Are the Constraints to SME Financing within ECOWAS? *Review of Development Finance, 7*(1), 18–28.

Rabie, C., Cant, M. C., & Wiid, J. A. (2016). Training and Development in SMEs: South Africa's Key to Survival and Success? *The Journal of Applied Business Research, 32*(4), 1009–1024.

Schreyer, P. (1996). *SMEs and Employment Creation: Overview of Selected Quantitative Studies in OECD Member Countries*. OECD Science, Technology and Industry Working Papers 1996/04. https://www.itu.int/dms_pub/itu-s/opb/gen/S-GEN-MSMES-2016-PDF-E.pdf

Shih, W. C. (2020). Bringing Manufacturing Back to the U.S. Is Easier Said Than Done. *Harvard Business Review*.

South Africa. (2003). *National Small Businessses Act of 2003*. South Africa.

Speldekamp, D., Knoben, J., & Saka-Helmhout, A. (2020). Clusters and Firm-Level Innovation: A Configurational Analysis of Agglomeration, Network and Institutional Advantages in European Aerospace. *Research Policy, 49*(3), 103921.

The Banking Association of South Africa. (n.d.). https://www.banking.org.za/what-we-do/sme

The Economist. (2021). Made in Ethiopia: Textiles with Chinese Characteristics.

Tsatsenko, N. (2020). SME Development, Economic Growth and Structural Change: Evidence from Ghana and South Africa. *Journal of Agriculture and Environment, 2*(14), 1–13. https://doi.org/10.23649/jae.2020.2.14.7
UNCTAD. (2019). *Technology and Innovation Report 2019: Leveraging Frontier Technologies for Sustainable Development*. United Nations.
United Nations. (2021). Economic Commission for Africa (UNECA)—COVID-19 in Africa: Protecting Lives and Economies.
United States International Trade Commission (USITC). (2010). *Small and Medium Sized Enterprises: Overview of Participation in U.S. Exports*. Investigation No. 332–508
UNWTO. (2019). Tourism in Africa: Harnessing Tourism for Growth and Improved Livelihoods.
World Bank. (2017). *Africa's Infrastructure: A Time for Transformation*. World Bank Publications.
World Bank. (2019). *World Bank Enterprise Surveys: Africa Regional Business Environment—Overview*. World Bank.
World Bank. (2021). Youth Employment in Agriculture in Sub-Saharan Africa.
World Economic Forum. (2018). *The Future of Jobs Report 2018*. World Economic Forum.
World Economic Forum. (2022). The African Start-Up Ecosystem: Progress, Challenges, and Opportunities.
Yoshino, N., & Taghizadeh-Hesary, F. (2016). *Major Challenges Facing Small and Medium-sized Enterprises in Asia and Solutions for Mitigating Them*. ADBI.

CHAPTER 5

Digital Technologies for SMEs and Job Creation in Africa

Sriram Divi

5.1 Introduction

African economies are in dire need of digital technologies and job creation (World Bank, 2023; Strydom, 2021). This view is based on the fact that by 2100, Africa's working population is anticipated to exceed 2.5 billion people, that is, more than three times the current working population (World Bank, 2023). Ironically, evidence shows a paradoxical relationship between the advancement of digital technologies and employment creation. To be specific, Brynjolfsson et al. (2018) showed that digital technological advancement such as machine learning has low correlation with jobs. Furthermore, Brynjolfsson et al. (2018) noted that few jobs are eligible for full automation and there is a high degree of variability in potential machine learning within jobs. At a country level, Strydom (2021) and Dauth et al. (2017) observed that for the period 1994–2014, because of

The original version of the chapter has been revised. A correction to this chapter can be found at https://doi.org/10.1007/978-3-031-69103-4_11

S. Divi (✉)
Department of Public Policy and Administration, Pandit Deendayal Energy University, Gujarat, India

Dept of Public Management and Economics, Durban University of Technology, Durban, South Africa

G. Mugano, N. Dorasamy, *SMEs Perspective in Africa*,
https://doi.org/10.1007/978-3-031-69103-4_5

automation, Germany experienced massive losses in the middle-skilled segment of the labour market.

Ironically, digital technological advancement in advanced economies were observed to be a key driver of high levels of productivity among large businesses in the OECD and EU countries (Di Bella et al., 2023).

This chapter presents the state of affairs in as far as the adoption of digital technologies is concerned, possible implications of digital technologies on jobs, binding constraints hindering full adoption of digital technologies in Africa and possible remedies.

5.2 The Puzzle on Digitalisation and Job Creation

The effect of technological progress on the job market is not a straightforward matter. Research on the impact of technological progress by Caprettini and Voth (2020) has shown conflicting outcomes on the labour market. For example, it was noted that during the Industrial Revolution in nineteenth-century Britain, in the spinning and weaving sector, the Luddites protested against technological progress by destroying machines because they believed that their manual labour was being replaced by machines (Caprettini & Voth, 2020).

Today, the debate on the implications of technological advancement on employment is complicated as it is now at the heart of domestic and international competitiveness and has continued to stimulate much debate (Parry et al., 2021). This is particularly so in the case of the contribution of advancement in computers. In this case, evidence shows that technological advancement which is computers-aided, by enabling them to perform various tasks more efficiently, have complemented the performance of highly skilled workers (Parry et al., 2021).

Ironically, various scholars have shown that the impact of digital technologies on employment is both massive and negative (Acemoglu & Restrepo, 2017; Autor, 2015; Autor et al., 2003; Baldwin, 2019; Brynjolfsson & McAfee, 2014). In line with this view, new technologies, such as automation, industrial robots, and artificial intelligence, which are often seen as a serious danger for both the existing jobs and future job creation prospects, have been seen to be promoting highly rewarding jobs. Various scholars observed that industrial robots and artificial intelligence will create new employment opportunities that did not exist in the past and increase the demand for labour in other sectors and which lead to higher wages and improvements in the standards of living (Acemoglu & Restrepo, 2017; Autor, 2015; Autor et al., 2003; Baldwin, 2019; Brynjolfsson & McAfee, 2014).

World Bank (2023) and Strydom (2021) studies have shown that historically technological advances have increased productivity, created more jobs than they have destroyed and generated sustained increases in the standards of living.

Of interest is the fact that technological progress has been accompanied by profound structural economic change which is characterised by creation of new sectors and new jobs and destruction of some sectors and jobs (World Bank, 2023; Strydom, 2021). These changes have massive dire consequences for low skilled workers.

In view of the fact that in African countries the bulk of workers are low skilled workers, it is important to review the nexus between technological progress and job creation in Africa. The following section presents technological progress in Africa and its impact on job markets.

5.3 State of Affairs of Adoption of Digital Technologies in Africa

In direct contrast of observation in advanced economies such as the United States and Germany where advancement in digital technologies results in significant losses of jobs as observed by Strydom (2021) and Dauth et al. (2017), the situation in Africa is very different (Strydom, 2021). Skills-displacing technologies have limited impact on job losses in Africa because, unlike developed economies which have a large share of the manufacturing sector, evidence shows that between 1995 and 2019, in Africa, only 11% of the total labour force was employed in the manufacturing sector (Strydom, 2021). Ironically, the agricultural sector is by far the most important sector in Africa since it created 52.9% of total jobs in 2019 albeit this is lower than 62.3% share of total jobs created in 1995 (Strydom, 2021). To make matters worse, in Africa, most SMEs in the agricultural sector are informal and experiences low productivity (Newman et al., 2016).

Evidence shows that, in Africa, SMEs in the agricultural sector have failed to transform themselves from low productivity in the agricultural sector to high-productivity manufacturing sector in line with the views by Newman et al. (2016), McMillan et al. (2014) and Rodrik (2016). Resultantly, Strydom (2021) argued that the African continent failed to foster economic transformation. However, transformation was noted in self-employment and informal services, which by nature suffer from low productivity making them weak in fostering sustainable employment (Strydom, 2021).

Resultantly, the internationalisation thrust of African economies has been curtailed by this situation because any meaningful internationalisation effort must be underpinned by a more diverse and value-added range of economic activities. In view of this quagmire, World Bank (2023) and Strydom (2021) argued that digital technologies present opportunities for African SMEs to leapfrog from a low productivity to high productivity. This is an a priori requirement for the continent to build resilience, build economic transformation, spur sustainable economic growth, and improve the quality of jobs which are needed to support local as well as export development.

Recent advancement of digital technologies in Africa which inter alia include improved access to internet has had a positive impact on job creation in African economies (World Bank, 2023). To be specific, evidence shows that in countries such as Tanzania, Nigeria, and Kenya advancement in digital technologies resulted in positive impact on job creation, productivity growth, and earnings (World Bank, 2023). On a refreshing note, in direct contrast with the establishing?? notion which says that new technologies disproportionately benefit highly skilled workers, these impacts helped to reduce poverty because they are inclusive of all population segments in most African countries (World Bank, 2023).

In addition, Onuoha (2022) underscored that digital innovations are likely to significantly impact on the socio-economic development of African economies. Within the spectrum of SMEs, sectors such as financial services, agriculture, and manufacturing sectors are expected to be major beneficiaries (Melia, 2020). The agricultural sector, which employs more than 60% of the working population from Africa, was distinctly identified by Onuoha (2022) as one of the major beneficiaries of digital innovations.

To be specific, in the African regions, digital innovations like machine learning (ML)-based technologies are widely used for early disease detection and improved yield prediction in Kenya, Malawi, Tanzania, Nigeria, and Zambia (Ly, 2021). The growing use of machine learning-based agricultural technologies in Africa is largely driven by a surge in investments in artificial intelligence (AI) startups that create services and commercial products for agribusinesses and farmers on the continent (Onuoha, 2022). Some of the agricultural–AI-based startups which are currently being used in Africa inter alia include DroneClouds, Aerobotics, and MySmartFarm (Ly, 2021; Onuoha, 2022).

Although the absorption of these digital technologies is still limited to a handful of countries as indicated earlier, the impact on productivity, food security and income is both positive and massive (Onuoha, 2022). Ly (2021) and Onuoha (2022) argued that most African countries have either failed to scale up or adopt these digital innovations due to absence of data and availability of technological skills.

With regards to the gig economy, the growth of the online labour sector in Africa is driven by the current surge in gig economy globally. For the African continent, with almost 70% of the population as youths, this is a key attraction for gig economy (Ly, 2021; Onuoha, 2022). Undoubtedly, in a digitally connected world, this emerging economic sector provides massive potential for increased job opportunities for young Africans (Ly, 2021; Onuoha, 2022).

One of the challenges of this type of digital technology is the likelihood of wage suppression which is caused by the absence of the standardised conditions of work and traditional social protections in a labour market with excess supply (Graham & Anwar, 2018; Jean-Paul & Mudavanhu, 2018). However, Onuoha (2022) argued that wage suppression still remains a better alternative to the lower-paying jobs which are prevalent in the African continent especially in the informal sector which is characterised with high levels of youth unemployment and underemployment.

Interestingly, notwithstanding the fact that digital technologies are skill-biased, World Bank (2020) observed that the advancement of digital innovations in Africa have positive employment reinstatement effects. In addition, in Africa, evidence shows that the rise in digitalisation propels increase in exports which has positive effects on African economies (World Bank, 2020).

Most importantly, studies by World Bank (2020) shows that increase in digital innovation is associated with cost reduction processes and high productivity which is key in fostering the competitiveness of SMEs. Most strikingly, World Bank (2020) revealed that advancement in digital technologies are effective in raising real income in Africa which is key in stimulating demand and increasing job creation across different sectors. Surprisingly, studies by World Bank (2020) shows that, contrary to the established view that digital technologies do not create employment for unskilled workers, in Africa, digital technologies successfully created employment for the unskilled workers.

In the absence of a well-developed financial system in Africa, mobile money is the most important digital technology application in most countries. Platforms such as M-Pesa and Ecocash are best examples of financial services offered in Kenya and Zimbabwe, respectively. These mobile platforms offer safe and secure ways to receive and send money, apply for short-term loans, and make payments (Strydom, 2021). Resultantly, in Kenya, through M-Pesa, evidence shows substantial employment mainly as new jobs in categories such as mobile payment agents (World Bank, 2019). Interestingly, from a gender perspective, to a larger?? extent, these new jobs were taken up by women (World Bank, 2019).

As noted by the World Bank (2019), most women in Kenya have moved out of subsistence agriculture into business and other service-sector occupations. This is a classic example of how digital technologies have been a driving force in fostering transformation from low-productivity to higher-productivity economic sectors.

Hjort and Poulsen (2019) carried out a study on the impact of digital technologies, specifically internet on African economies. In this regard, Hjort and Poulsen (2019) compared changes in employment patterns in areas with good and fast internet connectivity with areas with limited internet connectivity. In the study, Hjort and Poulsen (2019) used the three different data sets covering 12 African countries and confirmed that fast internet access fosters massive, new, strong, and direct employment creation. Hjort and Poulsen (2019) revealed that new firms starting operations, increased productivity, and rising exports were the major drivers of internet-related employment.

Hjort and Poulsen (2019) confirmed that internet-related job creation is heterogeneous across different countries on the globe. Of interest is the fact that, like other scholars such as Strydom (2021), Ly (2021) and Onuoha (2022) observed that in direct contrast of the standing view that digital technologies creates jobs for skilled workers, jobs are not at risk of displacement in Africa. Rather, Hjort and Poulsen (2019) confirmed that these jobs are beneficiaries of technological progress. This is particularly so because businesses in Africa accept low skilled workers into the production supply chain and undertake on-the-job training with a view to upgrade their skills (Hjort & Poulsen, 2019; World Bank, 2020). This is a similar experience which was noted in Germany by Dauth et al. (2017) where low skilled workers are retained and are requested to sign up for on-the-job training with a view to upgrade their skills and retain their jobs. Based on the observations by Hjort and Poulsen (2019), World Bank (2020), and Dauth et al. (2017), it can be argued that advancement of digital technologies is an important vehicle for transforming an economy to high-productivity from low-productivity endeavours.

The flexible manner in which digital technologies are applied in African countries, in the sense of introducing on-the-job training, allows employment opportunities to extend to those with varying educational backgrounds. Over and above this, digital technologies improve the generally poor quality of human capital in Africa and are well placed to make a large developmental footprint in Africa. One of the most important features of digital technologies discussed in this section is that they drive the shift from low-productivity to high-productivity economic activity, thus making them instruments of economic development. This promotes sustainable, quality jobs—particularly for women—as has been evident in Kenya with the help of mobile technology (World Bank, 2019).

5.4 Challenges Faced by Workers in Africa the Digital Economy

The risk of worsening existing structural inequalities prominent in gender differences in the African continent is one of the persistent hurdles affecting workers within the digital economy in Africa. To be specific, the current setting in Africa shows that, principally due to a lower digital literacy level, the participation of women in the digital labour force market is lower and if no radical and disruptive policy measures are implemented by African governments, this trend will remain the same for decades to come (Onkokame et al., 2018; WEF, 2020). Evidence shows that this digital divide is largely driven by lower uptake of science, technology, engineering, and mathematics (STEM) education by girls (Onkokame et al., 2018; WEF, 2020). Furthermore, the prevalence of gender stereotyping in work allocation with consequent income differences, in favour of males, exacerbates the digital divide in Africa (Onkokame et al., 2018; WEF, 2020).

Evidence shows that, in order to gainfully engage within the global digital economy, Africa's digital labour space, technical capacity of workers matters. Brynjolfsson and McAfee (2014), Strydom (2021), and Dauth et al. (2017) underscored that there are high chances of work being segregated towards high-skilled jobs because in a digital economy digital skills are becoming a critical factor of production.

As a result of this context, population growth in Africa is not matching with the supply of jobs to the labour market, resulting in excess supply notwithstanding emerging jobs within the digital economy in Africa (Gaus, 2015). This unfavourable labour market situation shifts bargaining power disproportionately in favour of digital companies. Gaus (2015) argued that digital firms will have more ability to lower wages and undermine the plausibility of collective bargaining. The risk of an economic model centred on cheap labour is that it creates a vicious cycle that politically disincentivises the need for larger-scale automation (Rapanyane & Sethole, 2020). In contrast, the manufacturing and service sectors stand to be major beneficiaries of digital innovations.

If this case is established, this will result in reduction in potential levels of industrialisation of the African continent.

However, in Africa, within the short to medium term, extensive automation in Africa is far-fetched particularly in the agricultural sector which is the backbone of most African economies (Onuoha, 2022). This is mainly because Africa faces acute shortage of technological skills. The situation is worsened by the ever-increasing numbers of emigration of skilled workers to developed countries (Rapanyane & Sethole, 2020).

In the gig space faces challenges associated with high dependence on technology devices such as mobile phones and computers and access to internet (Rapanyane & Sethole, 2020). In addition, Jean-Paul and Mudavanhu (2018) argued that erratic supply of electricity and affordability of internet, computers, and mobile phones are binding constraints on the growth of the digital economy in Africa. With respect to internet, on average, the African region has less than 30% internet penetration, that is, the lowest in the world (Mothobi, 2021 and IMF, 2018). In advanced economies such as the EU, internet penetration stands at 81% (Strydom, 2021).

In addition, the reliable, affordable, and effective supply of electricity is a key infrastructural support required for the digitalisation process (Strydom, 2021). Sadly, most African countries do not have adequate electricity supply networks and enough supply of power required to meet the necessary conditions for efficiency and effectiveness (Strydom, 2021). To be specific, as noted in Chap. 1, Abisuga-Oyekunle et al. (2019) cited reliable and regular supply of electricity as one of the major hindrances faced by SMEs in Africa. A study by Abisuga-Oyekunle et al. (2019) showed that 23.3% of small firms interviewed highlighted that their biggest challenge is access to reliable electricity. In the same vein, World Bank (2018) showed that 49% of SMEs in SSA considers electricity as the major impediment. In fact, Abisuga-Oyekunle et al. (2019) went further to argue that Africa is the only continent in the world where SMEs' capacity to innovate and develop is constrained by lack of reliable supply of electricity.

5.5 Possible Remedies to Challenges Affecting the Digital Process in Africa

However, notwithstanding that digital technologies have a positive and outstanding impact on jobs in Africa, there is need to address existing binding constraints if African countries are to realise long-term benefits of digital technologies. In line with the views of Hjort and Poulsen (2019), World Bank (2020), and Strydom (2021), African governments must come up with pragmatic and disruptive policy measures which inter alia include three policy measures presented below.

Firstly, there is need for African countries to establish an affordable and reliable supply of electricity. The availability of reliable and affordable electricity is an a priori requirement for the advancement of digital technologies and sustainable development. Hjort and Poulsen (2019), World Bank (2020), and Strydom (2021) argued that, in the absence of reliable supply of electricity, Africa will miss the opportunity to use digital technologies as an instrument for stimulating economic growth, which is a priori requirement for quality jobs and establishing an entrepreneurial middle class.

Secondly, in order to increase the application and access to appropriate digital technologies in Africa, there is need for policymakers to increase access to internet in line with global trends of at least 80% of the population having access to high-speed and good quality internet. In the preceding discussions, evidence shows that there is a positive causal relationship between access to internet and the country's productivity levels.

Thirdly, in view of the fact that the African region is marked as the continent with a high number of unskilled workers and the lowest human capital development, as noted by the World Bank (2020), African countries must build a skilled workforce focused on STEMs. Building a dynamic pool of skilled workforce is essential for African economies to tap into youth dividend which is close to 70% of the population. This is a plausible view since the youths have potential to learn and establish startups which are key for the continent's economic transformation.

5.6 Conclusion

This chapter shows that the impact of technological progress on the job market is not a straightforward matter. Research on the impact of technological progress by Caprettini and Voth (2020) has shown conflicting outcomes on the labour market. For example, it was noted that during the Industrial Revolution in nineteenth-century Britain, in the spinning and weaving sector, the Luddites protested against technological progress by destroying machines because they believed that their manual labour was being replaced by machines (Caprettini & Voth, 2020).

Technological advancement which is computers-aided, for example, has complemented the performance of highly skilled workers because they enable them to perform various tasks more efficiently (Parry et al., 2021). This view was supported by World Bank (2023) and Strydom (2021) who underscored that historically technological advances have increased productivity, created more jobs than they have destroyed and generated sustained increases in the standards of living.

As part of the complexity, in advanced economies, this book shows that technological progress has been accompanied profound structural economic change which is characterised by creation of new sectors and new jobs and destruction of some sectors and jobs (World Bank, 2023; Strydom, 2021). These changes have massive dire consequences for low-skilled workers.

In view of this quagmire, World Bank (2023) and Strydom (2021) argued that digital technologies present opportunity for African SMEs to leapfrog from low productivity to high productivity which is an a priori requirement for the continent to build resilience, build economic transformation, spur sustainable economic growth, and improve the quality of jobs which are needed to support local as well as export development.

Recent advancement of digital technologies in Africa, which inter alia include improved access to internet, has had a positive impact on job creation in African economies (World Bank, 2023). To be specific, evidence shows that in countries such as Tanzania, Nigeria, and Kenya advancement in digital technologies resulted in a positive impact on job creation, productivity growth, and earnings (World Bank, 2023). On a refreshing note, in direct contrast with the established notion which says that new technologies disproportionately benefit highly skilled workers, these impacts helped to reduce poverty because they are inclusive across population segments in most African countries (World Bank, 2023).

This is mainly because the African faces acute shortage of technological skills. The situation is worsened by an ever-increasing number of emigration of skilled workers to developed countries (Rapanyane & Sethole, 2020).

In addition, the reliable, affordable, and effective supply of electricity is a key infrastructure support required for the digitalisation process (Strydom, 2021). Sadly, most African countries do not have adequate electricity supply networks and enough supply of power required to meet the necessary conditions for efficiency and effectiveness (Strydom, 2021).

As part of the strategies which must be considered by African governments to expedite the rollout and effective use of digital technologies, this book argues for the development of key infrastructures such as electricity and internet and massive rollout of STEM programmes in schools and institutions of higher learning.

References

Abisuga-Oyekunle, O. A., Patra, S. K., & Muchie, M. (2019). SMEs in sustainable development: Their role in poverty reduction and employment generation in sub-Saharan Africa. *African Journal of Science, Technology, Innovation and Development, 12*(4), 405–419. https://doi.org/10.1080/20421338.2019.1656428

Acemoglu, D., & Restrepo, P. (2017). *Robots and jobs: Evidence from US labour markets*, NBER Working Papers 23285, National Bureau of Economic Research, Cambridge, MA.

Autor, D. H., Levy, F., & Murnane, R. J. (2003). The skill content of recent technological change: An empirical exploration. *Quarterly Journal of Economics, 118*(4), 1279–1333. https://doi.org/10.1162/003355303322552801

Baldwin, R. (2019). *The globotics upheaval: Globalisation, robotics and the future of work*. Weidenfeld & Nicolson.

Brynjolfsson, A., & McAfee, A. (2014). *The second machine age: Work, progress, and prosperity in a time of brilliant technologies*. Norton.

Brynjolfsson, E., Mitchell, T., & Rock, D. (2018). 'What can machines learn and what does it mean for occupations and the economy?', *American Economic Review Papers and Proceedings 108*, 43–47. https://doi.org/10.1257/pandp.20181019

Caprettini, B., & Voth, H. (2020). Rage against the machines: Labor-saving technology and unrest in industrializing England. *American Economic Review: Insights, 2*(3), 305–320. https://doi.org/10.1257/aeri.20190385

Dauth, W., Findeisen, S., Südekum, J., & Woessner, N. (2017). The rise of robots in the German labour market. *VOXEU CEPR*, 19 September, viewed 16 October 2020, from https://voxeu.org/article/rise-robots-german-labour-market.

Di Bella, L., Katsinis, A., Lagüera-González, J., Odenthal, L., Hell, M., & Lozar, B (2023). *Annual Report on European SMEs 2022/2023*, Publications Office of the European Union, Luxemburg. https://doi.org/10.2760/028705JRC134336

Gaus, A. (2015). Automation and the Future of Work in Sub-Saharan Africa. Konrad Adenauer Stiftung. Retrieved December 20, 2023, from https://www.gppi.net/media/Automation-and-the-Future-of-Work-in-Sub-Saharan-Africa.pdf

Graham, M., & Anwar, M. A. (2018). Two models for a fairer sharing economy. In N. Davidson, M. Finck, & J. Infranca (Eds.), *The Cambridge Handbook of the Law of the Sharing Economy* (pp. 328–340). Cambridge University Press. https://doi.org/10.1017/9781108255882.025

Hjort, J., & Poulsen, J. (2019). The arrival of fast internet and employment in Africa. *American Economic Review, 109*(3), 1032–1079. https://doi.org/10.1257/aer.20161385

International Monetary Fund (IMF). (2018). *The future of work in Sub-Saharan Africa*. International Monetary Fund, Washington, DC.

Jean-Paul, van B., & Mudavanhu, S. (2018). Digital Labor in Africa: A Status Report. Retrieved January 7, 2024, from https://diodeweb.les.wordpress.com/2018/01/digital-labor-in-africa-diode-paper.pdf

Ly, R. (2021). Machine Learning Challenges and Opportunities in the African Agricultural Sector—A General Perspective. arXiv preprint arXiv:2107.05101.

McMillan, M., Rodrik, D., & Verduzco-Gallo, I. (2014). 'Globalization, structural change and productivity growth: An update on Africa', *World Development 63*, 11–32. https://doi.org/10.1016/j.worlddev.2013.10.012

Melia, E. (2020). *African Jobs in the Digital Era: Export Options with a focus on Online Labour (No.3/2020)*. Discussion Paper.

Mothobi, O. (2021). Digital Labor in Africa: Opportunities and Challenges. https://www.africaportal.org/documents/20971/Digital-labor-in-Africa-Jan-2021.pdf

Newman, C., Page, J., Shimeles, A., Söderbom, M., & Tarp, F. (2016). *Made in Africa: Learning to compete in industry*. Brookings Institution Press.

Onkokame, M., Schoentgen, A., & Gillwald, A. (2018). What is the state of microwork in Africa? A view from seven countries. *Policy Paper, 5*, 55–76. https://researchictafrica.net/wp/wp-content/uploads/2018/09/After-Access_The-state-of-microwork-in-Africa.pdf

Onuoha, R. (2022). Digitalisation and Labour in Africa: A Regional Snapshot for Relevant Social Interventions. *EPR Journal, 20*(1), 46–54.

Parry, A., Jansen van Rensburg, A., Viviers, W., & Orkoh, E. (2021). Are digital advances and inclusive growth compatible goals? Implications for trade policy in developing countries. In M. Smeets (Ed.), *Adapting to the digital trade era: Challenges and opportunities* (pp. 88–91). WTO (World Trade Organization) Publications.

Rapanyane, M. B., & Sethole, F. R. (2020). The rise of artificial intelligence and robots in the 4th Industrial Revolution: implications for future South African job creation. *Contemporary Social Science, 15*(4), 489–501.

Rodrik, D. (2016). 'An African growth miracle?', *Journal of African Economics 216*, 1–18.

Strydom, P. D. F. (2021). Digital technologies, employment and labour-market polarisation in Africa. In W. Viviers, A. Parry, & S. J. Jansen van Rensburg (Eds.), *Africa's digital future: From theory to action (The future of international trade and development Volume 1)* (pp. 101–127). AOSIS. https://doi.org/10.4102/aosis.2021.BK199.04

WEF Global Gender Gap Report. (2020). http://www3.weforum.org/docs/WEF_GGGR_2020.pdf

World Bank. (2018). *The Global Findex Database 2017.* Washington, D.C.: Author. Retrieved from https://globalfindex.worldbank.org/

World Bank. (2019). *World development report 2019: The changing nature of work.* World Bank.

World Bank. (2020). *World development report 2020: The future of work in Africa: Harnessing the potential of digital technologies for all.* World Bank.

World Bank. (2023). *World Bank report Digital Africa: Technological Transformation for Jobs.* World Bank.

CHAPTER 6

SMEs' Access to Finance, Growth, and Jobs

Gift Mugano

6.1 Introduction

Evidence shows that unlike large businesses, SMEs are more constrained in their access to financial services (Beck et al., 2005; Ayyagari et al., 2007; Mugano, 2024). With respect to the SMEs and growth nexus, weak legal and financial institutions which are normally prevalent in developing countries are one of the major hindrances preventing SMEs from growing into large firms (Mugano, 2024). Ironically, from an empirical underpinning perspective, existing finance and growth literature shows that finance is critical for SMEs' growth and ultimately economic growth. For example, the first-generation studies which inter alia include Levine and Zervos (1998), Rajan and Zingales (1998), and Demirgüç-Kunt and Maksimovic (1998) used aggregate data to showcase that financial development affects economic growth.

This chapter discusses and assesses the nexus between access to finance, SMEs growth, and job creation in Africa. In view of this, the chapter is organised as follows: Sect. 6.2 unpacks SMEs access to finance, growth, and job creation; Sect. 6.3 discusses possible remedies to access to finance; Sect. 6.4 provides concluding remarks.

G. Mugano (✉)
Faculty of Management Sciences, Durban University of Technology, Durban, South Africa

G. Mugano, N. Dorasamy, *SMEs Perspective in Africa*,
https://doi.org/10.1007/978-3-031-69103-4_6

6.2 SMEs' Access to Finance, Growth, and Job Creation Unpacked

Access to finance is defined from two fronts, that is, internal financing and external financing (Goldhausen, 2017). Internal financing is a form of financing generated within the business through sales of assets and retained earnings or profits (Goldhausen, 2017; Rossi et al., 2016). On the other hand, external financing can be defined as financial resources obtained through third parties, that is, outside the business, which include loans from banks, trade credit profits, and sale of equity (Goldhausen, 2017; Rossi et al., 2016).

This chapter places emphasis on both internal and external sources of finance.

Penrose (1959) underscored that growth was defined from two perspectives. First, joint venture, acquisition, increase in output or sales, and expanding into new markets especially global markets can be used as variables describing SMEs' growth (Penrose, 1959). Second, the quality of internal processes of SMEs can be used to describe growth (Penrose, 1959; Davidsson et al., 2006). Evidence shows that small firms' growth is largely organic, that is, it is achieved gradually and internally over time (Rahaman, 2011). On the contrary, larger firms' growth is normally achieved through joint ventures, mergers, and acquisition (Davidsson & Delmar, 1997; Penrose, 1959; Davidsson et al., 2006).

Several studies which inter alia include Carpenter and Petersen (2002), Rahaman (2011), and Honjo and Harada (2006) revealed that SMEs' growth is severely hindered by access to finance. A study by Carpenter and Petersen (2002) observed that in instances where an SME uses internal financing and has no access to external financing, its growth is adversely constrained. In direct contrast with the observation of Carpenter and Petersen (2002), Rahaman (2011) observed that internal financing is a key driver on growth for SMEs with substantial resources. This view was supported by Degryse et al. (2012) who observed that Dutch SMEs used internal financing as the most reliable and cheapest source of financing especially during and after the financial crisis.

In explaining how internal financing impacts on SMEs' growth, Rahaman (2011) argued that access to internal financing impacts on SMEs in two ways. Firstly, internal financing serves as a proxy for the SMEs' capacity and provides additional signals to outsiders about the potential of the SME and future growth prospects. External stakeholders use this information in assessing the bankability of the firm when providing external credit. Secondly, internal financing is used as a primary source of finance and a priori requirement when considering the firm's application for external financing. Normally, as noted by Rahaman (2011), banks don't provide finance or credit to SMEs with no sufficient records of how the internal finances are being used. Ideally, banks should be providing external finance to close in the gap that the firm could not adequately fund on its own as opposed to meeting all the financial requirements of the firm (Rahaman, 2011).

However, in line with conventional wisdom on the finance–growth nexus, evidence shows that SMEs which have better access to external financing experiences massive growth (Carpenter & Petersen, 2002; Beck & Demirguc-Kunt, 2006).

In order to showcase a detailed analysis of the nexus between access to finance, SMEs growth, and job creation, a funnel approach will be used to unpack this discourse. In this regard, the succeeding section presents existing facts and evidence on access to finance, SMEs growth, and job creation from a global perspective, European Union perspective, Indian perspective, and African perspective.

6.2.1 SMEs' Access to Finance, Growth and Jobs: A Global Perspective

Grounded conventional wisdom shows that a combination of economic growth and employment is an a priori requirement for poverty eradication (Brixiova et al., 2020). In Africa, evidence shows that lack of access to finance is one of the major hindrances to economic growth, job creation, and poverty eradication (Brixiova et al., 2020; Blancher, 2019; Ghassibe et al., 2019). This is particularly so because SMEs constitute more than 90% of businesses in Africa (see Chap. 2).

Studies by the International Financial Corporation (2017) revealed that, in developing countries, at least 60% of SMEs are largely constrained by access to finance. In view of this observation, researchers and policymakers argued that financial sector is a strong driver of inclusive growth (Brixiova et al., 2020). Asongu and Odhiambo (2018) and Asongu et al. (2020) argued that access to finance complemented by training or enhancement of skills have positive correlation with job creation with women as major beneficiaries. Previously, Beck et al. (2005) revealed that relaxing improving access to finance has positive impacts on SMEs' employment growth. Dao and Liu (2017) argued the impact of access to finance on job creation is more defined in smaller firms whose production structure is labour-intensive.

Ayyagari et al. (2016) argued that the relationship between finance, growth, and employment is mostly subtle because it is not yet settled in literature if SMEs' access to finance results in incremental jobs. Most importantly, Ayyagari et al. (2016) underscored that access to finance, growth and job creation is not a straightforward matter. To be specific, it is not automatic that firms which access credit create new jobs. Rather, some firms, as noted by Ayyagari et al. (2016), automated their processes after accessing credit which resulted in job losses. In some instances, as noted by Ayyagari et al. (2016), access to finance without corresponding support such as training hasn't yielded significant impact on job creation. The relevance of this chapter is centred on the fact that although there is extensive literature on the nexus between SMEs' access to finance, growth, and jobs, in Africa, there is limited evidence in the continent. Ironically, the African continent is the poorest continent in the world which is characterised by high levels of informality, underdevelopment of its financial system, and massive financial exclusion (Brixiova et al., 2020).

The question is highly relevant as evidence suggests that up to one-third of private firms in Africa report limited access to finance as a major constraint, while the private sector generates estimated 90% of jobs on the continent (McKinsey & Company, 2012). Using available literature, this chapter examines the impact of access to finance, growth, and job creation by paying attention on how the impact differs by sectors such as manufacturing, agriculture, and services.

This view was supported by Ayyagari et al. (2016) who worked as the research team leader for the World Bank Enterprise Surveys and used firm-level data sets from two different sample sizes, that is, 52,231 firms in 70 countries and one million SMEs in 29 developing countries. In these surveys, Singh et al. established the relationship between access to finance and job creation or job growth was strong and positive. Based on evidence from the two data sets, Ayyagari et al. (2016) revealed that, overall, SMEs with access to loan show job growth ranging from 1 to 3 percentage points larger than SMEs with no access to credit. In countries with credit bureaus, Singh et al. established that countries with credit bureaus have the potential to increase jobs by an additional 5% more than countries which do not have credit bureaus.

6.2.2 SMEs' Access to Finance, Growth and Jobs: Evidence from the European Union

Considerable research by several scholars, which inter alia include Beck and Demirguc-Kunt (2006), Fowowe (2017), Quartey et al. (2017), Dao and Liu (2017), Asongu and Odhiambo (2018), Asongu et al. (2020) and Mugano (2024), lack of access to finance heavily constrain SMEs' productivity and entrepreneurship which both hinders SMEs growth and job creation.

Several reports on UK SMEs have emphasised the lack of competition in the supply of banking services to SMEs (Cruickshank, 2000; Independent Commission on Banking, 2011). Siedschlag et al. (2014) and European Commission (2014) documented that small and young firms in the EU have more difficulty than other firms to obtain bank credit, even if their financial performance is the same, pointing to inefficiencies in the market for bank credit. The limited access to credit hampers firms' long-term performance. Utilising an SME panel for 12 European countries during 2014–2016, Gomez (2018) showed negative effects of credit constraints on fixed asset investments, and a subdued impact on firm growth and working capital.

Berger and Udell (1998) and Galindo and Schiantarelli (2003) have shown that both in developing and advanced countries, small firms have a more limited access to finance and are more growth-constrained than their large firms counterparts. Using firm-level survey data, Ayyagari et al. (2008) found that access to finance is firmly linked to the performance of firms. They also evidenced that entities with access to formal financing grow faster than those with access to alternative sources of financing. This evidence is supported by other studies that show that financially included firms tend to have a more efficient allocation of their asset portfolio (Ayyagari et al., 2007). In the same vein, Beck et al. (2005) provided evidence that higher obstacles faced by smaller firms translate into a slower growth, with small firms' financing obstacles having almost twice the impact on their annual growth as compared with large firms.

Detailed study by Beck et al. (2005) on the impact of financial constraints on SMEs' growth revealed that financial hurdles are negatively and significantly linked to SMEs' growth rate. According to Beck et al. (2005) small firms are constantly being the most negatively impacted.

Studies by Schiffer and Weder (2001), Beck et al. (2005) and Beck and Demirguc-Kunt (2006) revealed that, in comparison with medium-sized

SMEs, small SMEs constantly report higher growth obstacles induced by lack of access to finance.

6.2.3 *SMEs' Access to Finance, Growth and Jobs: Evidence from India*

India is one of the highly populated countries in the world with similar resemblance to African economies with respect to the high level of poverty and dominance of SMEs. It is against this background that this section unpacks the impact of SMEs' access to finance on SMEs' growth and job creation. In this regard, previous studies by the International Finance Corporation (IFC) (2018) are reviewed with a view to draw less for Africa.

IFC (2018) assessed the impact of SMEs access to finance on SMEs growth and job creation in India, In this regard, IFC (2018) undertook a baseline study using firm-level data for 200 firms that received loans ranging from US $8000 to US $2 million for the 2013–2015 financial years. Out of the sample size of 200 SMEs, IFC (2018) used specific data variables which inter alia include initial capital invested, sales, women ownership status, gender breakdown, number of employees, income, assets, firm's age, first time borrower status, and use of financing. This quantitative data analysis was complemented by qualitative analysis where both the IFC and RBL team visited SMEs premises and discussed the impact of the loans as well as how their businesses have been performing.

After the baseline survey, IFC (2018) undertook end-line questionnaire with the same dataset used in the baseline survey as well as additional variables which inter alia include the impact of demonetisation, the impact of female management and employment, feedback from customers and future financing needs.

With respect to the relationship between SMEs' access to finance and job creation, over the study period, IFC (2018) revealed that an individual SME created additional jobs averaging 10–15 people annually. This outcome is significant considering the fact that SMEs in India are small in size employing a maximum of 99 workers (IFC, 2018).

Using a multiplier effect of 5.3 jobs per year for each million dollars in loan value, between 2013 and 2016, IFC (2018)'s extrapolation revealed that loans ranging from US $10,000 to US $2 million showed that SMEs created an estimated number of direct jobs ranging from 5600 to 7200 jobs at the SMEs, and several indirect jobs in downstream industries.

From a sectoral perspective, 24% of SMEs in the wholesale and retail sector created additional jobs after receiving loans, while in the manufacturing and service sectors, 28% and 31% of the SMEs created additional jobs, respectively (IFC, 2018).

To be specific, the wholesale and retail sectors witnessed a 6% growth in employment after receiving loans as compared to an average growth rate of 4% before being given the loan in India (IFC, 2018). Likewise, in terms of contribution to the country's GDP, a study by IFC (2018) revealed, between 2012 and 2015, that services' value add to GDP grew by an average rate of 8–10%, that is, higher than the manufacturing sector which recorded value add to GDP averaging 5% during the same period.

Strikingly, evidence shows that most jobs were created by small and young firms (IFC, 2018). To be specific, IFC (2018) revealed that SMEs which are at most five years old, their workforce grew by an average rate of 12% after securing the loan. Similarly, with respect to the responsiveness of job creation to the size of SMEs after acquiring a loan, IFC (2018) shows that 21%, 46%, and 8% of micro-, small-, and medium-sized SMEs created jobs, respectively. In addition, evidence shows that micro-, small-, and medium-sized SMEs' contribution to job creation stands at 6%, 8%, and 2%, respectively (IFC, 2018). This shows that small firms are the major contributors to job creation in India. Most importantly, this evidence convincingly confirms that access to finance has strong and positive correlation between?? SMEs' growth and job creation.

From a gender perspective, in India, IFC (2018) revealed that 22% of SMEs in the sample had women holding managerial position. These businesses which were run by women witnessed growth of employment by an average rate of 13% annually (IFC, 2018).

6.2.4 *SMEs' Access to Finance, Growth and Jobs: Evidence from Africa*

In Africa, for new firms in particular, access to credit is limited by lack of financial skills, absence of financial accounts, and weak property rights (Brixiova et al., 2020). Most strikingly, evidence shows that just like new firms, existing small firms face more hurdles on access to finance as compared to medium-sized or large firms (Brixiova et al., 2020).

Evidence shows that, in most African economies, access to credit is constrained by a weak legal framework, lack of financial literacy amongst SMEs, and lack of collateral (Brixiova et al., 2020).

A number of scholars such as Mugano (2024), Brixiova et al. (2020), Asongu and Odhiambo (2018), and Asongu et al. (2020) observed that lack of access to finance by SMEs is a binding constraint to firms' capital accumulation and entrepreneurship. In the absence of formal access to finance, Brixiova et al. (2020) noted that SMEs resort to informal finance which includes schemes such as loans from relatives and, friends and credit from suppliers.

Furthermore, over and above challenges associated with lack of access to finance, studies by Auriol (2014) and Brixiová (2010) show that productive SMEs in Africa which are formalised have been hampered by several non-financial constraints such as low sales revenue and lack of social protection.

Similarly, using firm-level data covering 30 African countries, Fowowe (2017) assessed the impact of access to credit on SMEs and established that access to finance is a key driver to SMEs' growth. At a regional level, Quartey et al. (2017) established that, in West Africa, access to finance for SMEs is influenced by firm ownership, size, managerial experience, firm's export orientation, the legal framework, and the depth of credit information.

Brixiova et al. (2020), using firm-level data on 14,047 SMEs in 42 African countries, assessed the impact of SMEs' access to finance on job creation and revealed that SMEs are severely constrained on access to finance. To be specific, only 9% of SMEs has access to financial loans while 26% of SMEs have access to overdraft facilities (Brixiova et al., 2020). In order to access finance, these SMEs were required to provide collateral valued at 135% of the loan size (Brixiova et al., 2020). In terms of loan tenure, Brixiova et al. (2020) observed that SMEs in Africa access short-term loans averaging 7.4 months which is not sufficient to cover normal business cycles.

Brixiova et al. (2020) confirmed that SMEs with access to finance albeit the terms and conditions were unfavourable, witnessed significant growth in sales and impressive employment creation. In contrast, SMEs with restricted access to credit were negatively affected with respect to SMEs' growth and job creation (Brixiova et al., 2020).

The succeeding section presents possible remedies aimed at improving access to finance for SMEs.

6.3 Improving Access to Finance: Showcasing Possible Remedies

Several scholars which inter alia include Mugano (2024), Ayyagari et al. (2017) and Runde et al. (2021) outlined the following as key interventions which must be implemented with a view to improve access to finance and foster SMEs' growth and job creation: role of state intervention, role of credit guarantee schemes, alternative financing instruments, use of blended finance, and improving human capital.

6.3.1 Direct State Intervention

Evidence has shown that in developed economies such as the European Union, governments have closed the credit gap by providing financial services directly to the SMEs through established development finance institutions and by improving the regulatory environment (Mugano, 2024; Ayyagari et al., 2017).

Albeit government intervention is important, evidence has shown that in several cases the impact and results of government intervention are sub-optimal, ineffective, and counterproductive (Ayyagari et al., 2017; Mugano, 2024). For example, Mugano (2024) observed that, in order to increase outreach, the Reserve Bank of India has used the branching regulations policy. As part of this policy, a commercial bank in India, in line with the requirements that it must open four branches in areas it has no presence led to overconcentration of banks in one area (Mugano, 2024).

Contrary to the view that increase in bank branches and access to finance in the rural areas reduces rural poverty, evidence shows that the impact of increase in banks' presence in rural areas in India on poverty was elusive (Ayyagari et al., 2017). Ayyagari et al. (2017) carried a study covering the period from 1980 to 2005 and showed that bank presence in India failed to trigger more jobs and ultimately reduce poverty because of high loan losses as commercial banks incurred large losses on the back of highly subsidised interest rates and low demand caused by overconcentration of banks.

In addition, scholars such as Mugano (2024), Ayyagari et al. (2017), Dinç (2005), La Porta et al. (2002), Cole (2009), Carvalho (2014) and Sapienza (2004) have shown that, in developing countries in particular, ownership of the banking sector has been problematic. There is consensus in literature to the effect that there is no evidence that supports the established view that increase in the presence of state-owned banks foster financial development and economic growth. Mugano (2024), Ayyagari et al. (2017), Dinç (2005), La Porta et al. (2002), Cole (2009), Carvalho (2014) and Sapienza (2004) observed that in several developing countries state-owned banks fall into political capture especially during elections because they are always directed to lend to institutions linked to political parties.

This explains why development finance institutions are less effective in improving credit access to SMEs. In view of the foregoing observation, World Bank (2006) argued that development financial institutions must be run on a commercial basis with no interference from governments so as to positively impact on SMEs' growth, job creation, and poverty alleviation. In addition, World Bank (2006) argued that development financial institutions have a positive impact on SMEs if and only if deposit services are activated in wide geographic areas where government post offices use them as tools of choice in the provision of savings products and basic payment in rural areas.

6.3.2 Credit Guarantee Schemes

In both developed and developing countries, evidence shows that credit guarantee schemes (CGSs), by covering a share of the default risk of the loans, are used as an effective vehicle aimed at alleviating financial constraints by providing full or partial guarantees on bank loans to SMEs (Ayyagari et al., 2017; Mugano, 2024).

Beck et al. (2008) studies show that, in countries with governments that respect property rights and rule of law, banks believe that the credit guarantee schemes guaranteed by governments, for example, Sinosure are effective instruments which can improve access to finance for SMEs ahead of regulatory subsidies, interest rate, and directed credit.

In support of Beck et al. (2008), Honohan (2010) outlined three potential impacts of CGSs. First, CGSs which are normally backed by government guarantees helps SMEs especially from poor rural areas without collateral to access finance or loans. According to Honohan (2010), in the absence of CGSs, SMEs from poor rural areas would not have access to finance.

Second, CGSs are effective in addressing market failure that arises from adverse selection and may result in lending being rationed due to undersupply of resources to levels that are below social optimum. Finally, CGSs can be used to promote spillover of information in markets where lending is underdeveloped due to information asymmetry. In this situation, CGSs present the opportunity for banks to learn-by-doing with minimum risks.

6.3.3 *Alternative Financing Instruments*

Ayyagari et al. (2017) underscored that asset-based finance such as asset-based lending, factoring, and leasing are effective instruments which can be used by SMEs to secure credit using an underlying asset it uses as part of its business. In addition, Mugano (2024) argues that additional instruments which inter alia include corporate bonds, securitised debt and bonds are effective vehicles which can be used to bolster access to finance for SMEs.

Evidence has shown that SME loan securitisation is widely used in both advanced and emerging markets and has been effective in improving access to finance for SMEs (Mugano, 2024). From a technical perspective, with securitisation of loans, the bank which originates the loans extends the loans to SMEs and pools the loan in a portfolio and uses a Special Purpose Vehicle (SPV) which is backed by the loan portfolio and sells it to capital market investors (Mugano, 2024). Through securitisation process, the bank's exposure to credit risk is reduced and transferred to the capital market as assets are taken off the balance sheet of the originator bank (Mugano, 2024). This helps in improving the capital to risk-weighted asset ratios of the bank in full compliance of the Basel III regulations.

In practice, Kraemer-Eis et al. (2010) underscored that securitisation of SME loans works well with smaller banks because transferring of risks to capital markets helps them to increase their lending capacity and they have competitive edge in lending to smaller companies.

With respect to equity finance, scholars such as Mugano (2024), Ayyagari et al. (2017), and Runde et al. (2021) argued that where debt finance is not an option, equity finance could be another beneficial source of financing for SMEs especially during early stages of establishment. This works well in markets with established financial system where second-tier SME stock exchanges, which allow Over-the-Counter-Exchange, as in the case of India, provide opportunity for SMEs to raise equity capital. However, as noted by Mugano (2024), developing countries especially in Africa lack institutional framework, demand, and the necessary infrastructures required to rollout such financial instruments.

Mugano (2024) argued that African SMEs face two significant financing challenges in accessing finance: accessibility and affordability. With respect to accessibility, African SMEs' access to finance is complicated by the fact that they are informal. As a result of informality, they can't access finance because they don't have formal identity, registered nor banked (Mugano, 2024). However, formalisation of SMEs doesn't guarantee access to finance as there are other impediments which inter alia include absence of collateral and lack of credit history especially for first time borrowers (Mugano, 2024; Runde et al., 2021). To amplify this observation, Runde et al. (2021) estimated that 28.3% in the African continent are credit constrained while between a third and a fifth of SMEs in Sub-Saharan Africa have a bank loan or line of credit.

With respect to cost of finance, Runde et al. (2021) observed that in Africa the cost of the loan is exorbitant as it attracts other costs such as establishment fees, insurance and legal fees over and above the interest rate. In Africa, this is a serious challenge as local interest rates are as high as 20–25% for commercial banks while microfinance institutions charge rates as high as 40–50% annually (Runde et al., 2021). At these high interest rates, SMEs are deterred from applying for loans which seriously hinders the growth of SMEs in Africa.

In view of the foregoing observations, blended finance has been successfully used as an effective instrument to improve access to finance for SMEs (Mugano, 2024). Blended finance is defined as strategic use of a combination of philanthropic funds and development finance with a view to avail finance to SMEs (Mugano, 2024 and Runde et al., 2021). According to Ayyagari et al. (2017) blended finance de-risks potential investments and takes away excessive risks, thereby paving way for the banks and other actors to participate in the scheme. Mugano (2024) argued that blended finance is used as an effective tool used to catalyse private or crowd—in investment from financial institutions that have a lower risk tolerance or seek a higher rate of return.

Bilateral donors and philanthropy funds make up a significant share of blended finance (Mugano, 2024 and Runde et al., 2021). To be specific, over US $152 billion have been mobilised through the blended finance schemes, that is, almost equal to official development assistant per year (Runde et al., 2021).

In view of the foregoing observation, there is a strong case for African countries to push for a widespread use of funds from both bilateral and philanthropy funds which make up blended finance. In this regard, in line with Mugano's (2024) views, there is need for African countries to undertake the following interventions: map the investment ecosystem, incorporate flexibility, develop an effective approach aimed at identifying areas of investment, work with local markets, and engage in investment facilitation.

6.3.4 *Human Capital*

Various scholars which inter alia include Bloom and Van Reenen (2007, 2010), Bruhn et al. (2010), Ayyagari et al. (2017), and Mugano (2024) argued that managerial capital and business skills are an important driver of SMEs' growth and productivity. In view of this observation, improving human capital could help SMEs in improving pricing strategies or marketing strategies as well as financial management, which, when combined, leads to greater impact of the access to finance (Bloom & Van Reenen, 2007, 2010; Bruhn et al., 2010; Ayyagari et al., 2017; Mugano, 2024).

In order to build effective human capital for SMEs, evidence has shown that business training together with field experiments or attachment have emerged as powerful forms of capacity building provided to SME across the world which African countries can adopt (Bloom et al., 2013; Mugano, 2024). For example, field experiments which were provided on modern management practices for a selected set of Indian textile firms revealed that such training programmes increase productivity and profitability of SMEs in India which made them attractive for lending (Bloom et al., 2013).

6.4 Conclusion

This chapter shows that empirical underpinning perspective, existing finance, and growth literature show that finance is critical for SMEs' growth and ultimately economic growth (IFC, 2018). For example, IFC (2018) observed that in India an individual SME created additional jobs averaging 10–15 people annually. This outcome is significant considering the fact that SMEs in India are small in size, employing a maximum of 99 workers (IFC, 2018).

Strikingly, evidence shows that most jobs were created by small and young firms (IFC, 2018). To be specific, IFC (2018) revealed that SMEs which are at most five years old grew their workforce by an average rate of 12% after securing the loan. Similarly, with respect to the responsiveness of job creation to the size of SMEs after acquiring a loan, IFC (2018) shows that 21%, 46%, and 8% of micro-, small-, and medium-sized SMEs created jobs, respectively. In addition, evidence shows that micro-, small-, and medium-sized SMEs' contribution to job creation stands at 6%, 8%, and 2%, respectively (IFC, 2018). This shows that small firms are the major contributors to job creation in India. Most importantly, this evidence convincingly confirms that access to finance has strong and positive correlation to SMEs' growth and job creation.

However, evidence shows that in developing countries especially in Africa, unlike large businesses, SMEs are more constrained in their access to financial services (Beck et al., 2005; Ayyagari et al., 2007; Mugano, 2024).

In improving access to finance, fostering economic growth and job creation, as well as building the required resilience for African economies, this chapter argues for the use of blended finance, credit guarantee schemes, use of development finance institutions with no interference from governments, and use of alternative financial instruments such as asset-based lending, factoring, and lease financing.

References

Asongu, S. A., & Odhiambo, N. M. (2018). ICT, Financial Access and Gender Inclusion in the Formal Economic Sector: Evidence from Africa. *African Finance Journal, 20*(2), 46–66.

Asongu, S. A., Nnanna, J., & Acha-Anyi, P. N. (2020). Inequality and gender economic inclusion: The moderating role of financial access in Sub-Saharan Africa. *Economic Analysis and Policy, 65*(March), 173–185.

Auriol, E. (2014). *Barriers to Formal Entrepreneurship in Developing Countries.* Toulouse School of Economics, Background Paper for the World Development Report 2014.

Ayyagari, M., Beck, T., & Demirgüç-Kunt, A. (2007). Small and medium enterprises across the globe. *Small Business Economics, 29*(4), 415–434.

Ayyagari, M., Demirgüç-Kunt, A., & Maksimovic, V. (2008). How Important are Financing Constraints? The role of finance in the business environment. *World Bank Economic Review, 22*(3), 483–516.

Ayyagari, M., Demirgüç-Kunt, A., & Maksimovic, V. (2017). *SME finance.* World Bank Group, Washington D.C., https://doi.org/10.1596/1813-9450-8241.

Ayyagari, M., Juarros, P., Peria, M. S. M., & Singh, S. (2016). *Access to Finance and Job Growth: Firm-Level Evidence across Developing Countries.* World Bank.

Beck, T., & Demirguc-Kunt, A. (2006). Small and medium-size enterprises: Access to finance as a growth constraint. *Journal of Banking and Finance, 30*, 2931–2943.

Beck, T., Demirgüç-Kunt, A., & Maksimovic, V. (2005). Financial and legal constraints to firm growth: Does firm size matter? *Journal of Finance, 60*, 137–177.

Beck, T., Demirgüç-Kunt, A., & Peria, M. S. M. (2008). Banking services for everyone? Barriers to bank access and use around the world. *World Bank Economic Review, 22*(3), 397–430.

Berger, A., & Udell, G. (1998). The Economics of Small Business Finance: The Roles of Private Equity and Debt Markets in the Financial Growth Cycle. *Journal of Banking and Finance, 22*(6–8): 613–673.

Berger, A., & Udell, G. (2006). A More Complete Conceptual Framework for SME Financing. *Journal of Banking and Finance, 30*(11): 2945–2966.

Blancher, N. (2019). *Financial Inclusion of Small and Medium-Sized Enterprises in the Middle East and Central Asia*. IMF Middle East and Central Asia Department, Washington DC.

Bloom, N., & Van Reenen, J. (2007). Measuring and explaining management practices across firms and countries. *Quarterly Journal of Economics, 122*(4), 1351–1408.

Bloom, N., & Van Reenen, J. (2010). Why do management practices differ across firms and countries? *Journal of Economic Perspectives, 24*(1), 203–224.

Bloom, N., Eifert, B., McKenzie, D., Mahajan, A., & Roberts, J. (2013). Does management matter: evidence from India. *Quarterly Journal of Economics, 128*(1), 1–51.

Brixiová, Z. (2010). Unlocking Productive Entrepreneurship in Africa's Least-developed Countries. *African Development Review, 22*(3), 440–451.

Brixiova, Z., Kangoye, T., & Yogo, U. T. (2020). *Access to Finance among Small and Medium-Sized Enterprises and Job Creation in Africa*. IZA Discussion Papers, No. 13708, Institute of Labor Economics (IZA), Bonn.

Bruhn, M., Karlan, D., & Schoar, A. (2010). What capital is missing in developing countries? *American Economic Review, 100*(2), 629–633.

Carpenter, R. E., & Petersen, B. (2002). Is the growth of small firm constrained by internal finance? *The Review of Economics and Statistics, 82*(4), 298–309.

Carvalho, D. (2014). The real effects of government-owned banks: Evidence from an emerging market. *The Journal of Finance, 69*(2), 577–609.

Cole, S. (2009). Fixing market failures or fixing elections? Agricultural credit in India. *American Economic Journal: Applied Economics, 1*(1), 219–250.

Cruickshank, D. (2000). *Competition in UK banking: A Report to the Chancellor of the Exchequer*. HMSO.

Dao, M. C., & Liu, Q. L. (2017). *Finance and Employment in Developing Countries: the Working Capital Channel*. IMF Working Paper, 17/189, Washington DC, USA.

Davidsson, P., & Delmar, F. (1997). High Growth Firms and their Contribution to Employment: the Case of Sweden 1987–96. In *OECD, High-Growth SMEs and Employment* (pp. 9–42). OECD.

Degryse, H., de Goeij, P., & Kappert, P. (2012). The impact of firm and industry characteristics on small firms' capital structure. *Small Bus Econ, 38*, 431–447. https://doi.org/10.1007/s11187-010-9281-8

Demirgüç-Kunt, A., & Maksimovic, V. (1998). Law, finance, and firm growth. *Journal of Finance, 53*(6), 2107–2137.

Dinç, S. (2005). Politicians and banks: Political influences on government—Owned banks in emerging countries. *Journal of Financial Economics, 77*(2), 453–479.

European Commission. (2014). Access to External Financing and Firms' Growth. In *European Competitiveness Report 2014: Helping Firms Grow*.

Fowowe, B. (2017). Access to finance and firm performance: Evidence from African countries. *Review of Development Finance, 7*(1), 6–17. https://doi.org/10.1016/j.rdf.2017.01.006

Galindo, A., & Schiantarelli, F. (Eds.) (2003). 'Credit Constraints and Investment in Latin America'. Inter-American Development Bank, Washington D.C.

Ghassibe, M., Appendino, M., & Mahmoudi, S. E. (2019). *SME Financial Inclusion for Sustained Growth in the Middle East and Central Asia*. IMF Working Paper No. 19/209.

Goldhausen, J. (2017). *Access to Finance and Growth: Evidence from Dutch SMEs*. University of Twente.

Gomez, G. M. (2018). *Credit Constraints, Firm Investment and Growth: Evidence from Survey Data*. European Central Bank Working Paper No. 2126.

Honjo, Y., & Harada, N. (2006). SME Policy. Financial Structure and Firm Growth: Evidence From Japan. *Small Bus Econ, 27*, 289–300. https://doi.org/10.1007/s11187-005-6703-0

Honohan, P. (2010). Partial credit guarantees: Principles and practice. *Journal of Financial Stability, 6*, 1–9.

Independent Commission on Banking. (2011). *Final Report—Recommendations*. http://bankingcommission.independent.gov.uk

International Finance Corporation. (2017). *MSME Finance Gap: Assessment of the Shortfalls and Opportunities in Financing Micro*. Small and Medium Enterprises in Emerging Markets, IFC.

International Finance Corporation. (2018). *SME finance and growth: evidence from RBL Bank*. World Bank.

Kraemer-Eis, H., Schaber, M., & Tappi, A. (2010). *SME loan securitisation. An important tool to support European SME lending*. Working Paper EIF Research & Market Analysis, European Investment Fund, Luxembourg.

La Porta, R., López-de-Silanes, F., & Shleifer, A. (2002). Government ownership of banks. *Journal of Finance, 57*(2), 265–301.

Levine, R., & Zervos, S. (1998). Stock Markets, Banks, and Economic Growth. *American Economic Review, 88*(3), 537–558.

McKinsey & Company. (2012). *Africa at work: Job creation and inclusive growth.* McKinsey Global Institute.

Mugano, G. (2024). SME Finance: Challenges and Options. In G. Mugano & N. Dorasamy (Eds.), *SMEs and Economic Development in Africa: Challenges and Policy Options.* Routledge.

Penrose, E. (1959). *The Theory of the Growth of the Firm.* Oxford University Press.

Quartey, P., Turkson, E., Abor, J. Y., & Iddrisu, A. M. (2017). Financing the growth of SMEs in Africa: What are the constraints to SME financing within ECOWAS? *Review of Development Finance, 7*, 18–28.

Rahaman, M. M. (2011). Access to financing and firm growth. *Journal of Banking & Finance, 35*, 709–723.

Rajan, R. G., & Zingales, L. (1998). "Financial dependence and growth". *American Economic Review, 88*, 559–587.

Rossi, M., Lombardi, R., Siggia, D., & Oliva, N. (2016). The impact of corporate characteristics on the financial decisions of companies: Evidence on funding decision by Italian SMEs. *Journal of Innovation and Entrepreneurship, 5*(2), 1–14.

Runde, D. F., Savoy, C. M., & Staguhn, J. (2021). *Supporting Small and Medium Enterprises in Sub-Saharan Africa through Blended Finance.* Center for Strategic and International Studies.

Sapienza, P. (2004). The Effects of Government Ownership on Bank Lending. *Journal of Financial Economics, 72*(2), 357–384.

Schiffer, M., & Weder, B. (2001). *Firm Size and the Business Environment: Worldwide Survey Results.* Discussion Paper No. 43, International Finance Corporation, Washington, DC.

Siedschlag, I., O'Toole, C., Murphy, G., & O'Connell, B. (2014). *Access to External Financing and Firm Growth.* Background Study for the European Competitiveness Report 2014: Helping Firms Grow.

The World Bank. (2006). *The role of postal networks in expanding access to financial services.* Washington, DC.

CHAPTER 7

SMEs' Information Infrastructure and Access to Finance

Nirmala Dorasamy and Eustache Tanzala Kikasu

7.1 Introduction

Many economies worldwide remain heavily dependent on SMEs, particularly for their role and contribution, which remains globally an important source of employment creation opportunities and poverty reduction (Kreslins et al., 2018; Ackah & Vuvor, 2011; Nejadirani et al., 2011). Despite these great prospects that SMEs provide in terms of socio-economic development, challenges facing Small and Medium Enterprises are many, whether globally or typically in the entire African continent. In

The original version of the chapter has been revised. A correction to this chapter can be found at https://doi.org/10.1007/978-3-031-69103-4_11

N. Dorasamy (✉)
Faculty of Management Sciences, Durban University of Technology, Durban, South Africa
e-mail: nirmala@dut.ac.za

E. T. Kikasu
Dept of Public Management and Economics, Durban University of Technology, Durban, South Africa

G. Mugano, N. Dorasamy, *SMEs Perspective in Africa*,
https://doi.org/10.1007/978-3-031-69103-4_7

general, challenges such as the ability to adapt to rapidly changing market demands; technological changes and capacity constraints relating to knowledge; innovation and creativity; lack of resources (limited access to finance, technology, skilled labour, market access, and market information); lack of economies of scale and scope; higher transaction costs relative to large enterprises; lack of networks that can contribute to a lack of information and experience of domestic and international markets; increased market competition and concentration from large multinational enterprises caused by globalisation and economic integration; inability to compete against larger firms in terms of R&D expenditure and innovation (product, process, and organisation); subject to churning and instability; lack of entrepreneurial zeal, capacity, and know-how; lack of databases; insufficient use of information technology; low R&D expenditures; and undeveloped sales channels and low levels of financial inclusion are amongst the critical barriers affecting the growth of SMEs in various world countries (Yoshino & Hesary, 2016).

Particularly, information infrastructure and difficulties in accessing finance for SMEs are examined in this chapter. Whilst several big enterprises list their shares on stock markets and issue securities in bond markets, most SMEs have no connection with capital markets. The lack of information infrastructure for SMEs exacerbates the information asymmetry problem (Yoshino & Hesary, 2016). Research and development based on information infrastructure seems to be a key critical remedial approach in addressing challenges affecting SMEs' sustainable competitiveness. In collateral-based lending, the provision of collateral could be the simplest way for SMEs and financial institutions to reduce the risk premium in loan formulations. However, many governments are expanding policy-based finance for SMEs to mitigate the constraints on SME finance as an urgent countermeasure. Under such a situation, efficient and lower cost credit risk evaluation tools are necessary for SME financing, especially for transaction-based lending. Thus, this chapter discusses challenges of information infrastructure on SMEs, its impact on accessing credit and remedial measures for mitigating these challenges. The next section provides the ontological consideration of the concept information infrastructure and its impact on SMEs.

7.2 Concept of Information Infrastructure

According to Araujo and Katy, the phrase "infrastructure" conjures up large arrays of collective equipment essential to human activity, such as structures, roads, bridges, rail tracks, canals, ports, and communications networks. Infrastructure includes things that are more abstract than pipes, bricks, and wires, like standards, memory, and human and computer protocols. Kurniawan et al. (2018) stated that information infrastructure plays a significant role in increasing interest in the production and dissemination of information. It refers to artefacts, tools, and resources that contribute to the acquisition, processing, storage, distribution, and use of information. This implies that infrastructure is a relational term that only takes on the characteristics of a structure when it is related to structured practices. Infrastructures can therefore be both tangible (such as a computer connection hooked into a data point) and intangible and challenging to understand (such as a data point connected to a broader system that includes electricity and data networks, cloud services). In order for a computer to function as a component of a larger system, these many levels must be mobilised. Depending on the perspective we choose (such as the user, the software specialist, or the communications engineer), we can choose what at any given time constitutes the suitable infrastructure, claim. Therefore, creating an infrastructure involves categorising a network and giving various stages of view priority. Nejadirani et al. (2011) asserts that the use of information infrastructure from mainframes to personal computers, from word processing to complex applications and systems has significantly impacted large, medium, and even small organisations. According to Kreslins et al. (2018), information infrastructure can be thought of as a computing approach that gives remote users access to scalable and adaptable IT facilities over the Internet. Therefore, SMEs can take advantage of electronic commerce (e-commerce), as a type of information infrastructure, in helping their businesses to expand. In this chapter, e-commerce relates to information infrastructure in action, which consists of any economic or business activity through Web storefronts to enable the buying and selling of products and services, and to facilitate the transaction of business and activities between and amongst individuals and organisations (Nejadirani et al., 2011).

However, Nejadirani et al. (2011) specified that information infrastructure is not limited to buying and selling products online only, an online business, which will also find its suppliers, accountants, payment services, government agencies and competitors online. Furthermore, these online partners demand changes in the way they do business from production to consumption. In this regard, Kurniawan et al. (2018) added that information infrastructure includes fundamental components such as hardware, software, and support staff. According to Cordella (2012), information infrastructure refers to information technology as a productive foundation. Therefore, information technology, rather than being a productive foundation, can be seen as a flexible means of communication, by which social structures are formed, re-formed, and dissolved in a continuous process of networking. Thus, information infrastructure can be defined by a dynamic and unstable set of relationships, summarised in the idea of networking, and conceived as a configuration of communication activities (Cordella, 2012). It is the outcome of a dynamic set of actions or relationships that explains and gives meaning to the complex phenomenon of the interaction between people and technology (Cordella, 2012).

Moreover, information infrastructures are hence considered more than the outcome of a dynamic set of relationships in action, meaning that they are not stable (dynamic) but performed in, by, and through relations. The concept "infrastructure" in the context of information infrastructure is a patterned network of heterogeneous relations of heterogeneous materials (Cordella, 2012). It is an emergent phenomenon that is dynamically generated and regenerated in open-ended relationships. Therefore, the concept "information infrastructure" applied for SMEs refers to the role played by information infrastructure in action, in leveraging business performance, which is the outcome of the process of negotiation among different information systems, work practices, and routines in the daily activities of organisations (Cordella, 2012). In addition, Cordella (2012) emphasised that information infrastructure is considered not as stable entities, but rather as entities performed in, by, and through relations. It can be seen as an investment made to achieve specific objectives, such as a strategic solution to save costs via economies of scale; or as a way to benefit from the life of the current strategy, or as a strategic solution to enable current and future flexibility (Cordella, 2012). Yoshino and Hesary (2016) aligned information infrastructure to institutional information-sharing schemes of capital markets by stating that it can facilitate access to a wide range of information, necessary to estimate the creditworthiness of small or big enterprises.

Gäre highlighted that information infrastructure aligned to information systems (IS), is the complex merge of heterogeneous IS artefacts with dependencies among them. Gäre also added that a complex, evolving, and heterogeneous socio-technical system is called an information infrastructure. In other words, it correspondingly refers to a shared, evolving, heterogeneous installed base of information and communication technology (ICT) capabilities with a set of user communities based on open and/or standardised interfaces. Therefore, an information infrastructure, when appropriated by a community of users, offers a shared resource for delivering and using information services in a set community (He et al., 2021). This implies that information infrastructure plays a significant role in supporting economic activities in contemporary society. Consequently, each new generation of technology and every major technological innovation are followed by strong prerogatives that organisations, businesses, and society in general would have to be radically and fundamentally transformed to consider the new opportunities offered by the innovations in technological capabilities (Cordella, 2012). The changes brought about by technologies in organisations help to reorganise work activities or improve their management. According to Cordella (2012), information infrastructures are characterised by the complex interplay of interconnected hardware, software, and procedural configurations. These artefacts are commonly deployed to support and enact pre-determined paths of behaviour in organisations and amongst users. However, information infrastructures involve the interplay between technologies and the organisations using them, and this interplay is regarded as the main force that shapes information infrastructures, and hence it is an important factor to be considered when trying to understand the complexity of these systems (Cordella, 2012). Considering the aforementioned, it can be argued that SMEs and big enterprises must relate to capital markets or financial industry towards dealing with financial information issues and procedures that generally involve suppliers and demanders of funds. Therefore, information infrastructure is indispensable towards remedying transactional problems that mostly occur between suppliers and demanders of funds. Kurniawan et al. (2018) and Gäre identified the following three types of information infrastructure.

- **Universal service infrastructure (IT knowledge)**: refers to potential application, service, or user's knowledge of communication information technologies (ICT), which is conceptualised as the extent to which an organisation has technical knowledge about objects such as computer-based systems. Thus, IT knowledge refers to a set of principles and techniques that are useful for bringing about change towards desired goals.
- **Business sector infrastructure (IT operations)**: refers to primarily companies within the sector, but also customers and suppliers. Technical operations, or techniques, consist of activities carried out to achieve specific objectives. Operational technicalities can be considered as the methods, skills, and processes needed to complete a focal assignment. In addition, the technique consists of heterogeneous processes, most of which are directed at the production of

goods and services of economic value. Thus, the idea of a technological process aligns with a set of steps used to achieve a goal (finished product). Technical operations are also considered as a manifestation of technical knowledge, so that the implementation of technical knowledge will result in technical operations or skills. However, skills not only represent a certain deep understanding of the "knowledge domain" but also reflect the ability to export. Therefore, information infrastructure operations are conceptualised as the extent to which a company uses IT to manage market and customer information, improve effectiveness and decision-making.

- **Corporate infrastructure (information infrastructure):** refers to departments and employees within a corporation, but also suppliers, customers, and partners. Information infrastructure also refers to artefacts, tools, and resources that contribute to the acquisition, processing, storage, distribution, and use of information. Therefore, information infrastructure includes elements such as hardware, software, and support staff.

These three types of information infrastructure relate to the action or application of connectivity (network) linking organisations with services or users of technologies that support suppliers, customers, and partners in business. Afzal (2012) considered information infrastructure as a global network of people, organisations, agencies, policies, processes, and technologies organised in a loosely coordinated system to enhance the creation, production, dissemination, organisation, storage, retrieval, and preservation of information and knowledge for people. This implies that the primary objective of this network is the diffusion of knowledge for society. In light of the aforementioned, the description of the concept information infrastructure emphasises the importance of people and technology, specifically that people are part of the information infrastructure (Afzal, 2012). In addition, information infrastructure emphasises that such infrastructure includes sociopolitical, organisational, and technological factors (all related with each other and interacting in a sphere, which transcends national boundaries and cultures). Thus, the objective of the information infrastructure at a national level is to create, communicate, and deliver useful information needed for the economic, social, and political activities of the country (Afzal, 2012). This objective describes the broader role of information infrastructure and the sector of information organisations, which such infrastructure supports.

7.3 Impact of Information Infrastructure on SMEs

Savrula et al. (2014) postulated that SMEs play foremost roles in terms of employment generation and economic development in both developing and developed economies. Okello-Obura and Matovu (2011) indicated that the development of the SMEs has long been regarded as crucial for the achievement of broader development objectives, including poverty alleviation, economic development, and the promotion of more democratic and pluralist societies. Considering these perceptions, the role of information structure on SMEs depends on how unstable or dynamic the foundation upon which organisational activities are established and exploited. Kreslins et al. (2018) and Nejadirani et al. (2011) highlighted that the adoption of information infrastructure can offer the following benefits to SMEs:

- Cost and time saving; increased efficiency; flexibility and scalability of resources; increased collaboration in innovation; quick recovery of data in case of emergencies; and better communication with a client.
- Communication and collaboration in technology innovation and data analysis; as well as improvements in sustainability can be highlighted among organisational benefits at a micro level.
- Information infrastructure offers unmatched savings in terms of transaction costs.
- New developments in the labour market, that is, creation of new jobs and reallocation of labour in the IT sector as well as change in government expenditures and indirect change in revenues due to taxes can be considered as main impact factors in the macroeconomic situation.
- The reduction of costs in advertising and promotion, as well as speed communication between buyer and seller are amongst the benefits of adoption of information infrastructure by SMEs.
- SMEs can shorten their traditional supply chains, minimise transport obstacles and reduce delivery costs. Physical limitations of time and space are removed.
- Cost efficiency, facilitation of labour flexibility and improvement of communication with clients and business partners can also be named as favourable aspects for the introduction of information infrastructure.

These benefits can be facilitated using internet software and services to link internet use with opportunities it offers SMEs. The strategic potential of internet use is that it allows exercising of control over the bounds of relationships and interfaces used in relationships between customers and the business, which are also related to the firm's strategies (Nejadirani et al., 2011). According to Modimogale and Kroeze (2011), information infrastructure can fulfil several business needs such as strategic operational or marketing needs, or a combination of all of them. The different needs of the business lead to the categorisation of the use of information infrastructure, which are grouped into general-user, production-integration, and market-oriented groups. Therefore, the general-user group is where the basic technologies are used such as the telephone, e-mail, and internet to carry out administrative functions of SMEs, while the production-integration group is where information infrastructure is tightly coupled with production of goods and functionality of the business. The market-oriented group is where information infrastructure is used to market or communicate with the outside world (Araujo & Mason, 2021).

Thus, the role that information infrastructure plays within an organisation (SMEs) may be influenced by innovation or technological change. Technology and its users co-define SMEs trajectories in a dynamic interplay that is constantly reshaped by its output. This interplay is what defines information infrastructure as an emergent phenomenon in a state of permanent action rather than being a stable and static organisational foundation. According to Cordella (2012), new infrastructure calls for changes and adaptations in the existing information infrastructure. These changes can be both technological and organisational. New standards must be designed to guarantee the interoperability of the new infrastructure with all systems in place (installed base). Changes in standards and the development of technological gateways increase the complexity of the technological systems and make future changes and adaptations more difficult and demanding. The implementation of an information infrastructure calls for changes in the internal organisation of processes and organisational routines. New information infrastructures facilitate the re-organisation of work processes and routines because the technological architecture redistributes and re-organises the information flow, and thus the interdependence among pre-existing organisation departments and functions (Aanestad et al., 2017). Cordella (2012) emphasised that every change in technology or in the organisation of work activities produces side effects. Groups of users as well as technologies are always affected by changes in the information infrastructure, but they are also forces that produce these changes. These effects can be either negative, so that changes leave angry orphans, or positive, making these actors reinforce their interests in the information infrastructures.

Accordingly, whether the effects are negative or positive, both cases generate forces that shape the information infrastructure. According to Kurniawan et al. (2018), information infrastructure has a significant and positive effect towards the growth of SMEs. Most importantly, the effects can be seen through the efficiency and effectiveness on the application/utilisation of information or knowledge management. Therefore, information infrastructure can assist towards improving the management of information/knowledge which supports the growth and development of SMEs. Thus, the understanding of the role of information infrastructure on SMEs was necessary in order to elaborate, discuss, and establish a clear view about challenges facing SMEs aligned to information infrastructure and the difficulties in accessing finance.

7.4 Challenges of Information Infrastructure for SMEs

It was significantly indicated in the preceding section that SMEs play foremost roles in terms of employment generation and economic development in both developing and developed economies and that the development of SMEs has long been regarded as crucial for the achievement of broader development objectives, including poverty alleviation, economic development, and the promotion of more democratic and pluralist societies (Savrula et al., 2014; Okello-Obura & Matovu, 2011). Despite this important role, challenges affecting Small and Medium Enterprises are many, whether globally or in the African continent particularly. These challenges are commonly aligned to the lack of in-house information infrastructure expertise and financial resources (Nejadirani et al., 2011). According to Yoshino and Hesary (2016), most barriers limiting SMEs expansion include the lack of ability to adapt to rapidly changing market demand; technological change and capacity constraints relating to knowledge; innovation and creativity; lack of resources (limited access to finance, technology, skilled labour, market access, and market information); lack of economies of scale and scope; higher transaction costs relative to large enterprises; lack of appropriate networks that contribute to a lack of information, and experience of domestic and international markets. Furthermore, Yoshino and Hesary (2016) emphasised that SMEs are facing challenges related to the increased market competition and concentration from large multinational enterprises caused by globalisation and economic integration; inability to compete against larger firms in terms of R&D expenditure and innovation (product, process, and organisation);

subject to churning and instability; lack of entrepreneurial zeal, capacity, and know-how; lack of databases; insufficient use of information technology; low R&D expenditures; undeveloped sales channels and low levels of financial inclusion.

These challenges are amongst the critical factors impacting on the slow growth of SMEs in various countries. Specifically, this section emphasises on the challenges of information infrastructure and difficulties in accessing finance for SMEs. According to Yoshino and Hesary (2016), whilst several big enterprises list their shares on stock markets and issue securities in bond markets, most SMEs have no connection with capital markets. The lack of information infrastructure for SMEs exacerbates the information asymmetry problem. Two important subsections discuss the challenges facing SMEs with regard to information infrastructure and the difficulties in accessing finance. Firstly, challenges facing SMEs associated with information infrastructure is examined, then the second subsection will consider SMEs' difficulties in accessing finance.

7.4.1 Challenges Facing SMEs Aligned to Information Infrastructure

Modimogale and Kroeze (2011) asserted that globalisation and digitalisation are changing the way businesses are done and competing in the marketplace. Information infrastructure that involves information communication technology (ICT) as an essential element which leads organisations to this change. However, changes caused by the rapid development of information infrastructure have resulted in the progressive innovative economy known as the knowledge economy. In the current way of doing business, information (knowledge) remains the most significant and imperative asset in this era of globalisation economy. Information or knowledge is one of the essential products that businesses buy and sell towards supporting effective and efficient competitive growth and development of various other related businesses. However, information infrastructure represents the foundation on which the knowledge of businesses (economy) is based and the driver of organisational (economic growth) competitive advantages. Also, Okello-Obura and Matovu (2011) detailed that SMEs are experiencing difficulties in achieving economies of scale in the purchase of inputs and are often unable to take advantage of market opportunities that require large production quantities, homogenous standards, and regular supply. Furthermore, SMEs are confronted with situations where decisions are made arbitrarily and not based on accurate business information (Okello-Obura & Matovu, 2011).

In addition, Yoshino and Hesary (2016) indicated that most SMEs in the developing countries are facing several challenges from increased competition, the inability to adapt to rapidly changing market demand, technological change, and capacity constraints relating to knowledge, innovation, and creativity. Moreover, for many SMEs, their potential is often not fully realised due to factors related to their small scale: lack of resources (finance, technology, skilled labour, market access, and market information); lack of economies of scale and scope; higher transaction costs relative to large enterprises; lack of networks that contribute to a lack of information, know-how, and experience of domestic and international markets; increased market competition and concentration from large multinational enterprises caused by globalisation and economic integration; an inability to compete against larger firms in terms of R&D expenditure and innovation (product, process, and organisation); being subject to disturbing and unstable situations; and a lack of entrepreneurial zeal, capacity, and know-how (Yoshino & Hesary, 2016).

Modimogale and Kroeze (2011) acknowledged that at the forefront of organisational performance is the recognition that information infrastructure (innovative technological asset which supports the distribution of information or communication process), knowledge and their intelligent application are the essential factors of success in the new economic environment where SMEs are intended to operate in taking advantage of information technology to achieve high levels of efficiency and effectiveness. Unfortunately, in most developing countries, the SMEs sector suffers from inadequacies in the provision of business information, which is only available from stand-alone institutions, and is often slow and cumbersome to access, limited in scope, and is not provided in an integrated manner. The lack of accessing adequate information which enhances productivity and facilitates market access remains a key barrier to the success of SMEs (Okello-Obura & Matovu, 2011). Therefore, it can be agreed that information/communication and information infrastructures are vital assets that support, promote, and give SMEs a competitive advantage in the innovative globalisation economy. However, in many developing countries, including South Africa, SMEs' access to information remains a real challenge, due to a lack of innovation and appropriate usage of information infrastructure.

According to Modimogale and Kroeze (2011), taking advantage of innovative information infrastructure and getting easy access to information plays a critical role in the informed decision-making process, thus making it easy for SMEs to make sound competitive decisions. In addition, the ability of SMEs to survive in an increasingly competitive global environment is largely dependent or based upon their capacity to leverage information as a resource. Thus, it is imperative for SMEs to strategically position information infrastructure within their organisation in such a way that they will maximise its benefits. Accordingly, to maximise the benefits of innovative information infrastructure, SMEs are required to promptly deal with different barriers that prevent them from adopting or implementing information infrastructure, ranging from socio-economic issues to technology-related issues.

Kreslins et al. (2018) indicated that in the context of African countries (developing countries), including South Africa, barriers affecting SMEs are related to the lack of access to financial support (money), power cuts, lack of knowledge, and possibility of fraud, technology intimidation and (perceived) high cost of information infrastructure. Hence, regarding barriers aligned with technology-related issues, Modimogale and Kroeze (2011) indicated that there are several things (technology perspective) that SMEs need to take into consideration when implementing technology. For instance, the organisational culture should be technology oriented; business processes must be flexible in order to consider technology; and the need to check the availability of IT skills needed for implementing the technology. Consequently, the lack of consideration of these factors might cause failures in the adoption of information infrastructure processes. Furthermore, regarding barriers aligned with socio-economic issues, Yoshino and Hesary (2016) specified that there are limitations which are related to the management and organisation of technology perspectives; limitations aligned to owners-managers of SMEs; barriers facing SMEs' adopting information infrastructure as a competitive tool; and environmental or geographical barriers. Table 7.1 discusses and reflects on elements that involve each of the aforementioned barriers.

Table 7.1 highlights elements of nonalignment to information infrastructure, potentially limiting the growth and development of SMEs, especially in developing countries, which endure management and organisation of technology challenges. This affects the owners-managers of SMEs adopting information infrastructure as a competitive tool. Relatedly, Modimogale and Kroeze (2011) acknowledged that one of the biggest

Table 7.1 Nonalignment to information infrastructure limiting the growth of SMEs

Nonalignment to the management and organisation of technology perspective	*Nonalignment by owners-managers of SMEs*	*Nonalignment to the adoption of information infrastructure as a competitive tool*	*Nonalignment of the environmental or geographical position of SMEs*
—The management and organisation of technology perspective places emphasis on the strategic approach to information infrastructure by SMEs and on the capabilities and structures of the SMEs. —Small firms and information infrastructure from the small-firm perspective: This view focuses on the SMEs and how they use technology as a tool to improve their competitiveness. This perspective takes into consideration the vision of the SME. —If they have a well-trained information infrastructure staff, SMEs are likely to adopt and use information infrastructure as a competitive tool successfully.	—The owner-manager, as a crucial part of the SME, makes all or most of the decisions regarding the business. This consistency in making rational decisions is critical. —Owners-managers may have the following limitations: # Capability gaps or knowledge gaps which prevent effective technology use and selection. # Intuitive and organic styles of management have important consequences for the way in which they evaluate and use technology.	—Everyone assumes that information infrastructure will successfully bring about benefits, but not all environments are the same. —The issues affecting successful implementation or adoption of information infrastructure are both socio-economic and technological: these barriers can be caused by factors external and/or internal to the organisation, which in this case is the SME. —Many underdeveloped economies exist below subsistence levels and remain impoverished because they have no access to basic infrastructure essential for economic growth and development. —SMEs may be prevented from adopting information infrastructure due to:	—Ever-changing information infrastructure environment: the information infrastructure environment is ever-changing, so constant learning and updating of technologies is needed. Technology is constantly evolving, getting faster, smaller, more powerful, or digital. There are two issues here: on the one hand, the SMEs need to monitor the kind of technologies that their clients are using and try to make sure that they are on par in order to serve them. On the other hand, the SMEs do not need to change every time there is a change in technology; this depends on the focus area of the SMEs.

(*continued*)

Table 7.1 (continued)

Nonalignment to the management and organisation of technology perspective	*Nonalignment by owners-managers of SMEs*	*Nonalignment to the adoption of information infrastructure as a competitive tool*	*Nonalignment of the environmental or geographical position of SMEs*
—Getting the right skills is part of the strategic function of the organisation, since understanding that information infrastructure plays a critical role in the business to help in planning the right budget, creating the right job description, and knowing how to interview for information infrastructure skills. —Perceived high setup costs: information infrastructure is perceived to be expensive by SMEs, so they often do not have a budget for it. The other problem regarding the cost of information infrastructure is that SMEs may invest in unnecessarily big solutions due to sale pitches, hype of specific products, or market patterns without considering their real need. There are different types of costs associated with information infrastructure: product/solution, development, connectivity, hardware, software, maintaining workforce, and hidden costs such as annual licence fees, upgrade fees, etc. —Fear of capital investment and associated complexities; lack of realising possible benefits; lack of technical resources as well as lack of time and IT skills; security issues, data ownership, and protection; and also the philosophy of managers and their subjective opinion may be hindrances. —Pressure of competitors, technology efficiency, and pressure from the business partners are the main factors which stimulate the introduction of new technologies in the companies.	# The owners-managers' personal skills and mind-sets influence their organisations' culture. This means that if the owner-manager is technology-averse, it will be difficult to adopt information infrastructure and use it as a tool. —The owner is at the centre of the business, making all or most of the decisions in the small business, so the adoption of information infrastructure by the small business depends on the owner's information infrastructure skills, personality, and attitude towards technology. —The owners-managers' attitude towards information infrastructure and its value to bring about change, as SMEs need such expertise to work with. —The ideal staff level for an SME that considers information infrastructure to be the core of its business strategy is that of a high-user group. Optimal use of information infrastructure in the economy depends on well-trained human resources for developing relevant applications and supporting and maintaining systems. —If the owner-manager has little concern towards the importance of information infrastructure strategy and planning within their business, then information infrastructure adoption can be affected.	# Lack of knowledge about the strategic use of information infrastructure (lack of knowledge about the potential benefits of information infrastructure and strategies to support SMEs in achieving their business objectives). # Strategic-level oversights regarding information infrastructure which needs to be considered as a key player for the SME in reaching its goals. —Lack of necessary IT skills-base. The IT skills problem forms part of the bigger problem of a shortage of specialists in IT/ ICT. —SMEs tend to use computers more as tools and less as a communication medium. —SMEs have considerably fewer resources available to implement information infrastructure solutions. —Security risks (if the service is dependent on internet technology, then a certain security risk is inevitable). —Lack of control, lack of customisation, economic disadvantages, and compliance are also drawbacks. —The security problems may emerge as the result of failing to verify the physical infrastructure, that is, location of information and methods used for data protection are often unknown for most SMEs. —Failure to use the latest information technology solutions. Many SMEs are not ready to invest in IT to increase performance and competitivenesscompanies.	—The information infrastructure strategy of the SME needs to take into consideration that technology changes at a rapid rate, the different technologies need to be monitored as they evolve into the future, and the staff needs to be excited enough to have an interest in the changes as they happen. —Geographical factors: most rural areas lack resources and infrastructure and have no proper address systems. Fixed-line connectivity in rural areas is still a huge problem, though the use of cell phones is high. Another major problem is the high rate of illiteracy in the rural areas.

Source: Adapted from Kreslins et al. (2018), Modimogale and Kroeze (2011) and Nejadirani et al. (2011)

problems affecting SMEs growth and development in Africa is the high cost of connectivity and the lack of infrastructure. In addition, difficulties in accessing finance remain a key factor for the emergence of SMEs in the continent. Thus, overall, SMEs possess significant problems in identifying the appropriate application of information infrastructure and its strategy due to the lack of knowledge and planning in information infrastructure (Nejadirani et al., 2011). The following subsection discusses challenges facing SMEs aligned to the difficulties in accessing finance.

7.4.2 Challenges Facing SMEs Aligned to the Difficulties in Accessing Finance

According to the European Union briefing (2021) and Yoshino and Hesary (2016), SMEs' challenges may be internal (intrinsic) or external (extrinsic). Mostly, internal barriers are related to the difficulties in raising or accessing finance. Therefore, financial barriers represent an important obstacle for SMEs, especially those that are not yet sufficiently developed. A study found that more than a half of SMEs report that the financial investment required to become more competitive is too large and thus discourages them to invest more resources on R&D (European Union, 2021). Financial barriers can occur in many ways. According to Yoshino and Hesary (2016), many banks prefer to allocate their resources to large enterprises rather than to SMEs because large enterprises have a lower risk of default and their financial statements are clear, while SMEs are riskier mainly from the point of view of lenders as they do not have clear accounting information. Therefore, in most cases financial barriers include the following (European Union, 2021; Ackah & Vuvor, 2011):

- When SMEs have a shortage of funds needed for researching new markets and adapting marketing strategies to local or international markets.
- When there is a shortage of funds needed to finance the necessary investments to start local or international operations.
- When there is a shortage of funds needed to insure products or assets in local or foreign markets.
- When there are requirements of collateral, which most SMEs cannot provide (lack of adequate collateral: usually in the form of landed property). Those who are able to provide the collateral and to access this credit are also facing the challenge of high interest rates and

short repayment periods, making it very difficult to embark on any developmental or expansion projects. The availability of collateral plays a significant role in the readiness of banks to meet the demand of the private sector. Collateral provides an incentive to repay and offset losses in cases of default.

- In most countries, especially developing nations, lending to small businesses and entrepreneurs remains limited because financial intermediaries are apprehensive about supplying credit to businesses due to their high risk, small portfolios, and high transaction costs (costs of transaction contribute to the inability of the SMEs to access finance). If transaction costs of lending are high, the net margin banks expect from loans operation do not compare favourably against safe investment represented by treasury bonds.

Furthermore, financial barriers can be particularly relevant to SMEs as they are linked to the size of the business (European Union, 2021). Certainly, compared to larger businesses, SMEs are usually at a disadvantage when seeking to obtain loans from banks due to their lower assets. In most cases, SMEs do not obtain the full bank loan for which they apply, and this clearly creates difficulties for SMEs to emerge or grow (European Union, 2021). In some other cases, the cost of borrowing may also be a strong barrier for SMEs to access financial support from banks. However, it is only when SMEs overcome their financial barriers and have access to sufficient capital that they can become competitive locally, nationally, or globally (European Union, 2021). Additionally, there exist other barriers which are associated with information. According to the European Union (2021), these barriers are internal (information, human resources, financial, and marketing barriers) and external (competitor, procedural, and governmental barriers). Table 7.2 specifies in detail some these internal and external barriers.

Table 7.2 illustrated some of the internal and external barriers affecting SMEs' growth and development, especially in developing countries. Therefore, in the process of providing remedial measures for mitigating challenges affecting SMEs, the value and impact of information structure on SMEs is examined by two schools of thought. According to Modimogale and Kroeze (2011), the two schools of thought about the issue of information infrastructure value include Porter's theories, which declared that information infrastructure adds value to SMEs, and the other, known as Millar's theories, which considered that information infrastructure does

Table 7.2 Internal and external barriers aligned to SMEs' difficulties in accessing finance

Internal barriers	**Informational barriers or lack of information infrastructure:** —The lack of information infrastructure for SMEs exacerbates the information asymmetry problem. The financial industry deals with information intrinsically. There is an asymmetric information problem between suppliers and demanders of funds in general. Information infrastructure is necessary to remedy this problem. Many big enterprises list their shares on stock markets and issue securities in bond markets. Institutional information-sharing schemes of capital markets can facilitate access to a wide range of information necessary to estimate the creditworthiness of big enterprises. However, most SMEs have no connection with capital markets. Financial institutions can closely and continuously observe borrowers, but it is costly to do so for borrowers of small loans. —Unclear final cost of cloud computing, utilisation, dependency on the internet connection, lack of speed, and lack of customisation are amongst the weaknesses of SMEs. But their strengths include cost saving; time saving; improved efficiency of resource utilisation; and scalability and flexibility of system capacity. —Low levels of business research and development (R&D) in the SME sector: business enterprise expenditure on research and development is an important driver of innovation and economic growth. An economy's R&D is generally concentrated in a limited number of large firms. In some economies, however, small- and medium-sized firms account for a significant share of the total business R&D effort. This may be due to a relatively large body of SMEs that perform a large amount of R&D (such as specialised R&D units that are part of a larger group). The share of SMEs in total R&D in some economies is low; this is one of the important reasons behind the slowed economic growth in certain countries. —Insufficient use of information technology by SMEs: information technology has developed rapidly. Household ownership of mobile phones, smartphones, tablets, and computers have also spread quickly in the recent years. Accordingly, more consumers have come to prefer internet sales to over-the-counter sales and the e-commerce market for individuals is expanding. SMEs have been unable to sufficiently utilise such opportunities. Most small enterprises do not have their own websites. Currently, in developed countries, SMEs are selling products and receiving orders via their own websites where they have their own online shops or market their goods on internet shopping sites. —Informational barriers may prevent SMEs from internationalising their operations. Informational barriers refer to the problems in identifying, selecting, and contacting local or international markets due to information inefficiencies. —Informational barriers arise from limited information to locate and analyse markets, which increases the difficulty in finding those national and international sources of information that are available to reduce the amount of uncertainty associated with local or foreign markets. —Informational barriers may arise from the lack of reliable data about the local or international market, which can be due to problems associated with the source, quality, and comparability of available information used to attempt to increase understanding of local or foreign markets. —Informational barriers may arise from strategically and/or proactively identifying and selecting opportunities in foreign markets (including customers, contacts, business partners, and joint ventures). **Human resource barriers:** —Most SMEs have concerns relating to the difficulties associated with the management of human resources. Managers of SMEs may not have developed (locally or internationally) their operations due to time and human resource constraints, affecting the identification of local or foreign markets and for the designing of an appropriate entry strategy. —The increased amount of work demanded by SMEs (locally or internationally) for operations may become overwhelming, especially if an SME's personnel have no prior experience in handling the required information (documentation), the logistical arrangements, and the communication with local or foreign customers. —SMEs often do not have the same resources for training employees as larger companies do. Often, the non-availability of skilled staff or experienced managers remains the most serious problem for SMEs. **Marketing barriers:** —Marketing barriers can prevent SMEs from promoting their operations, including the company's product, pricing, distribution, logistics, and promotion activities abroad. —SMEs may have to develop new products or adapt existing ones to the needs of specific local or foreign markets. At the same time, SMEs may also have to modify their pricing formula in order to match competitors' prices. These changes may reduce the potential for economies of scale associated with selling locally or internationally and affect overall profitability. —The difficulties that SMEs may encounter are when they must identify partners to help roll out their operations, but such partners may have different organisational and operational structures that make the partnership difficult or even more problematic, while local potential partners may already be engaged by competitors.

(*continued*)

Table 7.2 (continued)

External barriers	**Competitor barriers:** —Constrained with limited resources, SMEs are likely to be exposed to intense competition in the markets, both from incumbent domestic players and from large multinational corporations. SMEs may thus be discouraged from entering the markets while they will fear that their domestic competitive advantage could be lost abroad due to more complicated and intensive competitive scenarios. —Traditional strategies that work for multinational corporations may be ineffective for SMEs. Therefore, SMEs will need to develop their own unique competitive strategy when faced with competition from multinational companies. —To successfully compete in markets, SMEs are required to focus on specific, well-defined market niches, in which they can still hold a competitive advantage and thus deliver higher value to their customers. **Procedural barriers:** —SMEs can be prevented from conducting effective operations due to their unfamiliarity with the necessary procedures and required paperwork. For example, SMEs may have difficulties in understanding and managing the complexity of customs documentation or the bureaucracy associated with operations due to their more limited resources. This raises compliance costs and may cause delays, which may require SMEs to hold larger inventories and working capital. In some cases, procedural barriers are less direct, and they are often not visible. As a result, they are usually hard to identify and eliminate. **Governmental barriers:** —SMEs wishing to introduce their operations to local or international markets are also often confronted with governmental barriers, such as extensive requirements from exporters, document completion, and clearance. This impacts on costs, causes delays, and procuring of potential business on time. —The lack of government assistance/incentives to participate in local or national value chains has been identified as a main concern for SMEs. —Globalisation has greatly increased in recent years, and production is now more fragmented across businesses and countries. While multinational corporations have been at the forefront of this process, SMEs are increasingly confronted with opportunities, but also the challenges offered by global value chains. Participation in global value chains can be extremely beneficial for SMEs as it can provide access to global markets at lower costs, create opportunities to scale up the business, and accelerate innovation and managerial know-how. However, without the resources and accessing of relevant information, such benefits may be lost. —SMEs' awareness and understanding of the structure and the dynamics of global value chains is generally low, and most SMEs across different sectors are not able to identify their competitive strengths within the value chain. Such awareness requires access to information which is time-consuming to access, while networking extensively and continuously can be a challenge for SMEs. —The concerns about both the inadequacy of resources needed and the inability to protect the company's intellectual assets may hinder the opportunities for SMEs to successfully participate in global value chains. —Lack of practical information on the benefits of participating in global value chains and assistance on how to obtain access from government support sectors is a mitigating factor. —Security and confidentiality problems, loss of control over data, and intellectual property theft could be more expensive. Such threats can negatively affect enhanced communication with partners/clients, easier collaboration in innovation, fast recovery of lost data, and opportunities for 24/7 real-time management.

Source: Adapted from European Union briefing (2021), Kreslins et al. (2018) and Yoshino and Hesary (2016)

not really add any value since it is a commodity, just like electricity, available to everyone. However, the two schools of thought have agreed that competitiveness of an SME depends on the ways in which information infrastructure is used to support business processes. Therefore, it can be understood that having information infrastructure applied in a business may not necessarily give the business any competitive advantage, but having it linked to the business processes and strategy could most likely give a competitive advantage (Modimogale & Kroeze, 2011). Consequently, SMEs that employ information infrastructure may have a better opportunity of becoming commercially successful via some of the following ways (Modimogale & Kroeze, 2011):

- Owner motivation, experience, and management skills
- Expertise in managing growth
- Access to resources (money, technology, and people)
- Innovation as a means of competitive advantage and flexibility
- Close contact with customers
- A focus on profits rather than sales and
- Strong demand and operating in a growth market

7.5 SMEs' Prospects for Accessing and Boosting Financial Support

According to the World Bank Group (2018), the limitations faced by SMEs are the result of a lack of credit information because determining their creditworthiness is a difficult task. As they have less access to traditional sources of financing like banks and other financial institutions, whose data is normally utilised in the development of credit reports, SMEs may find it more challenging to establish a credit history than larger companies. Additionally, SMEs typically lack access to fixed assets like land or buildings that banks typically seek as collateral for loans. Instead, in order to secure financing, SMEs mostly rely on transportable assets. Accordingly, SMEs which produce employment, value added, and contribute to innovation are crucial to national economies all over the world (OECD, 2017).

The pursuit of environmentally sustainable development and more inclusive economic growth depends heavily on SMEs. But their contributions vary greatly between businesses, nations, and industries. According to the World Bank Group (2018), it is possible to increase the contributions of SMEs to global markets by improving their access to financial support networks, but this is countered by a lack of funding, trade and investment restrictions, and inadequate physical and ICT infrastructure. These factors make it difficult for SMEs to operate effectively and to access domestic and international markets at prices that are competitive. Earlier, it was asserted that due to a variety of factors, Small and Medium-Sized Enterprises (SMEs) frequently have trouble obtaining financial assistance (European Union briefing, 2021; Kreslins et al., 2018). Therefore, support from both within the company and from outside the company (Government and Banks) might be crucial in assisting SMEs in overcoming these obstacles. According to Chowdhury, for SMEs to expand and prosper in any nation, financial access is essential. The growth and productivity of this industry are directly influenced by the accessibility of outside financing. It is widely acknowledged that banks and governments are the primary external sources of funding for the SMEs sector in both developed and developing countries. Table 7.3 illustrates the way SMEs can internally and externally enhance or boost opportunities for financial support.

Table 7.3 indicates that SMEs who are experiencing problems obtaining finance require both internal and external support. According to Chowdhury:

- Internal support consists of SMEs to benefit from improving their internal structures and financial management practices as well as work on building a strong credit history, given that a good credit history can lead to better loan terms and access to more financing options, create a comprehensive business plan that outlines the company's financial needs and growth strategies, etc.
- External support consists of governments, banks, and other financial institutions to support SMEs' access to finance through mechanisms described in Table 7.3.

By improving their internal financial processes and employing outside tools and support, SMEs can boost their probabilities of acquiring the finance they need to grow and survive. Government support for Small and Medium-sized Enterprises (SMEs) is a common practice in many countries (specifics might vary greatly between nations) in order to promote the growth and sustainability of small businesses which are crucial to the economy (OECD, 2021). In addition to elements highlighted in

Table 7.3 SMEs' prospects for boosting financial support

Internal assistance	*External assistance*
Financial management: SMEs can benefit from improving their internal financial management practices. This includes budgeting, cash flow management, and financial planning. Proper financial management can make SMEs more attractive to lenders and investors.	**Government programmes:** Many governments offer various programmes and incentives to support SMEs' access to finance. These can include loan guarantee schemes, grants, and tax incentives. SMEs should explore these options and take advantage of them.
Creditworthiness: SMEs should work on building a strong credit history. This involves paying bills on time and maintaining a good credit score. A good credit history can lead to better loan terms and access to more financing options.	**Financial institutions:** Banks and other financial institutions often have specialised programmes for SMEs, including loans, lines of credit, and trade finance. Building relationships with these institutions can improve access to finance.
Business planning: Creating a comprehensive business plan that outlines the company's financial needs and growth strategies is essential. A well-structured business plan can help SMEs articulate their financing needs to potential lenders and investors.	**Venture capital and angel investors:** For SMEs with high growth potential, venture capital firms and angel investors can provide equity financing. These investors often offer not only capital but also mentorship and industry connections.
Cost management: Efficient cost management practices can free up cash for SMEs to reinvest in their businesses or to meet financial obligations, reducing their need for external financing.	**Crowdfunding:** Online crowdfunding platforms enable SMEs to raise funds from a large number of individual investors. Crowdfunding can be an effective way to access capital, especially for startups and innovative businesses.
Financial literacy: Enhancing the financial literacy of SME owners and managers can empower them to make informed financial decisions and navigate the complex world of finance more effectively.	**Peer-to-peer lending:** Peer-to-peer lending platforms connect SMEs with individual lenders. These platforms often have more flexible lending criteria than traditional banks.
Digitalisation: Small- and medium-sized businesses (SMEs) now have more opportunity to take part in the global economy due to digitalisation; however, many businesses are trailing behind and disruptive consequences need to be taken into account.	**Financial advisors:** Seeking guidance from financial advisors or consultants can help SMEs identify the most suitable financing options and prepare strong loan applications.

(*continued*)

Table 7.3 (continued)

Internal assistance	*External assistance*
	Trade associations and chambers of commerce: These organisations can provide networking opportunities, access to industry-specific information, and connections to potential financiers. **Mentorship programmes:** Engaging with mentors who have experience in finance and entrepreneurship can provide valuable insights and connections that can assist SMEs in accessing finance.

Source: World Bank Group (2018) and OECD (2017)

Table 7.3, explicitly, the following are different types of government support for SMEs' growth and development (World Bank Group, 2018; OECD, 2017):

- **Financial support:**
  - **Grants:** Governments often provide grants to SMEs for various purposes, such as research and development, technology adoption, and innovation.
  - **Subsidised loans:** Governments may offer low-interest or interest-free loans to SMEs to help them with working capital, expansion, or investment in new equipment or technologies.
  - **Loan guarantees:** Some governments provide guarantees to banks or financial institutions to encourage them to lend to SMEs, even if they have limited collateral.
- **Tax incentives:**
  - **Tax credits:** Governments may offer tax credits to SMEs that engage in specific activities like research and development, hiring in specific regions, or investing in eco-friendly technologies.
  - **Tax deductions:** Deductions for certain business expenses can help SMEs reduce their tax burden and increase their cash flow.
- **Training and education:**
  - **Workforce training programmes:** Governments often support SMEs by offering training programmes for employees to improve their skills and productivity.

  - **Business development training:** Providing SMEs with access to business development programmes and workshops can help them improve their management and operations.
- **Access to markets:**
  - **Export assistance:** Governments may offer programmes to help SMEs expand into international markets by providing market research, trade missions, and export financing.
  - **Public procurement opportunities:** Governments may set aside a portion of their procurement budgets for SMEs, helping them secure government contracts.
- **Technology and innovation support:**
  - **Research and development (R&D) grants:** Governments can provide financial assistance to SMEs engaged in R&D activities to stimulate innovation.
  - **Technology transfer programmes:** Facilitating the transfer of technology from research institutions to SMEs can boost innovation and competitiveness.
- **Regulatory support:**
  - **Simplifying regulations:** Governments can streamline regulations and reduce bureaucratic hurdles that often burden SMEs.
  - **Compliance assistance:** Providing guidance and resources to help SMEs comply with regulations can reduce their compliance costs.
- **Networking and support services:**
  - **Business incubators and accelerators:** Governments may fund or support these programmes to help startups and SMEs access mentorship, office space, and networking opportunities.
  - **Trade associations and chambers of commerce:** These organisations often receive government support to provide services and advocacy on behalf of SMEs.
- **Access to finance and investment:**
  - **Venture capital and angel investor support:** Governments can encourage private investors to support SMEs through tax incentives or co-investment programmes.
  - **Stock market listings:** Facilitating SME listings on stock exchanges can provide them with access to additional sources of capital.

Considering the above aspects, government assistance to SMEs is indispensable for fostering economic growth, job creation, and innovation (Abara & Banti, 2017; Gopaul & Manley, 2015). In Europe, small- and medium-sized businesses are supported by governments' financial assistance and make up 99% of companies in OECD nations, which are crucial growth engines because they promote the development and adoption of technologies that increase productivity, spur higher growth, and generate jobs (OECD, 2021). However, the effectiveness of government assistance to SMEs can vary depending on factors such as the country's economic conditions, the design of the assistance programmes, and the level of administrative efficiency in their implementation (OECD, 2021). This implies that external support (Governments, banks, and other financial institutions) plays a crucial role in providing assistance to Small and Medium-sized Enterprises (SMEs) by offering a range of financial products, services, and support. SMEs are the backbone of many economies, and their success is essential for economic growth and job creation. Here are some ways in which banks and other financial institutions assist SMEs (IMF, 2019; Abara & Banti, 2017):

- **Access to financing**: Banks provide SMEs with access to capital through loans, lines of credit, and other financing options. These funds can be used for various purposes, including working capital, expansion, purchasing equipment, or funding specific projects.
- **Credit facilities**: Banks offer credit facilities, such as overdrafts and revolving credit lines, to help SMEs manage their cash flow and short-term financial needs.
- **Business loans**: Banks offer various types of business loans tailored to the specific needs of SMEs, such as term loans, equipment loans, and trade finance. These loans can be used for growth, investment, or operational purposes.
- **Trade finance services**: Banks facilitate international trade for SMEs by offering trade finance services like letters of credit, export financing, and trade credit insurance. This helps SMEs engage in global markets and expand their customer base.
- **Payment processing services**: Banks provide payment processing solutions, including merchant services, online payment gateways, and point-of-sale systems, to help SMEs accept payments from customers efficiently and securely.

- **Savings and investment products**: Banks offer various savings and investment products, such as business savings accounts, certificates of deposit (CDs), and investment advisory services, to help SMEs grow their wealth and manage surplus funds.
- **Cash management services**: Banks assist SMEs in optimising their cash flow with services like cash concentration, disbursement services, and remote deposit capture, helping them efficiently manage their finances.
- **Financial advisory and consulting**: Some banks offer financial advisory and consulting services to SMEs, providing expertise on financial planning, risk management, and strategic decision-making.
- **Online banking and mobile apps**: Many banks offer user-friendly online banking platforms and mobile apps that enable SMEs to manage their accounts, make payments, and access financial information conveniently.
- **Government assistance programmes**: In collaboration with government agencies, banks may offer financing options that come with favourable terms, reduced interest rates, or government guarantees to support SMEs during challenging economic times.
- **Educational resources**: Some banks provide educational resources, workshops, and seminars to help SMEs improve their financial literacy and business management skills.
- **Networking opportunities**: Banks often host networking events and forums where SMEs can connect with other businesses, potential partners, and industry experts, facilitating business growth and collaboration.
- **Risk mitigation**: Banks offer services like credit analysis and risk assessment to help SMEs assess the creditworthiness of their customers and suppliers, reducing the risk of bad debt.

In light of the above features, it is critical to consider that banks and other financial institutions play a vital role in supporting the growth and stability of SMEs by offering a wide range of financial tools and services (OECD, 2015). SMEs should carefully assess their financial needs and work with their bank or financial institutions to develop a customised financial strategy that aligns with their business goals. Additionally, seeking guidance from financial advisors or business consultants can be valuable in navigating the complexities of managing a small or medium-sized enterprise.

7.6 Remedial Measures for Mitigating Challenges Affecting SMEs

Through the continuation and expansion of conventional banking financing and non-financing instruments (such as loans, overdraft facilities, credit, and business development support), the banking sector can continue to play a catalytic role in the financing and investment of SMEs. But, according to Adam and Alarifi (2021), all modern businesses must innovate if they wish to thrive in a world that is marked by competition, technological development, and recurrent crises. Currently the focus is moving towards determining the impacts of information infrastructure (relationship) on SMEs following the envisioned objectives of SMEs. Studies are currently giving more consideration on information infrastructure towards suggesting remedial measures for mitigating these challenges because they have understood the importance of information infrastructure in supporting the SMEs' growth and development process.

According to Yoshino and Hesary (2016), one of the solutions towards mitigating challenges affecting SMEs involve the development of collateral-based lending, given that the provision of collateral could be the simplest way for SMEs and financial institutions to reduce the risk premium in loan formulations. This will require governments to expand policy-based finance for SMEs to mitigate the constraints on SME finance as an imperative countermeasure. Under such a situation, efficient and lower cost credit risk evaluation tools could be necessary for SME financing, especially for transaction-based lending. Therefore, in addressing the critical credit constraints on SMEs, comprehensive information infrastructure requirements on risk management are needed. Thus, according to Yoshino and Hesary (2016), the following requirements may contribute as remedial measures for mitigating challenges affecting SMEs:

- Diversifying channels of financing (development of credit guarantee schemes, development of specialised private banks for SME financing, and development of turf investment trust funds for risky SMEs).
- Development of SME Database and Credit Risk Analysis of SMEs, including a large amount of data that can be used to rate SMEs through statistical analysis.
- Development of business R&D tax incentives: Collaboration is a key vector of innovation-related knowledge flows both for firms that use R&D (either internally developed or externally acquired) and for those that are not R&D active.

- SMEs should align their business needs with cloud computing technology, but also all technical, organisational, and legal aspects should be taken into account to mitigate possible risks of cloud computing.
- Utilising information for SMEs: Insufficient use of information technology for sales is one of the major challenges affecting SMEs. Therefore, it is possible that national governments (through societies of commerce and industry and chambers of commerce and industry) should provide close mentoring-style support to SMEs and small enterprises in teaching them how to use information technology in their business.

In addition, Modimogale and Kroeze (2011) postulated that most of these barriers affecting SMEs could possibly be overcome by learning more about information infrastructure and by SMEs employing knowledgeable information infrastructure tools. Additionally, Mazla et al. (2019) claimed that in order to reduce challenges that SMEs face, measures for doing so must take into account innovation in processes (which includes updating and changing practices that help increase activity, lower costs, and boost demand); innovation in goods or services (through this innovation, the effective demand rises, encouraging a growth in investment and employment); and management and work organisation innovation (this innovation calls for equitable participation from all members of the business in order to produce ideas that have the potential to boost competition and give the company a competitive edge).

Furthermore, Mazla et al. (2019) posited that entrepreneurship as a whole must be rooted on the exploration of new ideas and the creation of new things. A creative entrepreneur develops fresh ways to improve the business and produce new items for already-existing services and goods. There must be always room for improvement in an enterprise's deliverables. Innovation and creativity help find fresh approaches to enhancing already-existing goods or services in order to maximise the business. This enables business owners to develop novel ideas and alternatives to conventional problems. Through this prospect, a fresh, intriguing, and perhaps useful thought emerges. According to Adam and Alarifi (2021), innovation has become a necessity for all contemporary enterprises that want to survive in a world characterised by competition, technological change, and recurring crises. Therefore, the concept of innovation refers to the use of new technology or new management practices in an organisation to achieve a targeted improvement in its operations. Adam and Alarifi (2021) emphasised that for their growth and development (success), SMEs need to embark on the following:

- SMEs will have to define and develop a clear information infrastructure strategy that will govern the adoption process.
- SMEs need to make sure that their information infrastructure strategy is aligned with the business strategy, which means that the information infrastructure strategy must support and achieve business goals.
- SMEs should make sure that they employ the right skills (permanent or contracted) and identify the roles that these skills will play in making sure that the SMEs are successful in leveraging information infrastructure.

Consequently, there could be a huge advantage from using emerging information infrastructure technologies, particularly, emerging internet connectivity and mobility. This will help the business understand the potential of information infrastructure and outline the processes and methods to be followed during adoption. In order for SMEs to achieve their envisioned objectives, they have to recognise the impact of information infrastructure on their business and invest in efforts to take advantage of it, invest efficient resources and time in getting the relevant advice from information infrastructure experts and consultants in order to set up the information infrastructure strategy, based on their business strategy. By defining their strategic objective, SMEs can decide which strategic investment to make in information infrastructure. However, investment in information infrastructure can be successful when SMEs take one of the following two forms (Modimogale & Kroeze, 2011): providing efficiency and savings or enabling added value. According to Adam and Alarifi (2021), SMEs should also invest in information infrastructure following the two dimensions of the SME: strategic focus (cost reduction vs. value adding) and customer dominance (where the technology to be used is dictated mainly by the customers). Figure 7.1 illustrates and discusses a scenario related to the four quadrants.

7.6.1 Information Infrastructure and Efficiency

Cordella (2012) argued that information infrastructures (IIs) are put in place to support business strategies and boost a company's ability to compete. Therefore, implementing IIs can be viewed as a strategic reaction to

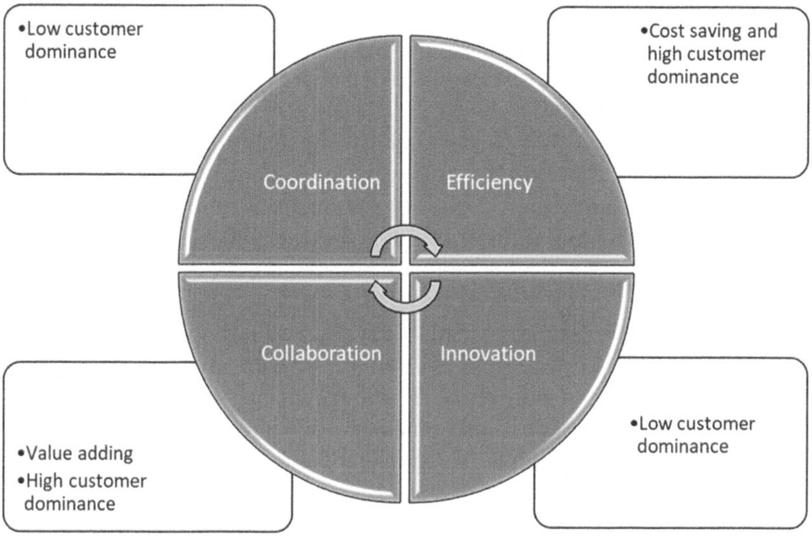

Fig. 7.1 Cost reduction versus value adding and customer dominance. (Source: Self-generated by the researcher)

outside market factors that exert pressure on businesses in cutthroat industries. Information infrastructures are used not just to meet business requirements but also to keep up with technology advancements that change the IT landscape of an organisation. According to Narcyz Roztocki et al. (2019), the nexus between information infrastructure and efficiency is a crucial aspect of modern business and society. Information infrastructure refers to the underlying framework of technology, communication networks, data storage, and software applications that enable the collection, processing, storage, and dissemination of information. In addition, Roztocki et al. (2019) argues that innovative technology alter how companies run their operations, which has a significant impact on corporate operations and the commercial basis. Therefore, enterprise information systems are employed in developing and transition economies to boost efficiency and speed up business processes. It provides an efficient relationship between technological dimension and the business dimension. Due to the demand for human resources and the opportunity to invest in social and human capital, the business dimension has an impact on society (Palvia et al., 2018). The business aspect has a direct impact on social growth as well because it increases income and employment, which raise living standards. Since technology is frequently the driving force behind social evolution, the technology dimension also has a significant impact on the society dimension.

Efficiency, on the other hand, relates to the ability to accomplish tasks or goals with minimal waste of time, resources, or effort. Here are some key points to consider when exploring the relationship between information infrastructure and efficiency (Roztocki et al., 2019 and Palvia et al., 2018):

- **Data accessibility and availability**: A well-developed information infrastructure ensures that data and information are readily accessible to those who need them. This accessibility allows for quicker decision-making and more efficient operations. For instance, in a business context, employees can access critical information in real time, enabling them to make informed decisions promptly.
- **Data integration:** Effective information infrastructure enables the integration of data from various sources and systems. When data can flow seamlessly between different parts of an organisation, it reduces duplication of effort and minimises errors. Integrated data systems are crucial for efficiency in supply chain management, customer relationship management, and other business functions.
- **Automation and process optimisation:** Information infrastructure supports automation of routine tasks and processes. Automation not only reduces the risk of human error but also increases the speed at which tasks are completed. This can lead to significant efficiency gains in industries such as manufacturing, logistics, and finance.
- **Scalability:** Information infrastructure should be scalable to accommodate growth in data volume and user demands. Scalability ensures that systems can handle increased workloads without a significant decrease in performance. This is particularly important for online services and businesses experiencing rapid growth.
- **Analytics and decision support:** Information infrastructure supports the collection and analysis of data, which can provide valuable insights for decision-making. Efficient data analytics can help organisations identify trends, opportunities, and areas for improvement, leading to more informed and effective decision-making.
- **Communication and collaboration:** Modern information infrastructure facilitates communication and collaboration among indi-

viduals and teams, regardless of geographical locations. Efficient communication tools and collaboration platforms enable remote work, reduce communication barriers, and enhance productivity.
- **Security and privacy:** Information infrastructure must also ensure the security and privacy of data. Efficient security measures protect sensitive information from unauthorised access, breaches, and data loss, which can be costly and damaging to an organisation's efficiency and reputation.
- **Cost reduction:** A well-planned information infrastructure can help reduce operational costs through the elimination of redundant systems, streamlined processes, and reduced manual intervention. Cost savings can be reinvested in other areas of the organisation.
- **Customer experience:** Information infrastructure can enhance customer service and satisfaction by providing faster responses to inquiries, personalised experiences, and better access to relevant information. This, in turn, can lead to increased customer loyalty and retention.

Roztocki et al. (2019) posited that information infrastructure plays a pivotal role in enhancing efficiency across various sectors, from businesses to government agencies and non-profit organisations. A robust and well-maintained information infrastructure can lead to improved decision-making, streamlined processes, reduced costs, and better overall performance, ultimately contributing to the success and competitiveness of an organisation in the digital age (Palvia et al., 2018).

7.6.2 Information Infrastructure and Value Adding

It was described earlier that information infrastructures can be seen as the product of negotiations between various information systems, working methods, and organisational practices, as well as the environment in which these negotiations take place (Cordella, 2012). As a result, the relationship between information infrastructure quality, availability, and use and its effect on generating extra value for businesses, organisations, and society as a whole is referred to as the nexus between information infrastructure and value-added. However, the phrase "value added" in business and economics refers to supplementary qualities that give a good or service something extra, enhancing their value to customers (Bartlett, 2016). In other words, value added refers to the additional worth or benefit created during a particular process or activity. It represents the increase in value or quality that occurs as a result of a specific action or transformation. Value added can be applied to various contexts, including economics, business, and production processes.

In economics and business, value added is often used to measure the contribution of a specific business or industry to the overall economy (Dieffenbacher, 2022). It is calculated by taking the difference between the total revenue generated by a business or industry and the cost of intermediate goods and services (goods and services purchased from other businesses to produce the final product). This calculation represents the value that the business or industry has added to the raw materials or components it has purchased. Mathematically, the formula for value added is **Value Added** = Total Revenue - Cost of Intermediate Goods and Services. According to Cain, the economic profit of a corporation is determined using the Economic Value-Added formula (EVA). The EVA is calculated as net operating profit after taxes minus invested capital times. As an illustration, Weighted Average Cost of Capital (WACC) is calculated using the economic value-added formula. An EVA computation would be like the one shown below:

For example, a company has a net profit of \$200,000 after taxes. They raised a total of \$70,000 for a project that year, with a weighted average cost of capital of 7%. Calculation is as follow:

EVA = \$200,000 - (\$70,000 × .07)

EVA = \$200,000 - \$4900

EVA = \$195,100

According to Subedi and Farazmand (2020) and Velnampy (2011), value added can also be used to assess the efficiency and productivity of a business or production process. A higher value added typically indicates that a business is effectively transforming inputs into outputs, creating more value in the process. Therefore, the nexus between information infrastructure and value-added refers to the relationship between the quality, availability, and utilisation of information technology infrastructure and its impact on creating additional value for businesses, organisations, and society as a whole. Information infrastructure encompasses a wide range of elements, including hardware, software, data, networks, and the human resources required to manage and use these resources effectively (Subedi & Farazmand, 2020). Value-added, in this context, signifies the benefits and advantages gained through the integration and effective use of information infrastructure. Here are some key aspects of the nexus between information infrastructure and value-added (Zeng et al., 2020; Subedi & Farazmand, 2020):

- **Efficiency and productivity:** Information infrastructure can enhance efficiency and productivity across various sectors. When organisations have access to reliable hardware and software, efficient data management systems, and high-speed communication networks, they can streamline operations, reduce manual processes, and automate tasks. This efficiency translates into cost savings and increased productivity.
- **Innovation and creativity:** Robust information infrastructure can enable innovation and creativity. Access to data and information tools can foster new ideas, drive research and development, and support the creation of new products and services. Value is added when innovation leads to a competitive edge and the development of products that meet evolving market demands.
- **Data-driven decision-making:** A well-developed information infrastructure allows organisations to collect, analyse, and interpret data effectively. This, in turn, supports data-driven decision-making processes. When decisions are based on accurate and timely information, organisations can optimise their strategies, respond to market changes faster, and improve their overall performance.
- **Market expansion and globalisation:** Information infrastructure facilitates market expansion and globalisation. Organisations can reach broader audiences, expand into new markets, and collaborate with partners worldwide. This increased market reach can lead to higher revenues and growth opportunities.
- **Customer experience:** Information infrastructure can significantly enhance the customer experience. It enables businesses to personalise services, provide real-time support, and gather feedback. Improving customer satisfaction can result in increased loyalty and repeat business, thereby adding value.
- **Supply chain optimisation:** Information infrastructure plays a crucial role in supply chain management. By integrating information systems across the supply chain, businesses can optimise inventory levels, reduce lead times, and enhance supplier relationships. This can lead to cost reductions and improved supply chain performance.

- **Risk management:** Effective information infrastructure also supports better risk management. Through data analytics and predictive modelling, organisations can identify potential risks and vulnerabilities early, allowing them to take proactive measures to mitigate these risks.
- **Competitive advantage:** Perhaps the most significant aspect of the nexus is the creation of a sustainable competitive advantage. Organisations that invest in and effectively utilise their information infrastructure are better positioned to outperform competitors in the long run.

In summary, the nexus between information infrastructure and value-added is a critical consideration for businesses and organisations in the digital age. By investing in and strategically leveraging information technology resources, entities can enhance efficiency, drive innovation, improve decision-making, and ultimately create additional value in various forms, such as increased revenue, cost savings, and competitive advantage. This suggests that "value added can increase in value, quality, or benefit created during a specific process or activity," often measured by the difference between revenue and the cost of intermediate goods and services. It is a concept commonly used in economics and business analysis to evaluate the performance and contribution of businesses and industries (Zeng et al., 2020; Subedi & Farazmand, 2020).

7.6.3 Infrastructure of Information and Cost Reduction

The understanding of the concept of information infrastructure was depicted further above. In order to draw the nexus between information infrastructure and cost reduction, it is vital to describe the concept of cost reduction. Cost reduction refers to the process of lowering the expenses and expenditures of a business or organisation while maintaining or improving the quality of its products or services (Ruparelia, 2023). Cost reduction is a key aspect of financial management and is often pursued to increase profitability, improve competitiveness, and enhance overall financial health. The common strategies and approaches for achieving cost reduction are the following (Kushner, 2022; Nikkeh et al., 2022; and Al-Maryani, 2015):

- **Cost analysis**: Begin by thoroughly analysing your current expenses and identifying areas where costs can be reduced. This can include reviewing financial statements, conducting cost-benefit analyses, and using financial ratios to pinpoint areas of concern.
- **Lean management**: Implement lean principles to eliminate waste in processes and operations. This involves streamlining workflows, reducing excess inventory, and minimising downtime.
- **Negotiating with suppliers**: Negotiate with suppliers to get better terms, discounts, or bulk purchase agreements. This can significantly reduce the cost of raw materials or goods.
- **Energy efficiency**: Invest in energy-efficient equipment and practices to lower utility bills. This includes using LED lighting, optimising heating and cooling systems, and reducing energy waste.
- **Labor optimisation**: Review your workforce and ensure that you have the right number of employees with the right skills. Automation and technology can often be used to increase efficiency and reduce labour costs.
- **Outsourcing**: Consider outsourcing non-core functions or tasks to specialised service providers who can often perform them more efficiently and cost-effectively.
- **Technology adoption**: Invest in technology solutions that can automate processes, improve productivity, and reduce the need for manual labour.
- **Inventory management**: Optimise inventory levels to reduce carrying costs and minimise the risk of obsolete stock.
- **Process improvement**: Continuously assess and improve your business processes to eliminate inefficiencies and reduce costs.
- **Marketing efficiency**: Evaluate your marketing strategies and focus on those that provide the highest return on investment (ROI). Digital marketing can often be more cost-effective than traditional advertising.
- **Supplier diversification**: Avoid over-dependence on a single supplier to reduce the risk of price fluctuations or disruptions in the supply chain.
- **Employee training**: Invest in training and development to enhance employee skills and productivity, which can lead to cost savings in the long run.
- **Waste reduction**: Implement strategies to reduce waste, whether it's material waste in manufacturing or time waste in processes.

- **Benchmarking**: Compare your costs and performance to industry benchmarks and competitors to identify areas where you can improve.
- **Customer feedback**: Listen to customer feedback and focus on delivering value where it matters most to your customers, which can help reduce costs associated with unnecessary features or services.

It's important to note that cost reduction should be pursued carefully to avoid negatively impacting product quality, customer satisfaction, or employee morale. It should be part of a larger strategic plan to ensure the long-term sustainability and growth of the business. Additionally, cost reduction efforts should be continuously monitored and adjusted as needed to adapt to changing market conditions and business goals. The nexus between information infrastructure and cost reduction refers to the relationship between an organisation's information technology (IT) systems, data management, and its ability to lower operational expenses (Avinir, 2023). Effective information infrastructure can offer competitive advantage and significantly impact cost reduction in several ways (Vagliasindi, 2022):

- **Efficiency and productivity:** Well-designed information infrastructure can streamline business processes and improve operational efficiency. Automated workflows, integrated systems, and data analytics tools enable employees to work more productively, reducing labour costs and the time required to complete tasks.
- **Data-driven decision-making:** A robust information infrastructure allows organisations to collect, store, and analyse data effectively. Data-driven decision-making can help identify areas where cost savings are possible. For example, analysing customer data may reveal opportunities for targeted marketing campaigns or product/service improvements.
- **Resource optimisation:** Information infrastructure can aid in resource optimisation. For example, supply chain management systems can help track inventory levels and demand, reducing overstocking or stockouts. This can lead to reduced carrying costs and improved cash flow.
- **Remote work and collaboration:** In an increasingly digital world, a well-established information infrastructure supports remote work and collaboration. Reduced reliance on physical office spaces can

lead to cost savings in terms of rent, utilities, and facilities management.
- **Energy efficiency:** Modern data centres and IT equipment are designed to be energy efficient. By upgrading and optimising IT infrastructure, organisations can lower their energy consumption, leading to reduced utility costs and a smaller carbon footprint.
- **Cloud computing:** Cloud-based infrastructure and services offer scalability and cost savings through a pay-as-you-go model. Organisations can scale up or down based on demand, avoiding the need for large upfront investments in hardware and software.
- **Security and compliance:** A secure information infrastructure can prevent costly data breaches and regulatory fines. Investing in cyber-security measures and compliance tools can protect the organisation from financial losses associated with data breaches or legal penalties.
- **Customer service and retention:** Information infrastructure can enhance customer service through improved communication channels, personalised experiences, and faster issue resolution. Satisfied customers are more likely to remain loyal, reducing the cost of acquiring new customers.
- **Predictive maintenance:** In sectors like manufacturing and utilities, information infrastructure can enable predictive maintenance by monitoring equipment health and performance in real time. This proactive approach reduces downtime and maintenance costs.
- **Supplier relationships:** Effective information infrastructure can help manage supplier relationships more efficiently. Timely communication, demand forecasting, and performance monitoring can lead to better negotiation terms and reduced procurement costs.
- **Regulatory compliance:** Compliance with industry regulations and standards often requires robust information infrastructure for data tracking and reporting. Non-compliance can result in fines and legal costs.
- **Reduction of paperwork:** Transitioning to digital document management and workflow automation can significantly reduce the costs associated with printing, storing, and managing paper documents.

Considering the above, a well-planned and maintained information infrastructure can have a profound impact on an organisation's cost reduction efforts by enhancing efficiency, data-driven decision-making, and overall business agility. However, it's important to note that the effectiveness of information infrastructure in reducing costs depends on how it aligns with an organisation's strategic goals and how effectively it is implemented and managed.

7.6.4 Information Infrastructure and Customer Dominance

According to Viana (2022), customer dominance is not a widely recognised term in business or marketing. It's known as a service-dominant orientation, customer-centricity, or customer-centric approach, which are concepts that emphasise the importance of focusing on the customer's needs, preferences, and satisfaction in all aspects of business strategy and operations (Viana, 2022;Reinartz et al., 2019). Customer-centricity involves:

- **Understanding customer needs:** Companies gather data and insights to understand what their customers want and need. This can involve market research, customer feedback, and data analysis.
- **Tailoring products and services:** Based on customer insights, companies adapt their products and services to better meet customer expectations. This may involve product customisation, design improvements, or the development of new offerings.
- **Customer experience:** Ensuring a positive customer experience is crucial. This includes everything from the usability of a website or app to the interactions customers have with company representatives.
- **Customer support:** Providing excellent customer support is a key aspect of customer-centricity. Companies aim to address customer issues and inquiries promptly and effectively.
- **Feedback loops:** Establishing mechanisms for ongoing feedback from customers helps companies continuously improve their offerings and customer experience.
- **Loyalty and retention:** By consistently meeting customer needs and providing a great experience, companies aim to build customer loyalty and encourage repeat business.
- **Long-term relationships:** Customer-centric companies prioritise building long-term relationships with their customers rather than focusing solely on short-term profits.

Overall, the idea is that by prioritising the customer and their satisfaction, a company can build a loyal customer base and achieve sustainable success (Reinartz et al., 2019). According to Heinonen and Strandvik (2020), customer dominance refers to the power of important clients, as many organisations are driven primarily by customer needs (where technology to be used is dictated mainly by the customers). The nexus between information infrastructure and customer dominance refers to the relationship between an organisation's information technology systems, data capabilities, and its ability to understand, engage, and retain customers effectively (Heinonen & Strandvik, 2020; Reinartz et al., 2019).

Customer dominance, in this context, means achieving a competitive advantage by focusing on customer-centric strategies and delivering exceptional customer experiences. Information infrastructure influences customer dominance through (Heinonen & Strandvik, 2020):

- **Customer data management:** Information infrastructure enables organisations to collect, store, and analyse vast amounts of customer data. This data includes customer preferences, behaviours, and interactions. By harnessing this information, businesses can gain insights into customer needs and tailor their products, services, and marketing strategies accordingly.
- **Personalisation:** With a robust information infrastructure, companies can create personalised customer experiences. By analysing customer data in real time, organisations can offer tailored recommendations, content, and offers that resonate with individual customers. Personalisation enhances customer satisfaction and loyalty.
- **Multichannel engagement:** Information infrastructure supports multichannel communication, allowing businesses to engage with customers through various touchpoints such as websites, mobile apps, social media, email, and more. This omni-channel approach ensures consistent messaging and a seamless customer experience, regardless of the channel.
- **Customer relationship management (CRM):** CRM systems, an integral part of information infrastructure, help manage and nurture customer relationships. They provide a centralised repository for customer information, history, and interactions, facilitating better communication and customer service.

- **Customer analytics:** Advanced analytics tools powered by information infrastructure enable businesses to segment customers based on behaviour, demographics, and preferences. These insights are crucial for targeted marketing campaigns, customer retention strategies, and product development.
- **Feedback and surveys:** Information infrastructure supports the collection and analysis of customer feedback through surveys, online reviews, and social media. This feedback loop helps organisations identify areas for improvement and refines their offerings to meet customer expectations.
- **Real-time response:** Modern information infrastructure allows organisations to respond to customer inquiries and issues in real time. Chatbots, AI-driven customer support, and instant messaging platforms can enhance responsiveness and customer satisfaction.
- **Predictive analytics:** Leveraging historical customer data and predictive analytics, businesses can anticipate customer needs and behaviour. This enables proactive customer engagement and product/service adjustments.
- **Customer loyalty programmes:** Information infrastructure aids in the management of customer loyalty programmes. By tracking customer interactions and purchases, organisations can reward loyal customers, incentivise repeat business, and reduce customer churn.
- **Competitive analysis:** Information infrastructure can help organisations monitor competitor activities and customer sentiment towards competitors. This information is valuable for adjusting strategies to maintain a competitive edge.
- **Compliance and data security:** Ensuring data privacy and compliance with regulations (e.g., GDPR, CCPA) are critical in maintaining customer trust. Information infrastructure plays a pivotal role in safeguarding customer data and ensuring legal compliance.
- **Scalability:** As businesses grow, their information infrastructure must scale to handle increasing volumes of customer data and interactions. Scalability is essential for maintaining high-quality customer experiences.

In summary, a well-developed information infrastructure is fundamental to achieving customer dominance by enabling data-driven insights, personalised interactions, efficient communication, and responsive customer service. Organisations that effectively leverage their information infrastructure can build strong customer relationships, foster loyalty, and outperform competitors in a customer-centric market. According to Modimogale and Kroeze (2011), coordination, efficiency, collaboration, and innovation create competitive scenarios. Therefore, SMEs would need to identify the quadrant (domain) into which it falls in the focus-dominance model, by determining whether its strategic focus is cost saving or value adding, and then determining whether the customer dominance is high or low. As an illustration, an individual organisation in the efficiency quadrant (where cost saving is important, and the customer dominance is high) will only need basic information infrastructures such as accounting and word processing programmes.

In addition, the SMEs that fit into the coordination quadrant (low customer dominance) will have to maintain a customer database to keep track of the clients' preferences. Since value adding is important in the collaboration quadrant, electronic data interchange and materials requirements planning should be facilitated due to a high customer dominance, while electronic business systems are typical of innovation SMEs (low customer dominance). When the strategic positioning is appropriately completed, the focus will be on getting the right tools and technology to achieve the envisioned strategy. Thus, aligning the information infrastructure strategy with SMEs strategy could ensure that information infrastructure is used to deliver on the SMEs' objectives. The information infrastructure strategy design should be based upon the business strategy, as SMEs should not be driven by technology needs, but by business needs (Reinartz et al., 2019).

The identification and adoption of information infrastructure tools or roles could help SMEs understand the nature of skills and knowledge needed to adopt information infrastructure. However, successful information infrastructure tools adoption (internet) depends on different roles of SMEs' employees. According to Modimogale and Kroeze (2011), the four main roles involve the following:

- Leader of the adoption process: Warrior
- Translator of technology into ordinary language so that everyone understands how to use it: Interpreter
- Administrator of technology seeing to it that the technology runs all the time: Clerk
- Technology specialist who is responsible to make sure that the right technology is used/selected and best practices are implemented: Priest

These four roles are not only important in the adoption of internet use but can be used in the adoption of technology in general. The group of high users of information infrastructure would have all four roles implemented, while the medium user of an information infrastructure group would have some of those roles but not necessarily all of them. Thus, according to Nejadirani et al. (2011), the success of information infrastructure (the internet) initiatives of a firm (SMEs) depends not only on its own effort to digitise its value chain, but also on the readiness of its customers, suppliers, and trading partners to engage in electronic interactions and transactions. Therefore, research and development should investigate the readiness practice requirements on the part of all players in the value chain, and about businesses that adopted information infrastructure or e-Business on how they invested efforts and resources in increasing their trading partners' readiness, so that other SMEs may use their example or experience.

Accordingly, information infrastructure application includes the use of many different types of online facilities to do business: order registration, electronic advertising, electronic billing system, electronic marketing, online delivery status and tracking, and customer services support. E-Business applications also include the use of many different types of online facilities to communicate and coordinate production planning, Just In Time (JIT) management, scheduling, outsourcing, and other business operation processes. In light of the aforementioned discussion, the remedial measures for mitigating challenges affecting SMEs should be considered in line with strategic focus (value addition vs. cost reduction) and customer domination (where consumers mostly determine the technology to be employed). Thus, competition for SMEs must be facilitated through coordination, effectiveness, teamwork, and invention. SMEs must determine which quadrant (domain) in the focus-dominance model they fall into by assessing whether their strategic focus is cost saving or value addition, and then whether or not customer dominance is high or low.

7.7 Conclusion

This chapter focussed on the challenges faced by SMEs regarding information infrastructure and difficulties in accessing finance. It is clear that SMEs face multiple barriers associated with information infrastructure and difficulties in accessing finance for their growth and development. Therefore, remedial measures for mitigating challenges affecting SMEs may increase, and create more opportunities for employment and economic growth, and contribute towards the achievement of broader development objectives, including poverty alleviation, and the promotion of more democratic and pluralist societies. Challenges facing SMEs, especially in developing countries, should be seen as opportunities for governments and SMEs to engage in more efficient and effective research and development operations, in order to understand the competitive advantages information infrastructure could offer by linking it to business strategies and objectives.

Consequently, SMEs should invest efforts and resources in educating their staff and management about information structure and its benefits. Cost reduction and time saving, improved labour flexibility, better customer service and communication with partners, as well as improved data analytics have been mentioned as the main economic advantages, including the main benefits regarding increased flexibility of resources. Decision-making with regard to information infrastructure needs to be addressed in order to give SMEs competitive capability. Also, SMEs should build a culture that is innovative and favourable to technology, by prioritising information infrastructure as a functional area. In addition, the business process should be more reliant on technology and less on manual processes and by continually exploring all the various and newest technological options with their possible benefits to the SME.

Future research work for SMEs' growth and development is critically needed in areas on how SMEs can diversify channels of financing through the development of credit guarantee schemes, the development of specialised private banks for SME financing, the development of turf investment trust funds for risky SMEs, the development of SME database and credit risk analysis of SMEs, and the development of R&D tax incentives (including collaboration on innovation and utilisation of information for SMEs). Access to such sources of information is pivotal for enhancing the performing of SMEs. Research on information infrastructure can increase and improve SMEs' competitiveness in order to keep them sustainable in the knowledge of global economy (information era). Thus, it is vital that critical research and development should be constantly undertaken towards providing innovative resolutions to challenges affecting SMEs, for them to be supportively assisted. Thus, it is vitally important for economies to have fully functioning support measures for the growth and development of SMEs. Prioritising efforts to financially sustain SMEs as a means of creating more employment; alleviating poverty; promoting economic growth and development; and contributing to socio-economic transformational processes are fundamentally important within the context of sound information infrastructural support.

References

Aanestad, M., Grisot, M., Hanseth, O., & Vassilakopoulou, P. (2017). *Information Infrastructures within European Health Care: Working with the Installed Base.* Springer. https://link.springer.com/chapter/10.1007/978-3-319-51020-0_3

Abara, G., & Banti, T. (2017). Role of Financial Institutions in the Growth of Micro and Small Enterprises in Assosa Zone. *Research Journal of Finance and Accounting, 8*(3), 36–40.

Ackah, J., & Vuvor, S. (2011). The Challenges faced by Small & Medium Enterprises (SMEs) in Obtaining Credit in Ghana. https://www.diva-portal.org/smash/get/diva2:829684/FULLTEXT01.pdf;The.

Adam, N. A., & Alarifi, G. (2021). Innovation practices for survival of small and medium enterprises (SMEs) in the COVID-19 times: The role of external support. *Journal of Innovation and Entrepreneurship, 10*(15), 1–22.

Afzal, W. (2012). Information Infrastructure. https://www.sciencedirect.com/topics/computer-science/information-infrastructure

Al-Maryani, M. A. H. H. (2015). The strategic impact of integration between target costing and continuous improvements techniques in achieving cost reductions and competitive advantage: An analytical study. *Merit Research Journal of Accounting, Auditing, Economics and Finance, 3*(4), 109–128.

Araujo, L., & Mason, K. (2021). Infrastructures and infrastructuring markets. *Springer* (AMS Rev) 11, 240–251. https://doi.org/10.1007/s13162-021-00212-0

Avinir, D. (2023). IT Cost Reduction Strategies—Solid Systems. https://www.solidsystems.co.za/blog/it-cost-reduction/

Bartlett, J. A. (2016). The Value-Added Organization: Beyond Business as Usual. *Library Leadership & Management, 30*(4), 1–4.

Cordella, A. (2012). Information Infrastructure an actor-Network Perspective. *International Journal of Actor-Network Theory and Technological Innovation, 2*(1), 27–53.

Dieffenbacher, S. F. (2022). Value Creation Definition, Model, Principles, Importance & Steps. https://digitalleadership.com/blog/value-creation/.

European Union Briefing. (2021). *Challenges and concerns for small and medium-sized enterprises (SMEs) doing business in third countries.* Policy Department for External Relations Directorate General for External Policies of the Union. www.imfbookstore.org/www.elibrary.imf.org.; https://www.europarl.europa.eu/RegData/etudes/BRIE/2021/653630/EXPO_BRI(2021)653630_EN.pdf

Gopaul, M., & Manley, L. L. (2015). SME perception of government assistance within South Africa. *Journal of Governance and Regulation, 4*(4), 306–314.

He, W., Zhang, Z. J., & Lia, W. (2021). Information technology solutions, challenges, and suggestions for tackling the COVID-19 pandemic. *Elsevier-PMC COVID-19 Collection*. https://www.ncbi.nlm.nih.gov/pmc/articles/PMC7724285/

Heinonen, K., & Strandvik, T. (2020). Customer-dominant service logic. https://www.taylorfrancis.com/chapters/edit/10.4324/9781351245234-4/customer-dominant-service-logic-kristina-heinonen-tore-strandvik

IMF. (2019). Financial Inclusion of Small and Medium-Sized Enterprises in the Middle East and Central Asia. https://www.imf.org/en/Publications/Departmental-Papers-Policy-Papers/Issues/2019/02/11/Financial-Inclusion-of-Small-and-Medium-Sized-Enterprises-in-the-Middle-East-and-Central-Asia-46335.

Kreslins, K., Novik, D., & Vasiljeva, T. (2018). 2018 Challenge of Cloud Computing for SMEs: A Case of Baltic Countries. *Journal of Innovation Management in Small & Medium Enterprises, 2018*, 1–10.

Kurniawan, A., Anwar, S. M., Suhardi, B. H., & Adam, S. (2018). The role of information technology in knowledge management in small medium enterprise. *Journal of Theoretical and Applied Information Technology, 96*(24), 8265–8278.

Kushner, A. (2022). Cost Reduction Process: Definition and Steps.. https://www.approve.com/blog/cost-reduction-process/.

Mazla, M. I. S. B., Jabor, M. K. B., Tufail, K., Yakim, A. F. N., & Zainal, H. (2019). The Roles of Creativity and Innovation in Entrepreneurship. *Advances in Social Science, Education and Humanities Research, 470*(2019), 213–217.

Modimogale, L., & Kroeze, J. H. (2011). The Role of ICT within Small and Medium Enterprises in Gauteng. *IBIMA Publishing: Communications of the IBIMA* 2011 (2011): 1–13

Nejadirani, F., Behravesh, M., & Rasouli, R. (2011). Developing Countries and Electronic Commerce the Case of SMEs. *World Applied Sciences Journal, 15*(5), 756–764.

Nikkeh, N. S., Hasan, S. I., & Flayyih, H. H. (2022). The role of costing techniques in reduction of cost and achieving competitive advantage in IRAQI financial institutions. *International Journal of Economics and Finance Studies, 14*(04), 62–79.

OECD. (2015). New Approaches to SME and Entrepreneurship Financing: Broadening the Range of Instruments. https://www.oecd.org/cfe/smes/New-Approaches-SME-full-report.pdf

OECD. (2017). Enhancing the contributions of SMES in a global and digitalised economy. https://www.oecd.org/industry/C-MIN-2017-8-EN.pdf

OECD. (2021). Government Support Has Helped Save Many SMEs but Challenges Remain. https://www.oecd.org/newsroom/government-support-has-helped-save-many-smes-but-challenges-remain-oecd.htm

Okello-Obura, C., & Matovu, J. (2011). SMEs and Business Information Provision Strategies: Analytical Perspective. *Library Philosophy and Practice (e-journal)*. https://digitalcommons.unl.edu/libphilprac/609

Palvia, P., Baqir, N., & Nemati, H. (2018). ICT for Socio-Economic Development: A Citizens' Perspective. *Information & Management, 55*(2), 160–176.

Reinartz, W., Wiegand, N., & Imschloss, M. (2019). The Impact of Digital Transformation on the Retailing Value Chain. *International Journal of Research in Marketing, 36*(3), 350–366.

Roztocki, Y., Soja, P., & Weistroffer, H. R. (2019). The Role of Information and Communication Technologies in Socioeconomic Development: Towards a Multi-Dimensional Framework. *Information Technology for Development, 25*(2), 171–183.

Ruparelia, A. (2023). Cost Reduction: How to Go About It Effectively.. https://agicap.com/en/article/cost-reduction/.

Savrula, M., Incekarab, A., & Sener, S. (2014). The Potential of E-commerce for SMEs in a Globalizing Business Environment. *ScienceDirect: Procedia—Social and Behavioral Sciences, 150*(2014), 35–45.

Subedi, M., & Farazmand, A. (2020). Economic Value Added (EVA) for Performance Evaluation of Public Organizations. *Public Organisation Review, 20*(2020), 613–630.

Vagliasindi, M. (2022). How Does Infrastructure Support Sustainable Growth? https://blogs.worldbank.org/digital-development/how-does-infrastructure-support-sustainable-growth.

Velnampy, T. (2011). Value Added, Productivity and Performance of few Selected Companies. *Indian journal of Commerce and Management Studies, 11*(2011), 1–15.

Viana, L. (2022). Infrastructuring the Foundations for a Service-Dominant Orientation. https://dl.designresearchsociety.org/cgi/viewcontent.cgi?article=2911&context =drs-conference-papers.

World Bank Group. (2018). Improving access to finance for SMES: Opportunities through Credit Reporting, Secured Lending and Insolvency Practices. https://www.doingbusiness.org/content/dam/doingBusiness/media/Special-Reports/improving-access-to-finance-for-SMEs.pdf

Yoshino, N., & Hesary, F. T. (2016). Major Challenges Facing Small and Medium-sized Enterprises in Asia and Solutions for Mitigating Them. https://www.adb.org/sites/default/files/publication/182532/adbi-wp564.pdf

Zeng, F., Lee, S. H. N., & Lo, C. K. Y. (2020). The Role of Information Systems in the Sustainable Development of Enterprises: A Systematic Literature Network Analysis. *Sustainability, 12*(8), 33–37.

CHAPTER 8

Nexus Between the Business Environment and SMEs' Performance

Nirmala Dorasamy

8.1 Introduction

The nexus between business and other environments, such as the economic, political, social, and technological contexts, can significantly impact the performance of Small and Medium-sized Enterprises (SMEs) in Africa. This interaction is multifaceted, and various factors can influence SME performance. As such, issues such as political instability, economic crises, and currency devaluations can negatively impact SMEs' business operations and planning (Senbet & Otchere, 2008).

Business organisations cannot succeed without conducive interacting environments. For example, the economic environment of any society, to a large extent, determines the direction and level of success of business enterprises. Thus, an enabling environment is crucial for the fortunes and the development prospects of business organisations such as SMEs. As such, part of the economic imperatives of development is a thriving business environment. In 2004, the Organization for Economic Co-Operation

N. Dorasamy (✉)
Faculty of Management Sciences, Durban University of Technology, Durban, South Africa
e-mail: nirmala@dut.ac.za

G. Mugano, N. Dorasamy, *SMEs Perspective in Africa*,
https://doi.org/10.1007/978-3-031-69103-4_8

and Development (OECD) identified provision of an enabling environment as a critical factor in the development of SMEs (OECD, 2004).

The United Nations' Economic and Social Commission for Asia and the Pacific (ESCAP) in its 2011 report noted the primacy of a sustainable environment for SMEs to accomplish the importance of their position as agents of inclusive economic growth and reduction of poverty in the annals of development (ESCAP, 2011). Alluding to the influence of various environments for the survival of SMEs, the report noted that the dearth of requisite environments has limited the capacities of the SMEs to compete successfully with their peers in the economic sector at the global scale (ESCAP, 2011). Scholarly business studies have shown the imperative of a conducive environment for successful and sustainable growth and development, especially for SMEs (Wruuck, 2015; Cepel, 2019). In other words, the fortunes of business activities that provide the necessary platforms for economic growth depend on the nature of incentives derivable from the environments. According to Wruuck (2015), the successful activities of business organisations are functions of the quality of the business environment because for the purpose of competitiveness, "their attractiveness for investments and ultimately growth (prospects)" are determined by the various environmental factors. The various conditions generated by these environments provide the necessary enablement in shaping the activities of the business organisation.

Environments that are unfriendly to business activities will retard the growth and development of SMEs. Global development agencies as well as regional economic organisations have recognised the importance of environmental factors to allow the space for SMEs to thrive in. Thus, the quality of the business environment has become a concern for different investment forums. Since 2003, the World Bank, in its Ease of Doing Business Index (EDBI), has been involved in the analysis of the quality and importance of business environment to national economic growth and development. The index considers a series of indicators that determine the success of business enterprises (World Bank Group, 2020). These indicators include factors surrounding starting a business, electricity, regulatory legislations, registration, acquisition of property, credit facilities, security, investment status, taxes and taxation, employment regulations and laws, accessing and acquisition of business locations, and finance routine operational requirements. All these issues are relevant components that define the business environment. The nature and characteristics of these issues determine the extent to which SMEs may attain sustainable growth and development.

The World Bank considers these issues and factors as components of doing business.

> Doing Business is founded on the principle that economic activity benefits from clear rules: rules that allow voluntary exchanges between economic actors, set out strong property rights, facilitate the resolution of commercial disputes, and provide contractual partners with protections against arbitrariness and abuse. Such rules are much more effective in promoting growth and development when they are efficient, transparent, and accessible to those for whom they are intended. (World Bank Group, 2020, p. 18)

Thus, these issues are contingent on the environments, which must be capable of driving the innovative ideas of enterprises for effective investment considerations and productivity. These environments would serve as incentives for businesses to engage in investment activities with a view to expanding, creating jobs, and making profits. Making these environments business-friendly requires effective policy direction of the government to encourage the growth and development of SMEs. According to Wruuck (2015, p. 2), "the growth of companies and economies" depends largely on "a good quality environment for doing business." In its earlier efforts to promote the growth of sustainable SMEs, the Organization for Economic Co-Operation and Development (OECD) noted three major factors that would generate sustainable environments conducive for the operation of SMEs, especially in developing economies within Africa. These are the "ability to integrate with the global economy through trade and investment; capacity to maintain sustainable government finances and sound money; and ability to put in place an institutional environment in which contracts can be enforced and property rights can be established" (OECD, 2004). The nature and characteristics of the business environment for SMEs created by these factors are dependent on the commitment of the government as well as the internal socio-economic and political dynamics of the country.

Creating a sustainable environment for economic development should be a priority of governments, because of the importance of commerce in societal growth and welfare. This becomes more critical for SMEs as an important domestic policy output aimed at promoting socio-economic development. A thriving environment where SMEs operate effectively would position them to function according to the objectives of their establishment. As such, SMEs are vital economic drivers for job creation and poverty alleviation (John-Akamelu & Muogbo, 2018; Kowo et al., 2019; Manzoor et al., 2019). SMEs contribute immensely to national and global economies. Thus, it is important that they operate in environments that would enhance their success and sustainability (Tsvetkova et al., 2020). The next section discusses the various factors that could determine the nature of environments that are available for business enterprises.

8.2 Nexus Between the Business and Various Environments

8.2.1 Political Environment

Government policies and political stability play a significant role in determining the success of SMEs. Political instability and conflict can have devastating effects on SMEs, as they may face physical threats, loss of assets, and disruptions to supply chains. Countries like Somalia have experienced prolonged conflict, which has severely impacted the ability of SMEs to operate (North & Weingast, 1989).

Every economic policy is a composite of political decisions. In other words, a country's economic policy is a derivative of political consideration within the context of the direction of the government. The political environment consists of the various influences and pressures from the various organs and institutions of government that shape the direction of the activities of economic activities (Hamiza et al., 2020). These influences and actions are patterned persistently and overtime as a routine component of the political administration of the state, within the context of the power and authority of public officials in these institutions of government. For example, in South Africa, the introduction of Broad-Based Black Economic Empowerment (B-BBEE) policies influenced SMEs' access to contracts and financing.

Additionally, the environment also includes the behaviour of governments, and the actions and inactions of the government that exert a series of pressure and influence on the activities of the various sectors of society. In addition, this environment itself is shaped by the nature and component of the political system, which most of the time defines the status of the state in the international environment. As such, the nexus between the business and political environment in Africa can significantly impact the performance of Small and Medium-sized Enterprises (SMEs). In this context, it's important to consider the unique challenges and opportunities that SMEs face in various African countries. For example, navigating through complex regulatory environments can be a significant burden for SMEs. Complying with tax regulations, industry-specific rules, and other legal requirements can be time-consuming and costly. Thus, SMEs that can effectively address these challenges through strategic planning, innovation, and resource management are more likely to thrive in the competitive business environment. Additionally, government policies and support programmes can play a significant role in helping SMEs overcome some of these challenges.

The unpredictability of the political environment makes it more pervasive, because it is defined by unexpected occurrences that could be triggered by unplanned events and actions with high magnitude impact. For example, the political protest in South Africa in July 2021 disrupted socio-economic activities in Kwazulu-Natal and Gauteng provinces. The unpredictable event in the country's political environment unsettled the economic environment, which suffered greatly with a loss of over which $14 billion (Smith, 2021). More than 50,000 traders in the informal sector with over 40,000 businesses were estimated to have been lost to the fracas. Protesters looted approximately 3000 stores and damaged more than 100 shopping malls, where more than 1200 retailers lost their outlets.

More specifically, an analyst predicted the future implication of the political unrest on the country's economy: "The medium to longer term impact of the unrest on the economy is expected to be more substantial than the immediate repercussions of the violence, which will drag down economic recovery prospects and potentially motivate higher rates of criminality and unrest, including copycat instances of looting" (cf. Smith, 2021). As a result, mostly affected in the fracas were SMEs as well as the informal sector business outlets that were struggling to break even. This sort of unpredictable political events create unwholesome environments that are not conducive for sustainable economic growth. Aside from the possibility of discouraging investments, victims of such political events would reconsider any long-term commitment to economic activities. Therefore, political stability is a crucial factor for SMEs. In countries with stable political environments, SMEs are more likely to thrive because they can plan for the long term and make investments with confidence. On the other hand, political instability, such as frequent changes in government or civil unrest, can disrupt business operations, deter foreign investors, and make it challenging for SMEs to operate effectively. Such examples are reflected in countries like Zimbabwe during times of political turmoil or in countries like Ghana with relatively stable political environments (World Bank, 2020).

The political environment can potentially provide both positive and negative business space for SMEs sustainability, depending on the change in the behaviours of stakeholders. As such, political factors can influence access to finance for SMEs. Government policies related to banking, interest rates, and financial stability can either facilitate or impede SMEs' access to capital. For example, in South Africa, government initiatives aimed at improving access to finance for SMEs have had a positive impact on their performance (ILO, 2019). More so, political decisions related to trade agreements and regional integration can affect SMEs engaged in cross-border trade. For instance, the African Continental Free Trade Area (AfCFTA) agreement has the potential to open up new markets for African SMEs. However, its successful implementation depends on political cooperation among member states (African Union, 2020).

However, where a society is characterised by weak coercive behavioural disposition of members, business enterprises are likely to benefit from the mass support. This support could ward off attempts by volatile political situations to prevent destruction or damage of economic activities. This presupposes that strengthening the supportive behaviour of citizens would prevent any unwholesome political events to disrupt economic activities in events such as public protests.

Thus, the survival of SMEs requires the support of the various political institutions (Zonouzi et al., 2021). The political exigencies for the establishment of SMEs and the subsequent support mechanisms from the environment are critical for creating sustenance pathways for the operation of these entrepreneurial adventures. In this regard, internal political developments influence the fortune of SMEs' operations. Zonouzi et al. (2021), in their study on SMEs in Iran, noted the importance of the country's political development and status for the sustainability of SMEs in the country. According to them, "one of the major challenges in the Iranian labor market is the closed, unchanged, and liberalized space of the laws and regulations as it annually observed a decline in its position and rank in the global business environment" (Zonouzi et al., 2021, 48). Thus, "removing the existing barriers, especially political factors, contributes to organising the business environment" (Zonouzi et al., 2021, 48). The implication of this is that an unwholesome political environment is antithetical to the sustainable operation of business ventures.

Further, political decisions are crucial to the organisation of every society because it is the structure upon which every other structure finds sustainability. The economic environment cannot be functional without political decisions, both domestic and international, in terms of appropriate relationships with major stakeholders. For example, the adoption of trade and economic policies, which provide the necessary guidelines for successful operation of SMEs, are clothed in the political decisions of government officials. Similarly, policy formulation processes are political activities that involve the political and bureaucratic elites. While policies are initiated by the political elites, the bureaucratic elites are charged with the administrative process that gives life to every policy. Thus, a synergy between the two sets of elites is necessary to provide a conducive policy environment for SMEs to thrive.

More so, business activities are susceptible to pressures arising from the challenge of constant change of regulatory measures occasioned by political consideration. When business owners or potential investors have interests in political development, depending on the side of the support, regulatory measures from government could stifle or promote the success of their business ventures (Hamiza et al., 2020). As an example, in Africa where the politics of vendettas is a characteristic of most ethnically or racially differentiated polities, business stakeholders are susceptible to political alignments which seek to promote their business interests. In many countries, nepotism and favouritism are the yardsticks for government support for business initiatives. This also implicates on attracting foreign investors or technical partners who might fall victims to the volatile ethnic and personalised politics.

Another political factor that could shape the operation of SMEs is the political behaviour of state in the international political system. In a globalised system, states are interconnected with networks of trading and economic activities. Thus, a behavioural disposition of a state defined by the political leadership, would determine the extent of benefits that could accrue to the domestic economic activities, in terms of exchange of ideas and technologies. For instance, a state under global economic sanction because of the political behaviour of its leaders would record lower economic development and growth. Zonouzi et al. (2021) note that the sanction on Iran created "an unfavorable situation for the business environment," a situation that made the country's policymakers to seek for interim policies while struggling to salvage the dwindling economy. This implies that the political behaviour of a state in the international system is potentially capable of stifling domestic economic growth and development. In Kenya, the government's commitment to improving the regulatory environment has eased business registration and licencing processes, fostering SME growth (Ikiara & Ndirangu, 2020).

Further, the state's political behaviour in the international system affects the national economy in different ways. Aside from stifling economic growth and development through SMEs' activities, multinational business organisations and conglomerates would be hampered from harnessing the comparative advantage of global economic transactions. Multinational organisations depend mostly on offshore markets for sales and procurement of raw materials. As superordinate competitors with the domestic industries and business organisations, rather than fold up, these organisations would secure the domestic economic space, thereby posing additional competition on the growth potentials of the SMEs.

In most cases where international sanctions have implications on domestic economic activities, governments usually adopt policies for the survival of SMEs and other economic activities with regulated enforceable rules. These policies include monetary control, currency, best practices in the period of uncertainties, intellectual capital, and political interactive policies, among others (Zonouzi et al., 2021). The essence of these policies is to contain the state from external infiltration in a manner that could constitute political and economic sabotage. Thus, a pariah state is often under economic siege, and often, a situation that hurts economic growth (Brandt & Erixon, 2013).

One of the consequences of international economic sanctions arising from the state's political behaviour is the export restrictions (Brandt & Erixon, 2013). In other words, sanctioned states would be locked up in the international trading transactions, thereby restricting economic activities of the state to its domestic environment. The domestic economy thrives when business organisations could transact economic activities across the borders. Similarly, the state would remain the consumer of its own product as well as raw materials. Even though this might lead to innovative strategies for the growth of SMEs, nevertheless, such growth would be stunted in view of saturated markets arising from competition from larger organisations with sufficient capital and resources to leverage on the consequence of the closed international economic market (Hamiza et al., 2020).

Additionally, in the aftermath of the COVID-19 pandemic, the Egyptian government provided the environment that motivated the World Bank to direct its investment support activities to the country's economy. In Egypt, government management of the pandemic has enabled it to secure the support of the World Bank in the area of job creation. With a population of 100 million, out of which 70% of citizens are below age 40, Egypt has a labour force of 30 million people. Unemployment in the pre-COVID-19 era stood at 8% but increased to 9.6% in the second quarter of 2020. Egypt's job creation ability has been facilitated by its large private sector firms with about 97% micro, small, and medium enterprises (MSMEs). This enabling environment has created the opportunity for interventionist programmes and measures by the World Bank to foster the growth of the private sector, more especially SMEs. The consequence of the above intervention is the expansion of the country's SMEs. About 97% of Egyptian enterprises today are micro, small, and medium enterprises (MSMEs), as well as large private sector firms, which are integral to the country's ability to create jobs. The COVID-19 pandemic's adverse effects on employment which had decreased to 8% before the pandemic only to increase to 9.6% in the second quarter of 2020, highlights the urgency of empowering entrepreneurs and private sector firms to enhance their competitiveness, flourish, and create more and better jobs. This underscores the need for an effective political environment for local business enterprises to benefit from financial and technical supports from international systems. In the age of globalisation, nations depend on each other for competitive advantages. Business enterprises, therefore, require conducive domestic, political environments to attract foreign partners for investments. Political decisions related to banking regulations in South Africa have influenced SMEs' access to credit. The South African government's support for SME financing has positively impacted the sector (Tchamyou, 2019). Additionally, the East African Community's efforts to enhance regional integration have opened up new markets for SMEs in member countries, such as Kenya and Tanzania (UNCTAD, 2020).

Institutional regulatory frameworks are crucial for sustainable growth of SMEs. According to the OECD (2017), uncertain institutional regulations characterised by inconsistency and complexity would disproportionately impact on the fortune and future of SMEs. As noted by the OECD (2017), "SMEs are typically less efficient than large firms in screening the regulatory environment and dealing with relevant norms." The problem generated by this environment often creates financial challenges in terms of indirect costs through payments to access necessary information, including expertise resources and training needed for compliance with the changing pattern of the regulations. Thus, the complexity of regulatory procedures and conditions for regulatory compliance are especially important for SMEs. However, administrative burdens that businesses, especially small ones, face can be overwhelming for SMEs' progress and success (OECD, 2017).

8.2.2 Economic Environment

The economic environment in Africa can greatly affect SME performance. African SMEs are increasingly interconnected with the global economy, so fluctuations in global markets and trade policies can influence their performance (HBR Staff, 2003). Political instability and conflicts in some African nations can disrupt supply chains, deter foreign investments, adversely affect economic activities, and create an uncertain business environment. For instance, currency fluctuations and inflation rates can disrupt the financial stability of SMEs. When Zimbabwe experienced hyperinflation in the late 2000s, many SMEs struggled to survive (Hanke & Kwok, 2009). SMEs as derivatives of the economic policies of every country need to enjoy favourable economic initiatives promoted by governments. As Wruuck (2015) has noted, a good business environment, especially in terms of conducive economic policies, is necessary to increase investment. Furthermore, in many African countries, exchange rates can be highly volatile due to factors such as fluctuating commodity prices and political instability. This can affect SMEs that import or export goods. For instance, SMEs in Nigeria often struggle to cope with exchange rate fluctuations, which can lead to increased production costs and uncertainty in pricing strategies (Wruuck, 2015).In the study on Eurozone economies, Wruuck (2015) noted the significant contributions of economic reforms for the creation of conducive environments for investments and growth of entrepreneurial organisations. Reforms in the areas of investments and fiscal consolidation were recorded as boosting the business environment (Wruuck, 2015). Further, government policies and regulations can significantly impact SMEs. For instance, high taxes, burdensome regulations, and corruption can hinder SME growth. High inflation rates in some African countries, such as Nigeria can erode the purchasing power of consumers and increase operating costs for SMEs. This negatively impacts the profitability and competitiveness of SMEs in Nigeria.

On the other hand, governments that implement pro-business policies, streamline regulations, and offer incentives can create a conducive environment for SME development. Some examples include Nigeria with complex regulatory environments, and countries like Rwanda with initiatives to ease the business environment (World Bank, 2020). Thus, the complexity and inconsistency of regulatory frameworks across African countries can be a barrier to SME growth; and may stifle innovation and investment among SMEs.

The survival of SMEs requires substantial economic reliefs from governments as well as opportunities to compete favourably in the domestic and external environments (Koirala, 2018). While SMEs usually operate mostly in the domestic environment, sustainable growth and development would provide them with opportunities to explore participation in the global economic environment. The ESCAP (2011) report noted the feasibility of SMEs at the domestic levels to access global markets through the available value chains systems, whether at the regional or global level. Such participation in the international economic environment would provide them with channels to access a wider range of economic and other business activities that could add value to their operational capacity and networks (Koirala, 2018). In such instances, this opportunity would be available through more conducive foreign trade and immigration policies of the country. As such, stringent cross-border trading activities should be relaxed to enable flexible interactions among SMEs across the borders. Rampant corruption in Nigeria has posed challenges to SMEs, requiring them to pay bribes for permits and licences, affecting profitability. In contrast, Botswana's strong anti-corruption measures have created a conducive environment for SMEs (Ndongko, 2018).

The importance of a conducive international economic environment for the success of SMEs cannot be overemphasised. With globalisation that has made the world a global village, the operation of SMEs within the context of the international economic system would promote indigenous economic activities. Globalisation promotes open access for countries to harness their economic potentials through constructive networks of experts in different fields of economic activities and trade. This facilitates new and emerging markets to be easily accessible; and new technologies and skills to be available for innovative and creative ventures for the growth of SMEs. In addition, international economic environments expose SMEs to startup capitals and assistance (ESCAP, 2011; Koirala, 2018). Political instability in countries like Zimbabwe has led to hyperinflation and economic turmoil, negatively affecting SMEs. On the contrary, Ghana's political stability has attracted foreign investments, benefiting local SMEs (Aryeetey & Fosu, 2019). Another common phenomenon in the global economic system is the growth in economic integration drives across regions and continents. Economic conditions can impact consumer purchasing power, which, in turn, affects SMEs' sales and profitability (Khanna & Palepu, 2010).

Economic cooperation among nations has provided SMEs with further opportunities to access other markets with comparative and competitive advantages, since most SMEs are like brand ambassadors of the country's industrial and economic potential, especially those in the agricultural sector. On the other hand, further economic integration brings with it a striking increase in competition from imports, the entry of new foreign investors and the strengthening of the domestic economic environment. Relatedly, the World Bank (2020) posited that most of the indicators of doing business relate to the economic environment, which is critical for the sustainability of SMEs.

Furthermore, the economic regulatory rules are factors that affect "productivity, growth, employment, trade, investment, access to finance, and the size of the informal economy" (World Bank, 2020, 30). For instance, the firm entry rules include startup regulations that determine the capacity of firms to invest in the economy (World Bank, 2020). As the World Bank (2020) noted, ease of new firm entry regulations "results in higher productivity through the reallocation of resources from old to new firms." Excessive startup regulations and registration are likely to generate unfriendly business environments, thereby stifling the capacity of SMEs to grow within the context of the nation's economic policies. Additionally, limited access to finance is a common challenge for SMEs in Africa. High interest rates, inadequate collateral, and strict lending requirements can hinder business growth, thus hampering the expansion and sustainability of SMEs in Africa.

Another variant of economic environments to boost the growth of SMEs is the entrenched entrepreneurship culture through carefully planned economic policies and incentives (Cepel, 2019). For example, recognition of successful enterprises that are contributing to economic growth and job creation with rewards such as incentives would signal the need for a more conducive culture of best practice. As such, the environments where these SMEs operate influence their growth and development. Furthermore, the development of a true entrepreneurship culture requires commitment to legislative frameworks that would curb unethical practices among entrepreneurs who enjoy political shield to access government supports. In addition, balanced support for SMEs should reduce the burdensome administrative procedures applicable to SMEs. As such, a sound business environment and a well-functioning entrepreneurial "ecosystem" for businesses, is vital for countries and regions to promote the participation of SMEs in a globalised economy (OECD, 2017). The imperative of a conducive business environment for sustainable growth and development of SMEs cannot be overemphasised in a contemporary globalised system. Globalisation and the increasing revolution in the information and communication technology (ICT) have increased the pace of competitive pressures in the quest for innovation and access to strategic resources. Thus, the framework generated by this technological drive has a diverse impact on the growth level of entrepreneurial activities (OECD, 2017). Therefore, different dimensions of investment, innovation, and growth of business enterprises across the globe necessitate congenial collaboration for competitive advantage.

Furthermore, regulatory requirements for tax and taxation often create an unwholesome economic environment for SMEs. For instance, the OECD (2017) noted that "a substantial fixed cost component of tax regulatory requirements and compliance costs" such as record keeping, filing, and payment processes in most countries often disadvantaged small businesses compared to large corporations. More so, high interest rates, inflation, and currency volatility can make it challenging for SMEs to secure affordable loans or attract investors.

Thus, attempts by the SMEs to comply with these regulatory directives would mean further financial burdens in the area of compliance. Relatedly, the OECD (2017) opined that many firms, which also tend to be small, face high compliance costs which can exacerbate their resource and cash-flow constraints which are often experienced in the early stages of business development and this may act as a deterrent to formalisation as well. In certain cases, tax compliance costs for SMEs may even exceed their tax cash payments. Thus, economic conditions in Africa can significantly affect SMEs' access to financing. As such, SMEs may be vulnerable to stunted growth or total failure in societies where tax regulatory instructions are at a variance with the financial capacity of SMEs. In the process of seeking compliance with a series of business taxation demands such as tax credits and other incentives, SMEs could be vulnerable to unintentional consequences that outweigh their capital capacity.

Also, SMEs are likely to experience stunted growth in an economy characterised by mismanagement of public resources. Where public integrity is poor and a weak culture of transparent business transactions characterises public administration, SMEs may experience low growth because of a public sector environment characterised by poor governance. While the lack of transparency and corruption in the public sector are detrimental to all businesses, it poses particular problems to SMEs as they often lack the capacity to cope with an opaque public sector, design and implement anti-corruption strategies, and lobby for their needs in the absence of an established framework for participation in public decision-making. Consequently, while public service delivery would be in jeopardy, SMEs that tend to survive would be encumbered by unethical demands and practices. As such, attempts to recoup resources expended through facilitating approval of documents through bribery may negatively impact productivity. As the OECD (2017) noted, SMEs endure higher administrative burdens and red tape compared to large firms.

8.2.3 *Infrastructural Environment*

The infrastructural environment in Africa is shaping the performance and growth opportunities for SMEs across various sectors. It is important to note that the impact of infrastructure such as technology can vary depending on factors such as sector, location, and the specific technology adopted by the SME in different countries. An infrastructural environment for accelerated economic activities is also crucial for the success of SMEs, such as access to operating space for SME operations. Poor infrastructure, such as inadequate transportation and energy systems, can increase operational costs and hinder SMEs' competitiveness. Additionally, inadequate infrastructure, such as unreliable power supply and poor transportation networks, can disrupt business operations and increase costs. As acknowledged by the World Bank (2020), infrastructure deficits in Africa can significantly impede the productivity and competitiveness of SMEs. However, to the contrary, e-commerce platforms like Jumia and Konga in Nigeria have allowed SMEs to expand their market reach beyond local boundaries, boosting sales and growth opportunities (Oloyede & Afolabi, 2019).

For instance, in their study of business enterprises in Russia, Karas et al. (2015) noted the impact of the land tenure system and security on the success of SMEs. According to the study, the rights of individuals to own land was facilitated through access to financial assistance from external investment sources. Thus, the nature of property rights determines the type of confidence investors would have in the acquisition of land for the establishment of their businesses. Unsecured property rights in societies where there is land expropriation or occupation without notice, would drive investors and entrepreneurs into making decisions that are antithetical to the success of their business (Karas et al., 2015). Thus, the fear of expropriation of land without compensation presents an economic environment characterised by uncertainty of investments. This will have consequences for the sustainability of SMEs. Political decisions on infrastructure development can impact SME logistics. For instance, Ethiopia's investments in infrastructure have improved connectivity, benefiting SMEs engaged in export-oriented businesses (Abebe et al., 2017).

Where land tenure and property rights guaranteed adequate security for investments, SMEs often experience accelerated growth and development, as revealed in a study in Benin Republic by Goldstein et al. (2018), which noted the need to strengthen individual land property rights as an incentive for the growth of SMEs. In most African societies, land rights regulations associated with land allocation and enforcement are embroiled in complex and diverse customary and traditional arrangements. Unlike developed countries in Europe and America, access to land in most African societies involve a multiple of traditions and customs held by local stakeholders such as chiefs and community heads. As noted by Goldstein et al. (2018, 50), "customary land tenure systems often coexist with formal land administration systems." Thus, SMEs need to understand the type of land tenure system applicable and the security associated with the ownership of land, to ensure the success of their enterprise activities. Thus it is imperative that investors and business owners operate in a society where access to land has a guarantee of sustainable regulation. The policies of government in land tenure are therefore critical for the survival of SMEs because unsecured land would drive away investments.

Another important aspect of the infrastructural environment for the success of SMEs is energy. Business enterprises, especially the manufacturing SMEs, require reliable supply of electricity. For example, in societies with irregular supply of energy, SMEs in the manufacturing sector incur higher operational costs arising from reliance on alternative sources of energy. The World Bank (2017) noted the importance of reliable electricity supply, arguing that electricity "outages represent a significant obstacle to doing business in economies worldwide." It claimed that unreliable and irregular power supply would "result in spoiled perishable goods, damage to sensitive equipment, and productivity losses" (World Bank, 2017). As such, access to affordable renewable energy solutions, such as solar panels and mini-grids, has reduced energy costs and improved reliability for SMEs in regions with unreliable power infrastructure (Gebreeyesus & Mohnen, 2019).

Thus, for business organisations to secure their equipment and preserve their perishable goods, they have to procure electricity generators and "other expensive equipment to protect sensitive inventory and machinery" (World Bank, 2017). In this regard, governments need to prioritise provision of energy for sustainable development and growth of SMEs.

Also, technological advancements are reshaping SMEs in Africa. Mobile technology has enabled innovative business models, like mobile banking in Kenya through M-Pesa, which has empowered many small businesses to conduct transactions more efficiently, reach a wider customer base, and access financial services (Kuria et al., 2019). Expanding access to high-speed internet in various African countries is enabling SMEs to engage in online marketing, collaborate with global partners, and access cloud-based services for improved efficiency (Oyelaran-Oyeyinka & Adeyeye, 2020). For example, Mobile apps and data analytics tools are helping agricultural SMEs in Kenya optimise crop management, increase yields, and reduce waste (Munyua & Mwangi, 2016). Another example is the government-backed programmes promoting technology adoption, such as South Africa's Technology for Women in Business initiative, where female-owned SMEs are helped to access technology and training, thereby improving their business performance (Tshabalala & Chilwane, 2019).

8.2.4 Geographical Environment

The geographic environment in Africa can have diverse and substantial effects on the performance of SMEs in the region, emphasising the importance of understanding and adapting to local geographical conditions for business success.

The location of industrial organisations and setups have attracted the attention of scholars of economic geography (Boschma & Frenken, 2006; Allen & Arkolakis, 2014; Chłon-Dominczak et al., 2020). The argument is that there is an expectation "that existing institutional infrastructure measured as industry density can generate spillovers that contribute to entrepreneurship development" (Chłon-Dominczak et al., 2020, 2). These scholars posit that the geography of society determines the location behaviour of industries. As such, they pay due attention to the ways geographical location of firms determines prices of commodities and products; as well as conditioning propensity for sustainable growth and development. They contend that the concentration of industrial activities in a particular geographical location could lead to an agglomeration of economies capable of fostering innovative startups that would eventually enable the establishment of other industries that are engaged in the production of complementary services and products (Chłon-Dominczak et al., 2020). Additionally, when industries are located within the precinct of a geographical location, it would generate healthy competition capable of increasing productivity and quality of products. It also has a way of fostering collaboration and cooperation, especially among firms providing complementary services, with a view to ensuring sustainability and continuity in time of economic challenges.

Another potential benefit of concentration of firms in a geographical location is the feasibility of the opportunities for collective action against developments which may be capable of jeopardising their common goals and business interests (Guo et al., 2016). Additionally, firms within the same area tend to develop an institutionalised culture of routinised innovative behaviours. Thus, SMEs in such a geographical cluster may potentially develop characteristics capable of supporting the direction of operations for the further development of an innovative enterprising culture.

Thus, geographic economic factors are essential for SMEs to thrive and experience innovative and sustainable development and growth. It is important, therefore that states should harness the geographical pattern of the different societies to develop sustainable environments for SME growth and development. In this regard, the establishment of designated areas such as industrial estates or parks would encourage proximity advantages sufficient for them to engage in interactive learning (Guo et al., 2016; Chłon-Dominczak et al., 2020). According to Chłon-Dominczak et al. (2020, 3), proximity of firms within a geographical cluster "may also stimulate the formation and evolution of institutions, such as norms and habits that may affect interactive learning and innovation." However, when such proximity is minimal, then it may lead to a lack of spatial externalities.

Further, the success of SMEs depends, partly, on the nature, size, and scope of local markets in terms of demand and supply of products and labour (Chłon-Dominczak et al., 2020). The market environment is determined by the location and the variety of size. Where local demand for products is buoyant, SMEs may not have a sustained competitive advantage of increased productivity and business. If, on the other hand, the local labour market environment is conducive for the operation of the business, SMEs may access the population for the necessary human capital at reasonable costs. This geographical environment created by the local demand-and-supply market is capable of influencing the success of SMEs. Where these variables are not adequate, business managers could adapt to the local peculiarities and adjust the scope of the business to suit the environmental demands. This is capable of mitigating the impact on the success of the business.

1. **Infrastructure challenges:** In many parts of Africa, inadequate infrastructure, including poor road networks and unreliable electricity supply, can hinder the transportation of goods and the operation of businesses. This can increase logistics costs and disrupt production schedules, affecting SMEs' competitiveness and profitability (Söderbaum, 2015).
2. **Access to markets:** The vast size of the African continent, coupled with varying degrees of regional integration and trade barriers, can pose challenges for SMEs in accessing wider markets. SMEs may find it costly and logistically challenging to expand beyond their immediate geographic area, limiting their growth potential (UNCTAD, 2019).
3. **Climate and agricultural production:** Many SMEs in Africa are involved in agriculture. The geographic environment plays a crucial role in agricultural performance. Droughts, floods, and other extreme weather events can lead to crop failures and impact the livelihoods of farmers and agribusinesses (Morton, 2007).
4. **Proximity to suppliers and customers:** SMEs often rely on local suppliers and customers. The geographic location of an SME can affect the availability of raw materials and the proximity to target markets. Remote or isolated locations may result in higher transportation costs and limited access to inputs (World Bank, 2017).
5. **Political stability and security:** The geographic location of an SME within a country or region can determine its exposure to political instability and security risks. Areas with a history of conflict or political unrest can disrupt business operations, increase insurance costs, and deter potential investors (Collier & Hoeffler, 2004).
6. **Natural resources and extractive industries:** SMEs involved in natural resource extraction industries, such as mining or forestry, may be heavily influenced by the geographic distribution of these resources. Access to and the sustainability of these resources can significantly impact business performance (Sachs & Warner, 2001).

8.2.5 *Social-Cultural Environment*

Africa is a continent with diverse cultures and languages. In a study by Hofstede (1980), it was found that cultural dimensions, such as individualism–collectivism and power distance, can influence communication styles in business. SMEs operating in Africa need to navigate these cultural differences to establish effective communication with employees, customers, and partners. Thus, the socio-cultural environment in Africa can significantly affect the business performance of SMEs, since entrepreneurs and businesses must be sensitive to these factors and must adapt their strategies accordingly to succeed in the African market. Social factors like cultural preferences and demographics can affect SMEs. For example, understanding consumer preferences and adapting products accordingly is crucial. In Nigeria, the rise of digital payment systems has been instrumental for SMEs catering to a tech-savvy younger population (Olusegun, 2018).

The social-cultural environment embodies people's attitude to work and wealth; role of family, marriage, religion, and education; ethical issues; and social responsiveness of business. Every society has its value attachments that define the nature and disposition of generation of people. Culture as a symbol of the general pattern of behaviour and ways of life of citizens is crucial in the identification of preference and values (Ijaz et al., 2012). For example, consumer preferences in Africa can be deeply influenced by cultural factors. For instance, preferences for traditional products or local brands may be strong in certain regions. Understanding these preferences is critical for SMEs to tailor their products and marketing strategies effectively (Okazaki, 2009).

Culture as "the transformation of learned behavior from generation to generation through language and imitation" defines the pattern of human behaviour and inclination towards established value preferences (Ijaz et al., 2012, 911). Cultural attachment shapes "the human cognition and motivational variables to guide choices, commitments and standards of behaviors" (Ijaz et al., 2012, 911). Overtime, this cultural inclination evolves as practices that define the individual cognitive ability. When these practices become entrenched in society, it influences the direction and pattern of socio-economic interaction. Thus, business organisations and enterprises that seek to operate within society have to adapt to the cultural environment. In other words, culture impacts social and economic institutions and is also a source for development. (Ijaz et al., 2012, 911).

For SMEs to thrive in an environment created by entrenched cultural practices and orientation, stakeholders have to adapt to the need for engaging in socialisation processes with respect to existing practices in social networking and societal supports. At times, these cultural practices and patterns evolved over time to define the national scope especially in societies characterised by homogeneity. In this regard, national culture would have consequences on the nature of entrepreneurial culture that would evolve. Thus, small business owners should explore the various unwritten rules, norms, nuances, and conduct that could shape their decision-making processes, since the cultural environment is often complex, depending on the composition of society.

Socially built reality is when individuals create a social framework for themselves and consequently develop it into an effective reality that shapes and influences their behavioural patterns. Social systems and the culture of people converge to form the socio-cultural business environment and consequently the entrepreneurs become moulded by it. Additionally, religion is a central part of the socio-cultural fabric in Africa. For example, during Ramadan, business activities may slow down in predominantly Muslim countries in Africa. Understanding and respecting these religious practices is essential for SMEs to maintain good relations with their employees and customers (Huntington, 1996).

The socio-cultural environment also refers to the set of basic common values which contribute to shaping the behaviour of people in a society and has a significant degree of influence on the entrepreneurial intention of individuals. People acquire their shared characteristics and pattern of behaviour through socialisation processes which involves factors like education, religion, and family background. These dimensions happen to be the most prominent in describing the socio-cultural environment. The social and cultural environments influence and are influenced by entrepreneurial activity (Cepel, 2019). Indeed, scholars have noted that profits and social climate are critical for the success of entrepreneurial activities (Powell & Rodet, 2012; Castano et al., 2015; Cepel, 2019). Profits and social climate constitute the economy as well as the sociological and institutional dimensions of a society. According to Cepel (2019, 67), it comprises a social dimension known as the social environment in which individuals engage in entrepreneurial activities and its growth. In such engagement, social values may be influential. In the view of this, it is essential that those involved in entrepreneurial activities are familiar with environmental influences.

Relatedly, unfriendly business environments may emerge in societies characterised by inequality, civil society protests, and social stress arising from civil unrests. Subsequent, punitive measures to quell the aggrieved may affect entrepreneurship negatively. For example, ethnic tensions or cultural conflicts can disrupt business operations and affect long-term planning. This social climate is interwoven with cultural orientation, especially in plural societies. This is supported by Cepel (2019, 67), who noted that the environment created by the interplay of socio-cultural factors and activity would "influence economic development through entrepreneurship and innovation" and "motivate individuals to engage in entrepreneurial activity."

Societal movements and trends are also social environmental factors that could influence the growth and development of SMEs. Changes in societal preference and values, attitudinal dispositions of citizens as well as societal reactions to certain conditions would determine the extent of success of small businesses operating in such environments (Bouazza et al., 2015; Cepel, 2019). As such, in many African countries, traditional gender roles and social norms still play a significant role. This can affect the composition of the workforce in SMEs and their ability to access diverse talent pools. A study by Kabeer (1999) highlighted the importance of understanding these social norms in the context of female entrepreneurship in Africa (Kabeer, 1999).

When consumption habits of people change, it creates an unwholesome social environment for SMEs to thrive. While the government cannot effect any change in this direction, SMEs should strategise to recognise societal trends and preferences as they unfold so as to blend and adapt their business operations to explore alternative measures to operate during the flux. Thus, SMEs should always maintain a good public image to attract the patronage of citizens whose value preference could be influenced by the courtesy of incentives offered by SMEs.

In addition, the behavioural character of management could bolster the social environment capable of influencing the growth of SMEs (Castano et al., 2015). The character traits of business managers could make or mar the fortunes of the organisation amid societal trends and changes in value preferences in the social environment. Attitudinal disposition, personality traits, and nuances are personal attributes that could influence the nature of the social environment capable of attracting stakeholders for patronages. Relatedly, in many African communities, trust and relationships are crucial for business success. SMEs often rely on local networks and community ties for support and business opportunities. Understanding and participating in community activities can be vital for SMEs, as highlighted by Osei-Kojo and Amoako (2016) in their research on Ghanaian SMEs.

This is part of the public image that SMEs should maintain to blend and adapt to the various social changes within the environment. A congenial social environment created by the behavioural disposition of managers and employees are crucial for the success of SMEs, even if other factors are not so favourable.

Thus, the socio-cultural environment in Africa can affect the performance of SMEs; and important for SMEs operating in Africa to conduct thorough cultural analyses and adapt their strategies to the specific cultural context of the region in which they operate.

8.3 Conclusion

The aforementioned discussion demonstrates how the business environment for SMEs in Africa is intricately linked to other environments. Policies, political and economic stability, regulations, and corruption levels all play a pivotal role in shaping the performance and growth prospects of SMEs in the region. As such, SME performance in Africa is clearly linked to the broader business environment, including the economic, political, social, and technological spheres. This highlights the complex interplay between these environments and SME outcomes in the region. Thus, adaptation and strategic responses to these external factors are crucial for SMEs to thrive in African markets.

Further, good governance should be paramount, as a way of stimulating the evolution of more conducive environments for the operations of SMEs. When government officials recognise and respect the importance of adherence to extant rules and regulations as instruments of governance, society would embrace the culture of best practice capable of engendering a conducive social environment needed for SMEs to explore the diverse culture for their business activities. Further, insecurity and threats of political instability should draw the attention of governments for the need for inclusive administration that would cater for the interests of all segments of the society.

References

Abebe, G., Asrat, S., & Ketema, M. (2017). *Transport Infrastructure and the Performance of Manufacturing Firms in Ethiopia.* Harvard Business School Working Paper.

African Union. (2020). *Agreement Establishing the African Continental Free Trade Area.* African Union.

Allen, T., & Arkolakis, C. (2014). Trade and the Topography of the Spatial Economy. *The Quarterly Journal of Economics, 129*(3), 1085–1140.

Aryeetey, E., & Fosu, A. (2019). *Ghana's Political and Economic Development: An Assessment.* Harvard Kennedy School Faculty Research Working Paper Series.

Boschma, R. A., & Frenken, K. (2006). Why is economic geography not an evolutionary science? Towards an evolutionary economic geography. *Journal of Economic Geography, 6*, 273–302.

Bouazza, B., Ardjouman, D., & Abada, O. (2015). Establishing the Factors Affecting the Growth of Small and Medium-sized Enterprises in Algeria Asma. *American International Journal of Social Science, 4*(2), 101–115.

Brandt, L., & Erixon, F. (2013). *Pariah in the World Economy: How Should Countries Respond to Argentina's Return to Economic Nationalism?* Policy Briefs No. 1/2013, The European Centre for International Political Economy (ECIPE).

Castano, M. S., Mendez, M. T., & Galindo, M. A. (2015). The effect of social, cultural, and economic factors on entrepreneurship. *Journal of Business Research, 68*(7), 1496–1500.

Cepel, M. (2019). Social and Cultural Factors and their Impact on the quality of Business Environment in the SME Segment. *International Journal of Entrepreneurial Knowledge, 7(1), 65–73.*

Chłon-Dominczak, A., Fiedukowicz, A., & Olszewski, R. (2020). Geographical and Economic Factors Affecting the Spatial Distribution of Micro, Small, and Medium Enterprises: An Empirical Study of The Kujawsko-Pomorskie Region in Poland. *International Journal of Geo-Information, 9*(426), 1–28. https://doi.org/10.3390/ijgi9070426

Collier, P., & Hoeffler, A. (2004). Greed and grievance in civil war. *Oxford Economic Papers, 56*(4), 563–595.

ESCAP. (2011). *Enabling Environment for the Successful integration of small and Medium Scale Enterprises in Global Value Chains.* Studies in Trade and Investment, No. 70.

Gebreeyesus, M., & Mohnen, P. (2019). Innovation performance and embeddedness in networks: Evidence from the Ethiopian footwear cluster. *World Development, 115*, 78–93.

Goldstein, M., Houngbedji, K., Kondylis, F., O'Sullivan, M., & Selod, H. (2018). Formalization without Certification? Experimental Evidence on Property Rights and Investment. *Journal of Development Economics, 132*(May), 57–74.

Guo, Q., He, C., & Li, D. (2016). Entrepreneurship in China: The role of localisation and urbanisation economies. *Urban Studies., 53*(12), 2584–2606.

Hamiza, O., Francis, T. M., & Rashid, T. (2020). The Role of Socio-Political Environment in Business Success: A Case of Small Businesses in Uganda. *International Journal of Academic Research in Business and Social Sciences., 10*(10), 783–799.

Hanke, S. H., & Kwok, A. K. (2009). On the Measurement of Zimbabwe's Hyperinflation. *Cato Journal, 29*(2), 353–364.

HBR Staff. (2003). What Globalization Means for Your Business. Harvard Business Review.

Hofstede, G. (1980). *Culture's Consequences: International Differences in Work-Related Values.* Sage Publications.

Huntington, S. P. (1996). *The Clash of Civilizations and the Remaking of World Order.* Simon & Schuster.

Ijaz, M., Yasin, G., & Zafar, M. J. (2012). Cultural Factors Effecting Entrepreneurial Behaviour Among Entrepreneurs: Case Study of Multan, Pakistan. *International Journal of Asian Social Science, 2*(6), 908–917.

Ikiara, M., & Ndirangu, L. (2020). Small and Medium Enterprises (SMEs) and Regulatory Environment in Kenya. *Harvard International Law Journal, 61*(2), 57–71.

ILO. (2019). *Access to Finance for Small and Medium Enterprises in South Africa.* International Labour Organization.

John-Akamelu, C. R., & Muogbo, U. S. (2018). Role of Small & Medium Enterprises in Poverty Eradication in Nigeria. *European Journal of Research and Reflection in Management Sciences, 6*(2), 33–49.

Kabeer, N. (1999). Resources, Agency, Achievements: Reflections on the Measurement of Women's Empowerment. *Development and Change, 30*(3), 435–464.

Karas, A., Pyle, W., & Schoors, K. (2015). A 'de Soto Effect' in Industry? Evidence from the Russian Federation. *Journal of Law and Economics, 58*(2), 451–480.

Khanna, T., & Palepu, K. (2010). *Winning in Emerging Markets: A Road Map for Strategy and Execution.* Harvard Business Press.

Koirala, S. (2018). *SMEs: Key Drivers of Green and Inclusive Growth. Issue Paper.* OECD.

Kowo, S. A., Adenuga, O. A. O., & Sabitu, O. (2019). The Role of SMEs Development on Poverty Alleviation in Nigeria. *Insights into Regional Development, 1*(3), 214–226.

Kuria, D., Nyambane, G. A., & Njeru, A. (2019). The role of mobile banking on small and medium-sized enterprises (SMEs) performance in Kenya: A case of Nakuru town. *International Journal of Scientific and Research Publications, 9*(2), 258–268.

Manzoor, F., Wei, L., Nurunnabi, M., & Abdul Subhan, Q. (2019). Role of SME in Poverty Alleviation in SAARC Region via Panel Data Analysis. *Sustainability, 11*(22), 6480. MDPI AG. https://doi.org/10.3390/su11226480

Morton, J. F. (2007). The impact of climate change on smallholder and subsistence agriculture. *Proceedings of the National Academy of Sciences, 104*(50), 19680–19685.

Munyua, H. S., & Mwangi, W. M. (2016). Factors influencing the adoption of mobile phone based agricultural information services among farmers in Kenya: A field study. *International Journal of Scientific and Research Publications, 6*(2), 133–143.

Ndongko, M. J. (2018). Corruption and Its Effects on Small and Medium-Sized Enterprises in Africa: Evidence from Botswana and Nigeria. *Harvard Journal of African American Public Policy, 24*(1), 65–84.

North, D. C., & Weingast, B. R. (1989). Constitutions and Commitment: The Evolution of Institutions Governing Public Choice in Seventeenth-Century England. *Journal of Economic History, 49*(4), 803–832.

OECD. (2004). *Promoting SMEs for Development. Report of the 2nd OECD Conference of Ministers Responsible for Small and Medium-Sized Enterprises (SMEs Promoting Entrepreneurship and Innovative SMEs in a Global Economy: Towards a More Responsible and Inclusive Globalization.* Istanbul, Turkey 3–5 June 2004.

OECD. (2017). *Enhancing the Contributions of SMES in a Global and Digitalized Economy.* Meeting of the OECD Council at Ministerial Level Paris, 7–8 June. https://www.oecd.org/industry/C-MIN-2017-8-EN.pdf

Okazaki, S. (2009). Determinants of Export Performance in Small and Medium-Sized Enterprises: A Review. *International Marketing Review, 26*(6), 642–674.

Oloyede, O. S., & Afolabi, A. O. (2019). E-commerce adoption and SMEs performance in Nigeria. *Journal of African Business, 20*(4), 444–460.

Olusegun, O. (2018). Impact of E-Payment System on Small and Medium-Scale Enterprises in Nigeria. *International Journal of Economics, Commerce, and Management, 6*(6), 46–57.

Osei-Kojo, A., & Amoako, G. K. (2016). Network Ties and Growth of Small and Medium-Sized Enterprises in Ghana. *European Journal of Business and Innovation Research, 4*(6), 16–28.

Oyelaran-Oyeyinka, B., & Adeyeye, D. (2020). Digital technology adoption in Africa: Lessons from the informal economy. *World Development, 127*, 104–115.

Powell, B., & Rodet, C. (2012). *Praise and profits: Cultural and institutional determinants.* Palgrave.

Sachs, J. D., & Warner, A. M. (2001). The curse of natural resources. *European Economic Review, 45*(4–6), 827–838.

Senbet, L., & Otchere, I. (2008). *The Modernization of Stock Exchanges in Emerging Economies: Challenges and Opportunities.* Harvard Business School Note, 209–101.

Smith, E. (2021). *South Africa unrest and Covid measures are starting to derail its economic recovery.* CNBC, August 2.

Söderbaum, F. (2015). *The geography of African development: Making sense of the issues and actors.* Routledge.

Tchamyou, V. S. (2019). The Role of Information Sharing in Modulating the Effect of Financial Access on Inequality. *Harvard Data Science Review, 1*(1), 171–189.

Tshabalala, Z., & Chilwane, R. (2019). The Technology for Women in Business (TWIB) initiative: A socio-economic impact analysis of SMMEs. *South African Journal of Business Management, 50*(1), 1–10.

Tsvetkova, D., Bengtsson, E., & Durst, S. (2020). Maintaining Sustainable Practices in SMEs: Insights from Sweden. *Sustainability, 12*(10242). https://doi.org/10.3390/su122410242

UNCTAD. (2020). *Economic Development in Africa Report 2020: Tackling Illicit Financial Flows for Sustainable Development in Africa.* United Nations.

United Nations Conference on Trade and Development (UNCTAD). (2019). *Economic Development in Africa Report 2019: Made in Africa—Rules of Origin for Enhanced Intra-African Trade.* United Nations.

World Bank. (2017). *Doing Business 2017: Equal Opportunity for All.* World Bank Group.

World Bank. (2020). *Doing Business 2020: Comparing Business Regulation in 190 Economies.* World Bank Publications.

Wruuck, P. (2015). *The business environment in the eurozone: Why it is worth paying attention to the details.* Deutsche Bank Research. https://www.dbresearch.com/PROD/RPS_ENPROD/PROD0000000000463934/Research_Briefing%3A_The_business_environment_in_the.pdf?undefined&realload=V9~l3JhB0gW~0rxckK/jRPctng38R0tWFN1UOgnK4YWefZ/IZIl0oex53IrQk9D8

Zonouzi, M. K., Hoseyni, M., & Khoramshahi, M. (2021). Political factors affecting the survival of SMEs case study: An empirical study in Tehran Grand Bazaar. *Asia Pacific Management Review, 26*(1), 47–56.

CHAPTER 9

Internationalisation of SMEs: Challenges and Remedies

Gift Mugano

9.1 Introduction

Evidence shows that although SMEs from the African continent face several challenges as a result of the forces of globalisation, the increased need for internationalisation has been considered as a driver of competitive advantage and international performance of SMEs (Mutalemwa, 2015). As argued by Doole and Lowe (2008), globally SMEs have used internationalisation as a growth strategy as well as a vehicle to build resilience and sustainability. International strategies which are regularly used by SMEs with notable successes inter alia include licencing, exportation, and joint venture businesses (Guili, 2018).

In Africa, undisputable evidence shows that SMEs experience massive challenges which constrain their capability to internationalise globally and raise their competitiveness (Ocloo et al., 2014). Notable binding constraints which hinder African SMEs to internationalise inter alai include limited government support, trade restrictions, shortage of physical infrastructure including operating space, weak institutions, poor governance, and economic instability (Benzing & Chu, 2009; Guili, 2018).

G. Mugano (✉)
Faculty of Management Sciences, Durban University of Technology, Durban, South Africa

G. Mugano, N. Dorasamy, *SMEs Perspective in Africa*,
https://doi.org/10.1007/978-3-031-69103-4_9

In view of the fact that research focusing on the internationalisation of African SMEs is limited, this chapter discusses the impediments to internationalisation for African SMEs. In the same vein, building on evidence from the globe, the chapter provides a comprehensive understanding of activities linked with successful internationalisation of SMEs.

9.2 Internationalisation of SMEs Unpacked

Internationalisation is defined as a strategy used by firms to enter the global market (World Trade Organisation, 2016). Internationalisation of SMEs can be categorised from two perspectives, that is, the first view and second view.

Using the first view, World Trade Organisation (2016) identified four forms of internationalisation which can be adopted by SMEs, that is:

1. Foreign direct investments, through greenfield investment (i.e., where a firm establishes a new venture in a foreign country). The FDIs also include joint ventures, mergers, and acquisitions.
2. SMEs may use non-equity contractual agreement to enter global markets using vehicles such as licencing, franchising, or structural alliances through export consortia.
3. Direct exports: SMEs can enter international markets through the use of direct exports to final consumers or distributors located in foreign markets.
4. Indirect exports: SMEs may undertake indirect internationalisation strategy by selling their products in foreign land through various schemes which inter alia include regional or global value chains (GVCs) and export intermediaries such as brokers, export buying agents, and wholesalers who are located in their respective countries.

With respect to the second view, internationalisation of SMEs stresses on the importance of networks as an evolution of the first view rather than a radical departure from it (International Trade Centre (ITC) and World Trade Organisation (WTO), 2014). In this regard, networks are defined as the set of established relationships a business has with its customers and suppliers (ITC and WTO, 2014).

Based on this view, ITC and WTO (2014) underscored that there are two types of firms and two types of networks which are both differentiated by their level of internationalisation. For instance, a company may participate in a highly internationalised network and actively participate in national production only. On the contrary, an enterprise can actively participate within a predominantly national network and participate in massive foreign trade.

In view of these distinct differences on how firms participate in global trade, ITC and WTO (2014) argued that the challenges and opportunities presented to companies in these various categories are different and, as such, in order to foster internationalisation of SMEs, distinct support programmes are required.

When referring to internationalisation of SMEs, economists argued that there is need to consider importing and exporting as companies can use their experience of importing goods to enter export markets (Welch & Luostarinen, 1988). This view resonates well with the perceived importance of integrating SMEs in GVCs. A study by ITC and WTO (2014) using over 7500 SMEs from Italy revealed that when SMEs are involved in production supply chains, they can become competitive in the backdrop of existing economies of scale which increases their chances to export notwithstanding the fact that they are initially small and less productive firms (Giovannetti et al., 2014). Based on this observation, ITC and WTO (2014) observed that for companies which are part of the supply chain and employs between 1–9, 10–49, and 50–249 workers, the likelihood of being an exporter, respectively, increased by 98%, 34%, and 34%.

Because it allows SMEs to access international markets without having to meet upfront costs associated with scouting for new clients and negotiating contracts, WTO (2016) argued that indirect export can be easily used by SMEs to enter international markets because it is normally considered to be the least risky entry into global markets. Likewise, benefits such as negotiation skills, market knowledge that allow business risks to be diversified and pooled which result in reduction in searching and matching costs related to export business accrues to export intermediaries or companies which carry out sales in international markets on behalf of SMEs (WTO, 2016).

However, evidence shows that the contribution of SMEs in exports varies from region to region (WTO, 2016). For example, in Asia SMEs accounts for 8.7% of total exports, in Developing Europe SMEs account for 28% of total exports while in the Middle East SMEs account for 16% of total exports and only 3% of Africa's exports are SMEs-driven (WTO, 2016).

9.3 Internationalisation of African SMEs

The African continent has in recent years, that is, from the turn of the new millennium, made progress in building strong institutions, fostering good governance and political stability and economic reforms which are key in promoting business growth (Noman & Stiglitz, 2014). Of interest is the fact that over two-thirds of the African population are youths which present massive demographic dividends (UN, 2015). The factors, combined, provide the impetus for massive opportunities for growth and new business creation in Sub-Saharan Africa (Nyuur et al., 2016).

Evidence shows that the participation of African SMEs in international business and trade remains weak and discouraging (Benzing & Chu, 2009; Guili, 2018). Benzing and Chu (2009) and Guili (2018) cite institutional and infrastructural barriers, limited government support, trade restrictions, shortage of physical infrastructure including operating space, weak institutions, poor governance, and economic instability as major impediments that weaken the ability of African SMEs to participate in the global economy.

Notwithstanding the lacklustre performance of SMEs in the global economy, the scope, scale, and speed with which African multinational enterprises have been investing in the African continent and the global economy at large in the last two decades has been exceptional (Ngwu et al., 2015). To be specific, in the last 20 years, several South African companies have increased speed and shaped international commitment and international growth (Guili, 2018).

For example, South African companies such as MTN, Telkom, and Standard Bank have operations in 24 countries, 38 countries, and 20 countries, respectively. Interesting examples of African companies which have internationalised inter alia include Ecobank, Mali's Bank of Africa, Dangote, and Nigeria's UBA which have presence in 40 countries, 18 countries, 15 countries, and 20 countries, respectively (Ibeh, 2015). These new ventures are propelled by dramatic changes in the demographic and socio-economic landscape in Africa which have come with its massive business opportunities and new markets across the continent and which are key drivers of growth (Amankwah-Amoah, 2018).

Guili (2018) underscored that although the resurgence and rapid internationalisation of African firms has been phenomenal, the penetration of SMEs in the continent has been sluggish due to infrastructure deficit.

Studies by the World Bank (2013) revealed that a firm's productivity in Africa is normally slowed by an estimated 40% as a result of weak infrastructure. Likewise, Aker and Mbiti (2010) and Mugano (2022) argued that the African continent has dismally failed to attract significant foreign direct investment beyond 2% of world investment due to inadequate transportation infrastructure. In the absence of robust foreign direct investment, growth of SMEs is curtailed by their capacity to penetrate regional markets. The absence of key infrastructures, that is, energy, information communication technologies, water and sanitation and transport, has been singled out as major impediments to industrialisation and internationalisation of SMEs in Africa (Guili, 2018).

However, in the last decade, significant progress has been made in the development of key transport infrastructures especially rail and air transport. Strikingly, with a financial aid of US $4 billion from the Chinese government, African markets along 466 miles Djibouti and Ethiopia corridor are now linked after the development of the new railway line (Morlin-Yron, 2017; Jacobs, 2017). According to Amankwah-Amoah et al. (2018), the new railway line is anticipated to reduce the cost of transport as well as increase the connectivity of African markets which foster internationalisation of SMEs.

Notwithstanding the existing hurdles related to infrastructure deficits, evidence shows that there is a good business case for SMEs to go international (Devine & Kiggundu, 2016). Studies by Omer et al. (2015) show that internationalisation accelerates growth of SMEs. The view of Omer et al. (2015) is grounded on the fact that internationalisation allows SMEs to engage in foreign markets and also to create an important information network to make export activities easier (Gimede, 2004). Nevertheless, while African firms can overcome some difficulties in their home countries through internationalisation, lack of government support is more likely to hurt their export efficiency (Omer et al., 2015).

To be specific, existing evidence shows that SMEs that internationalise maximise profit, have enlarged market, diversify sales, tap into new opportunities in the foreign markets, raise brand equity and reputation, and enable growth of the firm (Matanda, 2012).

It is important to note that major drivers of internationalisation by African SMEs inter alia include managers' education, experience in international trade, access to technology, competitiveness of local firms in both the local and the foreign markets, and an ability to adapt to environmental changes (Misati et al., 2017; Matanda, 2012). In addition, Misati et al. (2017) argued that factors such as business networks, support of formal institutions and development partners which inter alia include financial support and capacity building are key drivers of internationalisation for SMEs.

Strikingly, Misati et al. (2017), Omer et al. (2015) and Matanda (2012) underscored that internationalisation of SMEs in Africa is slowed by lack of capital and international marketing skills, poor technology, information asymmetry, weak legal and regulatory frameworks, macroeconomic instability, and high tariffs.

Justifiably, SMEs in Africa face high cost of doing business, produce limited range of products, and don't benefit from the economies of scale (Okubadejo, 2014). Resultantly, African SMEs failed to secure the benefits of internationalisation which inter alia include improvement in productivity, increase of sales volumes, job creation, foreign exchange generation, and local industry developments (Matanda, 2012).

9.4 Impediments to Internationalisation of SMEs

Due to their size, SMEs face numerous challenges (Dinh et al., 2010). The survival rate of SMEs' exporters was observed to be quite low as some of these binding constraints are amplified in international markets (ITC and WTO, 2014). In line with this argument, a study by the ITC (2014) shows that the exporter failure rate for a sample of 17 least developing countries (LDCs) stood at 41%, with an average failure rate of 29% in Bangladesh and 67% in The Gambia.

Furthermore, to amplify this observation, a study by the ITC (2014) revealed that most firms in LDCs export for just one year, meaning that SMEs' exports are driven by opportunistic circumstances as opposed to permanent relationships with clients. This, together with the challenges faced by SMEs in establishing long-standing relationships with customers, combined, contributes to the low survival rates of SMEs in the export markets (World Bank, 2009).

Evidence has shown that, in comparison with larger firms, SMEs find it difficult to internationalise notwithstanding rapid evolution of globalisation which has seen increasing use of e-commerce and GVCs as effective vehicles to enter global markets (ITC and WTO, 2014). Extensive research on the bottlenecks of SMEs to internationalise have been centred around the following factors: lack of investment in foreign market research; access to finance and technology; lack of managerial time to deal with internationalisation; and lack of adequately trained personnel (OECD, 2009; ITC and WTO, 2014).

Studies carried out by the OECD (2009) rank top ten barriers affecting SMEs from accessing international markets (see Table 9.1).

Table 9.1 Barriers ranked by SMEs using the top ten ranking method

Rank—weighted factor	*Description of barrier*
1	Shortage of working capital to finance exports
2	Identifying foreign business opportunities
3	Limited information to locate/analyse markets
4	Inability to contact potential overseas customers
5	Obtaining reliable foreign representation
6	Lack of managerial time to deal with internationalisation
7	Inadequate quantity of and/or untrained personnel for internationalisation
8	Difficulty in matching competitors' prices
9	Lack of home government assistance/incentives
10	Excessive transportation costs

Source: OECD (2009)

9.4.1 Access to Finance

Globally, SMEs are perceived by banks as a diverse, large, and complex segment with high risk spectrum (Beck & Demiurgic-Kunt, 2003). Evidence shows that SMEs find it very difficult to secure the initial loan which is critical in establishing a credit history profile (ITC and WTO, 2014). To make matters worse, as noted by the International Finance Corporation (IFC), in cases where banks lend to SMEs, in many cases they provide smaller loans with short tenures with a view to mitigate risk until the SMEs build sufficient credit history required to warrant larger volumes of lending. In view of this observation, for low- and middle-income countries, access to finance is argued to be a major obstacle to growth and development for SMEs.

The severity of the difficulties in accessing financing is more defined in LDCs especially on the African continent (ITC and WTO, 2014; WTO, 2012 and Mugano, 2024). To qualify this view, evidence shows that on average banks serving SMEs in non-OECD countries topped 20% of formal SMEs while in Sub-Saharan Africa they serve less than 5% of SMEs (ITC and WTO, 2014; WTO, 2012; Mugano, 2024).

An important subset of access to finance which has an effect on exporters is access to trade finance. In practice, trade finance involves the exporter, the importer, and an intermediary, a bank, to agree to a contract which allows the movements of goods across borders (ITC and WTO, 2014).

SMEs' managers normally lack basic understanding of financial planning and trade finance instruments such as factoring, hence they find it difficult to leverage on the existing trade finance infrastructure. This explains why the participation of small firms in global chains is limited. Strikingly, in the absence of trade finance, SMEs find it difficult to finance their production cycle as importers take up to around 90 days to settle the first shipment or order (OECD, 2007; ITC and WTO, 2014).

In addressing the challenges associated with access to finance, OECD (2007) argued that financial tools such as reverse factoring and factoring have been used as effective vehicles in unlocking finance for SMEs especially in providing working capital to small suppliers. The OECD (2007) argued that, in advanced economies where factoring has been extensively used, SMEs have succeeded in alleviating challenges associated with access to finance.

9.4.2 *Difficulties in Entering New Markets*

In order to enter new markets, firms must make substantial investment in information gathering. Critical information which inter alia include distribution channels and market information such as consumer preferences, foreign prices, standards and testing requirements, is required to lower downside risks when exporting (ITC and WTO, 2014). In line with this view, a study on the effect of information on exporting SMEs by ITC and WTO (2014) shows that information on business opportunities and trade contacts is ranked as the top binding constraint for SMEs, followed by information on relevant regulations and export support measures.

As is always the case, cash-strapped SMEs find it very difficult to make the required investments to close these information gaps. This situation is complicated in instances where there are disincentives on the first movers especially in circumstances where information gathered on foreign demand as well as foreign distribution channels secured ends up benefitting competing enterprises (Lattimore et al., 1998).

In extreme cases where SMEs from countries with a reputational barrier or bad image, as in many African countries, require substantial investments in branding and marketing, which would end up benefiting competing firms. In view of the existence of free-riding opportunities by competing firms, individual SMEs are generally reluctant to make these investments that are necessary to enter into new markets (Lattimore et al., 1998; Bacchetta & Jansen, 2003).

In addressing challenges arising from information asymmetry and costs associated with acquiring information in foreign markets, Copeland (2007) argued that there is need to set up institutions that undertake reputation building and centralise the collection and dissemination of information on market intelligence. Copeland (2007) underscored that such institutions can take various forms such as diplomatic representations abroad, trade promotion organisations, and business associations such as chambers of commerce.

Evidence shows that these institutions can be effective in fostering internationalisation of SMEs by closing up the information gap (ITC and WTO, 2014). For example, Rose observed that exports are likely to rise by 6–10% if a diplomatic mission is added in a foreign land. In Latin America, Volpe Martincus et al. (2009) find that export promotion agencies and diplomatic missions are more successful in fostering exports of new products rather than increasing exports of existing products which is key in enhancing export diversification. Likewise, Lederman et al. (2006) noted that for the median export promotion agency, for each US dollar of export promotion, exports surge by US $40.

These findings provide for a well-oiled argument for the need for developing countries to use trade promotion organisations, foreign missions, and business associations as effective vehicles which can be used to enhance internationalisation of SMEs.

9.4.3 Difficulties in Defending Their Interests

Because of their small size, SMEs find it difficult to defend their interests. This normally happens in situations where SMEs may need to bargain with buyers and suppliers as well as lobbying for policies or regulations that favour their interests (ITC and WTO, 2014).

This is particularly so because in global markets concentration of market power is a common phenomenon. This phenomenon affects governance and functioning of global value chains (GVCs) because different actors in the value chains have different bargaining power (ITC and WTO, 2014). In the food supply chain, for example, this is one of the reasons why providers at the bottom of the value chain only retain an insignificant share of the final retail price power (ITC and WTO, 2014).

With respect to policymaking, SMEs find it hard to defend their interests in policy issues such as price controls on agricultural products (Cheong et al., 2013). Cheong et al. (2013) argued that smallholders in agriculture face exerting influence on trade policymakers.

In building capacity of SMEs required to defend their interests, World Bank argued that there is need for the establishment of business associations which can bargain on behalf of the SMEs with policymakers or suppliers within GVCs.

9.4.4 *Access to Technology and Scope for Innovation*

Because SMEs have limited financial capacity to employ technical specialists and don't have financial resources required to regularly update technology or buy new technology, unlike large enterprises, SMEs struggle to keep up with technological change (McCormick & Maalu, 2011; Chatterji et al., 2013).

In LDCs and African countries, in particular, simple information and communications technology (ICT) solutions such as the creation of a business website and access to the internet represent a serious challenge for SMEs.

Cluster policies such as innovation hubs have proven to be effective remedies to this challenge by providing access to SMEs located in the cluster (McCormick & Maalu, 2011; Chatterji et al., 2013).

In addition, in instances 'e' where SMEs are incubators of new technology, the challenges associated with protection of their intellectual property. To be specific, Zhang and Xia argued that SMEs find it hard to make use of national intellectual property (IP) systems as they tend to favour established and larger businesses with enough financial muscle and expertise to go through the burdensome processes.

The World Intellectual Property Organization (WIPO), in order to address this challenge, in 2000, created a division focusing on SMEs with a view to raise awareness among SMEs on IPR-related issues, and to bolster the capacity of public and private institutions involved in the provision of IP-related services.

9.4.5 *Availability of Skills*

As a result of globalisation, global production is increasingly characterised by the need to respond to consumer demand and rapid changes in technology. In such an environment, access to a skilled workforce is crucial because skilled workers adapt quickly to changes in the business environment (ITC and WTO, 2014). Jansen and Lanz (2013) reaffirmed that in global markets, skilled workforce is an important asset for both expansive and defensive enterprise strategies.

In established companies, the reality is that in an evolving environment it is difficult for companies to regularly improve workers' skills through in-house training or to hire staff with the right skills (ITC and WTO, 2014). These challenges are even more daunting for SMEs which by nature of their size have limited financial resources required to re-train their employees (Okada, 2004). Because SMEs lack both the capacity and resources to assess future skills needs, they lose competitiveness over time (Cedefop, 2012).

In addressing this challenge, McCormick argued that in high-tech sectors like ICT, industry clusters can be used to facilitate labour market pooling which is key in fostering access to skilled labour.

9.4.6 *Trade Costs*

In recent decades especially from the 1980s the global economy underwent massive trade liberalisation which saw tariff phase down and elimination of non-tariff measures (NTMs). However, SMEs are still disproportionally affected by both tariffs and NTMs, because, unlike large companies, they don't have in-house trade experts who have expertise required to facilitate trade efficiently. The situation is worsened by the fact that SMEs normally trade in smaller quantities, which means that fixed trade costs per unit are higher as compared to rivals exporting larger volumes.

In South Africa, exporters ranked exchange rate volatility as the largest constraint to exports. According to Aron, the unpredictable nature of the exchange rate coupled with existing trade costs presents significant disincentive to both the existing and potential SME exporters.

9.4.7 *Business Environment*

The ITC and WTO (2014) argued that because SMEs have limited resources and as such have limited capacity to carry the regulatory burden, the quality of the business environment is extremely important for SMEs. In instances where there are excessive regulations, when compared with large firms, SMEs are severely affected. To be specific, proportionate compliance costs range between 10 and 30 times greater for SMEs than for larger enterprises (ITC and WTO, 2014). This amplifies the challenges faced by SMEs when dealing with government regulations and possible impact on their competitiveness.

In view of this, OECD argued that there is need to remove superfluous Acts and Regulations as well as implementing information systems and digital reporting and rationalising conflicting regulations.

9.5 Bottlenecks for Internationalisation for SMEs in Africa

Over and above the discussions presented in the previous sections, this section provides bottlenecks for internationalisation for African SMEs in Africa from a regional perspective (see Box 9.1).

Internationalisation of African SMEs faces several challenges notwithstanding the massive campaigns aimed at promoting African products

Box 9.1 Bottlenecks for Internationalisation for SMEs in Africa: A Regional Perspective

Southern Africa

For landlocked LDCs such as Lesotho and Malawi, trade costs are singled out as a major impediment to SME internationalisation. Challenges associated with trade facilitation in Lesotho were identified as a major hurdle for its SMEs. In both countries, access to finance and the quality of the business environment are singled out as major constraints derailing the internationalisation of SMEs. To make matters worse, in Lesotho the internationalisation agenda of SMEs is further complicated by lack of physical facilities needed to ensure internet facilitates for logistics services, quality and hygiene, and linkages with supermarket chains. In order to foster internationalisation of SMEs and diversify the countries' exports, simplification and streamlining customs of documentation and rules of origin is of paramount importance.

Eastern Africa

In Rwanda, Burundi, Tanzania, and Uganda, access to finance, access to technology and innovation, and quality of the business environment are the main challenges affecting SMEs. Interestingly, these countries took steps to create an enabling environment for SMEs.

(*continued*)

Box 9.1 (continued)

Tanzania, for example, promulgated Small and Medium Enterprise policy which is aimed at improving the performance, participation of existing small enterprises and job creation. In Rwanda, in order to improve access to finance, awareness campaigns and programmes on existing financial support and exporters' credit and trade financing schemes are being rolled out. In Uganda, the Ugandan Revenue Authority is undertaking training on trade facilitation measures to SMEs.

Central Africa

In Chad and for the Democratic Republic of Congo (DRC) the quality of the business environment, access to finance, and access to technology topped as major challenges affecting SMEs in these countries. In Chad, in particular, the absence of enabling infrastructure especially ICT which facilitates economic activities, is making it difficult for the SMEs to formalise. In addressing this challenge, the Government of Chad is implementing several institutional reforms and policies with a strong emphasis on access to technology and innovation for SMEs as an effective vehicle to promote economic activity. These measures include provision of incentives to SMEs which invest in ICT and elimination of all taxes on all ICT import products. In the DRC, access to finance and power outages are singled out as major constraints on SMEs.

Western Africa

Access to finance and the quality of the business environment topped as the largest constraints to SMEs in the Western African countries, that is, Guinea-Bissau, The Gambia, Republic of Cabo Verde, Liberia, Senegal, Sierra Leone, and Togo.

Western African countries are undertaking formalisation of SMEs as an effective strategy to expand the tax base. The Gambia, for example, is focusing on SME development and is placing emphasis on streamlining of business registration and has set up a help desk for SMEs. Likewise, the government has set up The Gambia Investment and Export Promotion Agency whose mandate is to support micro-businesses and SMEs to penetrate international markets.

(*continued*)

Box 9.1 (continued)

In improving access to finance, Senegal adopted a Charter of SMEs whose mandate is to facilitate access to finance by setting up venture capital and regional Stock Exchanges focused on SMEs. These initiatives are funded by sovereign wealth fund. In Liberia, the Central Bank launched a Credit Stimulus Initiative for Liberian-owned SMEs with a view to improve access to finance. Ministry of Commerce and Industry is using the Bureau of Small Business Services to institutionalise support to SMEs focused on capacity building and access to information in foreign markets.

Source: ITC and WTO (2014)

under the banner "Proudly Made in Africa" (Boso et al., 2018). As a result of the heterogeneity of the African continent, Guili (2018) argued that poor technology, globalisation challenge, infrastructure deficit and non-price competition.

A combination of a growing middle class in Africa and increasing globalisation, there is an ever-growing need of foreign goods and global brands in Africa and outside the continent (Ojaide, 2018).

Mutalemwa (2015) argued that, as a result of globalisation, the spread of SMEs' operations and activities in Africa and outside the continent has given pressure to African SMEs to internationalise. According to Mutalemwa (2015), advances in technology, policy changes and competition driven by trade liberalisation have become building blocks for entering global markets. Thus, via foreign direct investment, globalisation encourages the creation of new competitors and allows influx of foreign products in domestic markets though imports.

However, Adeleye and Esposito (2018) argued that globalisation and global competitiveness remain a challenge for African SMEs both at a corporate and national level. This view was further amplified by Amankwah-Amoah (2018) who underscored that the competitiveness of African SMEs is hindered by the absence of economies of scale, burdensome regulations, and absence of basic infrastructure such as water, ICTs, energy, and transport. These factors, together with challenges which come with the smallness and newness of SMEs, African SMEs find it difficult to compete with more established and stronger firms in the global markets (Ogbechie et al., 2014).

Although the revolution of internet has created efficient bridges for trade amongst firms across the globe by reducing the gap by diminishing distance and providing instant access to information, most African countries have limited access to internet due to shortage of key infrastructures such as internet network and electricity supply (Mutalemwa, 2015).

References

Adeleye, I., & Esposito, M. (2018). *Africa's Competitiveness in the Global Economy*. Springer.

Aker, J. C., & Mbiti, I. M. (2010). Mobile Phones and Economic Development in Africa. *Journal of Economic Perspectives, 24*(3), 207–232.

Amankwah-Amoah, J. (2018). Why Are So Many African Companies Uncompetitive on the Global Stage? Insights from the Global Airline Industry. In *Africa's Competitiveness in the Global Economy* (pp. 195–216). Springer.

Bacchetta, M., & Jansen, M. (2003). *Adjusting to Trade Liberalization: The Role of Policy, Institutions and WTO Disciplines*. WTO Special Studies 7, Geneva: World Trade Organization.

Beck, T., & Demiurgic-Kunt, A. (2003). *Small and Medium-Size Enterprises: Access to Finance as a Growth Constraint*. https://doi.org/10.1016/j.jbankfin.2006.05.009

Benzing, C., & Chu, H. M. (2009). A Comparison of the Motivations of Small Business Owners in Africa. *Journal of Small Business and Enterprise Development, 16*(1), 60–77.

Cedefop. (2012). *Skill Mismatch: The Role of the Enterprise*. Cedefop Research Paper No. 21, Luxembourg: Publications Office of the European Union.

Chatterji, A., Glaeser, E. L., & Kerr William, R. (2013). *Cluster of Entrepreneurship and Innovation*. NBER Working Paper 19013.

Cheong, D., Jensen, M., & Peters, R. (2013). *Shared Harvests, Agriculture, Trade and Employment*. UNCTAD-ILO..

Copeland, B. (2007). *Is There a Case for Trade and Investment Promotion Policy?* Trade Policy Research 2007, Department of Foreign Affairs and International Trade, Canada.

Devine, R. A., & Kiggundu, M. N. (2016). Entrepreneurship in Africa: Identifying the Frontier of Impactful Research. *Africa Journal of Management, 2*(3), 349–380.

Dinh, H., Mavridis, D., & Nguyen, H. (2010). *The Binding Constraint on Firms' Growth in Developing Countries*. Policy Research Working Paper 5485. World Bank.

Doole, I., & Lowe, R. (2008). *International Marketing Strategy: Analysis, Development and Implementation*. Cengage Learning EMEA.

Gimede, V. (2004). Export Propensities and Intensities of Small and Medium Manufacturing Enterprises in South Africa. *Small Business Economics, 22*(5), 379–389.

Giovannetti, G., Marvasi, E., & Sanfilippo, M. (2014). *Supply Chains and the Internalization of SMEs: Evidence from Italy*. EUI Working Papers, RSCAS 2014/62

Guili, H. E. (2018). Internationalization of African SMEs: Context, Trends and Challenges, Research Association for Interdisciplinary Studies, 144–152.

Ibeh, K. (2015). Rising Africa and Its Nascent Multinational Corporations. In *The Changing Dynamics of International Business in Africa* (pp. 123–147). Springer.

International Trade Centre. (2014). *50 Years of Unlocking SME Competitiveness*. ISBN 978-92-9137-418-2.

International Trade Centre (ITC) and World Trade Organisation (WTO). (2014). *SME Competitiveness and Aid for Trade: Connecting Developing Country SMEs to Global Value Chains*. ITC and WTO.

Jacobs, A. (2017). Joyous Africans Take to the Rails, with China's Help. *New York Times*. www.nytimes.com/2017/02/07/world/africa/africa-china-train.html

Jansen, M., & Lanz, R. (2013). *Skills and Export Competitiveness for Small and Medium-Sized Enterprises*. Joint ILO and WTO Publication.

Lattimore, R., Madge, A., Martin, B., & Mills, J. (1998). *Design Principles for Small Business Programs and Regulations*. Staff Research Paper, Productivity Commission, Australia, August.

Lederman, D., Olarreaga, M., & Payton, L. (2006). *Export Promotion Agencies: What Works and What Doesn't*. World Bank Policy Research Working Paper 4044.

Matanda, M. (2012). Internationalization of Established Small Manufacturers in a Developing Economy: A Case Study of Kenyan SMEs. *Thunderbird International Business Review, 54*(4), 509–519.

McCormick, D., & Maalu, J. (2011). *Innovation Hubs and Small and Medium Enterprises in Africa: Setting the Policy Agenda*. Mimeo Institute for Development Studies and University of Nairobi.

Misati, E., Walumbwa, F. O., Lahiri, S., & Kundu, S. K. (2017). The Internationalization of African Small and Medium Enterprises (SMEs): A South-North pattern. *Africa Journal of Management, 3*(1), 53–81.

Morlin-Yron, S. (2017). All Aboard! The Chinese-Funded Railways Linking East Africa. *CNN Report*. http://edition.cnn.com/2016/11/21/africa/chinese-funded-railways-in-africa/

Mugano, G. (2022). Trade Liberalisation and Economic Development in Africa. *Routledge Studies in Development Economics*, ISBN 9780367749088. https://www.routledge.com/Trade-Liberalisation-and-Economic-Development-in-Africa/Mugano-Brookes/p/book/9780367749088 (Edited by Michael Brookes).

Mugano, G. (2024). SME Finance: Challenges and Options. In G. Mugano & N. Dorasamy (Eds.), *SMEs and Economic Development in Africa: Challenges and Policy Options*. Routledge.

Mutalemwa, D. K. (2015). Does Globalisation Impact SME Development in Africa? *African Journal of Economic and Management Studies, 6*(2), 164–182. https://doi.org/10.1108/AJEMS-01-2015-0012

Ngwu, F., Adeleye, I., & Ogbechie, C. (2015). Africa-to-Africa Internationalization: Rhetoric, Reality and Risks of Intra-African Regional Expansion. *The Routledge Companion to Business in Africa, 12*, 9–31.

Noman, A., & Stiglitz, J. E. (2014). Economics and Policy: Some Lessons from Africa's Experience. In C. Monga & J. Y. Lin (Eds.), *The Oxford Handbook of Africa and Economics, Vol. II: Policies and Practices* (pp. 830–848). Oxford University Press.

Nyuur, R. B., Ofori, D. F., & Debrah, Y. A. (2016). The Impact of FDI Inflow on Domestic Firms' Uptake of CSR Activities: The Moderating Effects of Host Institutions. *Thunderbird International Business Review, 58*(2), 147–159.

Ocloo, C. E., Akaba, S., & Worwui-Brown, D. K. (2014). Globalization and Competitiveness: Challenges of Small and Medium Enterprises (SMEs) in Accra, Ghana. *International Journal of Business and Social Science, 5*(4), 109–128.

OECD. (2009). *Top Barriers and Drivers to SME Internationalisation*. Report by the OECD Working Party on SMEs and Entrepreneurship, OECD, Paris.

Ogbechie, C., Adeleye, I., & Ngwu, F. (2014). Africa-to-Africa Internationalization: Rhetoric, Reality and Risks of Intra-African Regional Expansion. In *The Routledge Companion to Business in Africa* (pp. 37–59). Routledge.

Ojaide, T. (2018). Literature in Colonial Africa. In *The Palgrave Handbook of African Colonial and Postcolonial History* (pp. 413–428). Springer.

Okada, A. (2004). Skills Development and Inter-firm Learning under Globalization: Lessons from the Indian Automobile Industry. *World Development, 32*(7), 1265–1288.

Okubadejo, D. (2014). Financing for the Future: How Can Financial Services Best Support Inclusive Growth in Africa. World Bank, Washington DC.

Omer, N., Van Burg, E., Peters, R. M., & Visser, K. (2015). Internationalization as a 'Work-Around' Strategy: How Going Road Can Help SMEs Overcome Local Constraints. *Journal of Developmental Entrepreneurship, 20*(02), 1550011.

Organisation for Economic Co-operation and Development. (2007). *Enhancing the role of SMEs in Global Value Chains*. OECD.

United Nations. (2015). *Population Facts, Youth Population Trends and Sustainable Development*. United Nations.

Volpe Martincus, C., Carballo, J., & Gallo, A. (2009). *The Impact of Export Promotion Institutions on Trade: Is It the Intensive or the Extensive Margin?* IADB, Mimeo.

Welch, L. S., & Luostarinen, R. K. (1988). Internationalization: Evolution of a Concept. *Journal of General Management, 14*(2), 36–64.
World Bank. (2009). *Breaking into New Markets: Emerging Lessons from Export Diversification*. World Bank.
World Bank. (2013). *Fact Sheet: Infrastructure in Sub-Saharan Africa*. World Bank.
World Trade Organisation. (2016). *SMEs in International Trade: Stylized Facts*. World Trade Organisation Report, World Trade Organisation, Geneva.
World Trade Organization. (2012). *Trade and Public Policies: A Closer Look at Non-tariff Measures in the 21st Century*. World Trade Report.

CHAPTER 10

Using SMEs to Building Resilience and Sustainability of African Economies

Gift Mugano and Nirmala Dorasamy

10.1 Introduction

This book provided an emphatic argument which shows that SMEs are the bedrock of the global economy. For example, on average, 60% of the global gross domestic product (GDP) is contributed by SMEs (Organisation for Economic Cooperation and Development (OECD), 2017a). Most importantly, SMEs contribute to economic development through a number of channels which inter alia include exports, job creation, reduction in inequality, and poverty eradication which are key elements of inclusive growth (OECD, 2017a). Studies by Beck et al. (2005), after controlling other determinants of economic growth, revealed a robust positive relationship between economic growth and the relative size of the SME sector and economic growth.

However, notwithstanding the role of SMEs on economic development, in African economies in particular, SMEs are faced with multiple challenges which inter alia include lack of technology, access to markets (that is,

G. Mugano (✉) • N. Dorasamy
Faculty of Management Sciences, Durban University of Technology, Durban, South Africa
e-mail: nirmala@dut.ac.za

G. Mugano, N. Dorasamy, *SMEs Perspective in Africa*,
https://doi.org/10.1007/978-3-031-69103-4_10

domestic and international markets), access to finance, lack of information infrastructure, lack of physical infrastructures, macroeconomic instability, and ease of doing business. This book provides grounded hands-on and evidence-based solutions to these challenges with a view to use SMEs as effective vehicles for building resilient and sustainable economies in Africa.

In this regard, this chapter provides a summary and concluding remarks based on the submissions made in previous chapters as follows: Sect. 10.2 provides concluding remarks and key recommendations on the nexus between SMEs and economic development; Sect. 10.3 presents concluding remarks and recommendations arising from a discussion on the contribution of job creation; Sect. 10.4 provides concluding remarks and policy options arising from a discussion on the contribution of SMEs on job creation; Sect. 10.5 provides concluding remarks on the nexus between digital technology and job creation; Sect. 10.6 provides key insights on the nexus between access to finance, SMEs' growth, and job creation; Sect. 10.7 summaries discussion on information infrastructure and access to finance; Sect. 10.9 presents key observations on internationalisation of SMEs, challenges, and remedies.

10.2 SMEs and Economic Development: Global and African Perspectives

In this chapter, various scholars who inter alia include Mugano (2024a), Runde et al. (2021), Beck et al. (2005), OECD (2017a), OECD (2017b) and Oyekunle and Sirayi (2018) underscored that SMEs are the bedrock of the global economy. These scholars argued that SMEs contribute to economic development through a number of channels which inter alia include exports, job creation, reduction in inequality, and poverty eradication which are key elements of inclusive growth.

In line with this view, this chapter showed that SMEs contribute up to about 60% of the global gross domestic product (GDP) (Organisation for Economic Cooperation and Development (OECD), 2017a; Mugano, 2024a).

Of specific concerns, as exhibited in this chapter, is the fact that the contribution of SMEs to national economies across the world, in terms of job creation, value addition, economic growth, and social well-being, is diverse (Mugano, 2024b).

In advanced economies like OECD countries which has 99% of businesses as SMEs, SMEs account for approximately 70% of jobs and generate between 50% and 60% of value-added goods. In direct contrast, in

Africa, evidence shows the contribution of SMEs to the value-added goods is elusive notwithstanding the fact that 90% of businesses both in rural and in urban areas are made up of SMEs (Akugri et al., 2015; Runde et al., 2021). However, notwithstanding this observation, in terms of employment creation and contribution to economic growth, approximately 80% of jobs across the continent and at least 50% of GDP are contributed by SMEs (Runde et al., 2021).

In developing countries, especially the African continent, SMEs' potential for job creation, poverty eradication, and economic growth is largely constrained by a number of binding constraints which inter alia include lack of right technologies, access to markets, lack of innovative culture, ease of doing business, poor access to electricity and finance (Oyekunle & Sirayi, 2018; UNECE, 2022; Mugano, 2024a).

In order to strengthen the capacity of SMEs, build resilience for African economies, and foster deeper role of SMEs in economic development, policies such as improving access to finance, access global markets and knowledge networks, improving the business environment, improving access to information communication technologies, and training should be considered by African governments.

10.3 SMEs and the Prospect of Poverty Reduction in Africa

Evidence shows that as of May 2021, more than 50% of the global population living in extreme poverty (people living on US $1.90 per day) are domiciled in Africa (Saleh, 2021). Africa leads poverty in the world with an estimated 490 million (36% of the total population) citizens living in extreme poverty, as against 481 in 2019 (Human, 2021). Even though it is estimated that the poverty rate was declining, the number of poor people has been increasing. While the economy of North Africa has been favourable to the reduction in poverty, Sub-Saharan Africa (SSA) has the worst poverty phenomenon (Human, 2021). Nigeria, the largest economy in the continent, described as the global poverty headquarters in 2020 (Panchal, 2020), has an estimated 90 million people, representing 46% of the country's over 200 million population, living in extreme poverty (Human, 2021). South Africa has 16 million people, representing 26% of its estimated 58 million population, living in extreme poverty. In 2021, the poverty rate in Burundi, the Central African Republic, Madagascar, Republic of the Congo, and the Democratic Republic of Congo (DRC) were 80%, 79%, 75%, and 74%, respectively (Human, 2021).

This book revealed that the poverty situation in Africa is worsened by external shocks such as the COVID-19 pandemic. In line with this, UNECA (2021) estimated that an additional 40 million Africans could be pushed into extreme poverty as a result of the COVID-19 pandemic, thereby compounding the crisis of governance associated with poverty in the continent.

Evidence from South Asia shows that SMEs can be effective vehicles for poverty eradication through job creation (Abisuga-Oyekunle et al., 2020). This view is supported by Yoshino and Taghizadeh-Hesary (2016) who underscored that in Asia, SMEs contribute over 90% of total enterprises in each country, thereby generating more employment than the public sector. Invariably, SMEs in Asian countries are avenues for wealth creation and depletion of poverty among citizens. When an economy witnesses increased productivity, public welfare will be enhanced thereby reducing the level of poverty among the people. SMEs, therefore, complement the role of industrialisation in the promotion of a strong and stable economy that has its impact on the welfare of citizens.

This book provides a powerful argument that a stable and prosperous national economy is an antidote to poverty (Manzoor et al., 2019). This view is well pronounced in developing countries where SMEs are the major source of employment and income generation in the face of the failing government infrastructure to support the yearnings of the majority of citizens. For example, about 85% of the manufacturing employment in Ghana is provided by the SME sector. This sector consists of 92% of businesses and contributes 70% of the GDP in Ghana whereas, in South Africa, this sector contributes up to 52–57% of the GDP and provides 61% of employment (Abor & Quartey, 2010). SMEs constitute 91% of the formal business in South Africa. Thus, it can be argued that with concerted strategies to improve the sustainability of SMEs as an avenue for poverty alleviation, SMEs can play a prominent role in national socio-economic growth and development.

In this book, in Chap. 3 in particular, authors showcased that in line with the views of Yoshino and Taghizadeh-Hesary (2016) SMEs in developing countries especially in Africa face numerous challenges that impede them from realising their full potential, foster job creation and poverty eradication. Key challenges identified in this book which needs a whole-system approach inter alia include access to finance; lack of technical skills and mastery; access to market information and research; and innovative creativity; "lack of economies of scale and scope; higher transaction costs relative to large enterprises; and the lack of networks that can contribute to a lack of information, know-how, and experience of domestic and international markets" (Yoshino & Taghizadeh-Hesary, 2016, p. 5).

10.4 Small and Medium Enterprises as a Pathway to Job Creation

This book provided a grounded argument that SMEs are an effective tool for job creation and poverty reduction. In South Africa, for example, Dhanah (2016) observed that SMEs are more labour-intensive than large firms and thus the growth of the SMEs could result in higher levels of employment, with considerable implications for economic policies and the nation's ability to create jobs. Al-Haddad et al. (2019) and Dhanah (2016) emphasised that the promotion and development of SMEs was considered by the World Bank and other multilateral agencies as a key policy in the process of poverty reduction, social growth, and economic development.

Globally, SMEs are the major avenues for job creation. Studies have shown that more than 80% of the global workforce is employed by SMEs (Kamunge et al., 2014; ITU, 2016; ILO, 2019). The International Labour Organisation (ILO, 2019) described SMEs as engines of global development, with a 70% contribution to the global GDP. SMEs in the service industry, which is more prevalent in Southern African countries, account for over 60% of the GDP of the world's developed economies (ILO, 2019). In the Middle East and North African (MENA) regions, SMEs are the backbones of employment opportunities. SMEs in the MENA region constitute over 62% of the total workforce in the formal sector (Baduel et al., 2019). They also account for larger sales, thereby constituting a major source of economic growth.

As part of the resilience building strategies, in this book, authors underscored that policies that promote infrastructural development are needed for the development of SMEs and creation of jobs. One pivotal infrastructural development that could accelerate job creation prospects is the ICT environment. The explosion of ICT in the digital economy in the last years has bolstered the mode of operation of organisations across the globe. Indeed, ICT and its revolution in the digital economy have promoted globalisation and encouraged global interconnectedness in business activities (ITU, 2016). This has rendered SMEs to occupy the position as drivers of national economic growth. While knowledge-based SMEs have thrived in this venture, it has further increased the skills of youth who have explored ICT, thereby creating employment opportunities in different forms. Globally, SMEs have proven to be a source of employment. Developed economies such as the European Union have leveraged the opportunities of job creation provided by SMEs, and the consequential impact on their economic growth (Schreyer, 1996; Cant, 2012; OECD, 2017c).

This book shows that innovative strategies that characterise SMEs in Europe and emerging markets such as China, India, Brazil, and South Asia represent the causal driver for the leap in economic growth and thus reduce the unemployment rate. On the contrary, in African countries such as South Africa's scenario looks quite the different, as in recent years while the number of SMEs has been on the rise, unemployment has also been on the rise simultaneously (Dhanah, 2016).

As part of the strategies proffered by this book in building resilience for SMEs, authors call for the need to strengthen the infrastructural base of African countries, necessary to support the growth of SMEs in the technology, agriculture, enterprises, customer experience, and automation sectors. These require adequate funding in an environment characterised by a need for adequate infrastructural support such as electricity, good roads, water supply, security, conducive public policies, and legislative frameworks that encourage SMEs' startup and operations.

10.5 Digital Technologies for SMEs and Job Creation in Africa

This book shows that the impact of technological progress on the job market is not a straightforward matter. Research on the impact of technological progress by Caprettini and Voth (2020) has shown conflicting outcomes on the labour market. For example, it has been noted that during the Industrial Revolution in nineteenth-century Britain, in the spinning and weaving sector, the Luddites protested against technological progress by destroying machines because they believed that their manual labour was being replaced by machines (Caprettini & Voth, 2020).

Technological advancement which is computer-aided, for example, has complemented the performance of highly skilled workers because they enable them to perform various tasks more efficiently. This view was supported by World Bank (2023) and Strydom (2021) who underscored that historically technological advances have increased productivity, created more jobs than they have destroyed, and generated sustained increases in the standards of living.

As part of the complexity, in advanced economies, this book shows that technological progress has been accompanied by profound structural economic change which is characterised by the creation of new sectors and new jobs and the destruction of some sectors and jobs (World Bank, 2023; Strydom, 2021). These changes have massive dire consequences for low skilled workers.

In view of this quagmire, World Bank (2023) and Strydom (2021) argued that digital technologies present an opportunity for African SMEs to leapfrog from low productivity to high productivity which is an a priori requirement for the continent to build resilience, build economic transformation, spur sustainable economic growth, and improve the quality of jobs which are needed to support local as well as export development.

Recent advancement of digital technologies in Africa which inter alia include improved access to internet has had a positive impact on job creation in African economies (World Bank, 2023). To be specific, evidence shows that in countries such as Tanzania, Nigeria, and Kenya advancement in digital technologies resulted in positive impact on job creation, productivity growth, and earnings (World Bank, 2023). On a refreshing note, in direct contrast with the established notion which says that new technologies disproportionately benefit highly skilled workers, these impacts helped to reduce poverty because they are inclusive across population segments in most African countries (World Bank, 2023).

This is mainly because the African continent faces acute shortage of technological skills. The situation is worsened by the ever-increasing number of emigration of skilled workers to developed countries (Rapanyane & Sethole, 2020).

As part of the strategies which must be considered by African governments to expedite the rollout and effective use of digital technologies, this book argues for the development of key infrastructures such as electricity and internet and massive rollout of STEM programmes in schools and institutions of higher learning.

10.6 SMEs' Access to Finance, Growth, and Jobs

This book shows that empirical underpinning perspective, existing finance, and growth literature show that finance is critical for SMEs' growth and ultimately economic growth (IFC, 2018). For example, IFC (2018) observed that in India an individual SME created additional jobs averaging 10–15 people annually. This outcome is significant considering the fact that SMEs in India are small in size employing a maximum of 99 workers (IFC, 2018).

Strikingly, evidence shows that most jobs were created by small and young firms (IFC, 2018). To be specific, IFC (2018) revealed that SMEs which are at most five years old, their workforce grew by an average rate of 12% after securing a loan. Similarly, with respect to the responsiveness of job creation to the size of SMEs after acquiring a loan, IFC (2018) shows that 21%, 46%, and 8% of micro-, small-, and medium-sized SMEs created jobs, respectively. In addition, evidence shows that micro-, small-, and medium-sized SMEs' contribution to job creation stands at 6%, 8%, and 2%, respectively (IFC, 2018). This shows that small firms are the major contributors to job creation in India. Most importantly, this evidence convincingly confirms that access to finance has strong and positive correlation to SMEs' growth and job creation.

However, evidence shows that in developing countries especially in Africa, unlike large businesses, SMEs are more constrained in their access to financial services (Beck et al., 2005; Ayyagari et al., 2007; Mugano, 2024a).

In improving access to finance, fostering economic growth and job creation as well as building the required resilience for African economies, this book argues for the use of blended finance, credit guarantee schemes, use of development finance institutions with no interferences from governments, and use of alternative financial instruments such as asset-based lending, factoring, and lease financing.

10.7 SMEs' Information Infrastructure and Access to Finance

This book reviews the existing SMEs information infrastructure in Africa and difficulties in accessing finance for SMEs. This book shows that unlike big enterprises which list their shares on stock markets and issue securities in bond markets, most SMEs have no connection with capital markets. This book observes that lack of information infrastructure for SMEs exacerbates the information asymmetry problem. In the absence of information, collateral-based lending was noted as simplest which could be used by financial institutions to reduce the risk premium in loan formulations.

In view of this observation, in line with the views of World Bank (2018) and OECD (2017c), this book argues that SMEs should invest efforts and resources in educating their staff and management about information structure and its benefits. Cost reduction and time saving, improved labour flexibility, better customer service and communication with partners as well as improved data analytics have been mentioned as the main economic advantages, including the main benefits regarding increased flexibility of resources. Decision-making with regard to information infrastructure needs to be addressed in order to give SMEs competitive capability. Also, SMEs should build a culture that is innovative and favourable to technology, by prioritising information infrastructure as a functional area. In addition, the business process should be more reliant on technology and less on manual processes and by continually exploring all the various and newest technological options with their possible benefits to the SME.

10.8 The Business Environment and Its Effect on SMEs

This book argued that a conducive business environment is an a priori requirement for the success of SMEs and businesses in general. The economic environment of any society, to a large extent, determines the direction and level of success of business enterprises. Thus, an enabling environment is crucial to the fortunes and the development prospects of a business organisation. Part of the economic imperatives of development is a thriving business environment. This is more important in the areas of Small and Medium Enterprises (SMEs), where local economic support is critical to their success. In 2004, the Organization for Economic Co-Operation and Development (OECD) identified provision of an enabling environment as a critical factor in the development of SMEs (OECD, 2004).

In this book, authors argued that environments that are unfriendly to business activities will retard the growth and development of SMEs. Global development agencies as well as regional economic organisations have recognised the importance of environmental factors to allow the space for SMEs to thrive. In line with the observations of the World Bank (2020), this book submits that governments and policymakers must pay extra attention to the following factors surrounding starting a business: electricity, regulatory legislations, registration, acquisition of property, credit facilities, security, investment status, taxes and taxation, employment regulations and laws, accessing and acquisition of business locations, and finance routine operational requirements. All these issues are relevant components that define the business environment. The nature and characteristics of these issues determine the extent to which SMEs could attain sustainable growth and development.

10.9 Internationalisation of SMEs: Challenges and Remedies

This book shows that globally SMEs have used internationalisation as a growth strategy as well as a vehicle to build resilience and sustainability. However, on the contrary, in Africa, indisputable evidence shows that SMEs experience massive challenges which constrain their capability to internationalise globally and raise their competitiveness (Ocloo et al., 2014). Notable binding constraints which hinder African SMEs from internationalising inter alia include limited government support, trade restrictions, shortage of physical infrastructure including operating space, weak institutions, poor governance, and economic instability (Benzing & Chu, 2009; Guili, 2018). Justifiably, SMEs in Africa face high cost of doing business, produce a limited range of products, and don't benefit from the economies of scale (Okubadejo, 2014). Resultantly, African SMEs failed to secure the benefits of internationalisation which inter alia include improvement in productivity, increase of sales volumes, job creation, foreign exchange generation, and local industry developments (Matanda, 2012).

In line with the views of Doole and Lowe (2008), this book singles out internationalisation of SMEs as an effective strategy which can be used by African countries as a growth strategy as well as a vehicle to build resilience and sustainability. International strategies which are regularly used by SMEs with notable successes inter alia include licencing, exportation, and joint venture businesses (Guili, 2018). These strategies must be complemented with measures aimed at addressing the identified bottlenecks to internationalisation which inter alia include limited government support, trade restrictions, shortage of physical infrastructure including operating space, weak institutions, poor governance, and economic instability.

In the same vein, respective chapters of this book provide grounded policy options for African governments with a view to unleash the potential of SMEs as well as building resilience against exogenous shocks such as climate change, global pandemics, and macroeconomic instability. Some of the policy measures proffered in this book inter alia include the need to provide decent operating space for SMEs, improving access to finance, digitalisation and e-commerce, improving access to markets, ensuring economic stability, and good governance.

10.10 Conclusion

Evidence presented in this book shows that SMEs are the engines of economic growth, job creation, and poverty alleviation. In Africa, SMEs have massive potential to create jobs, unleash economic growth for African economies, and contribute to poverty reduction in African economies.

However, this is not a straightforward matter. SMEs are faced with multiple challenges which inter alia include lack of technology, access to markets (that is, domestic and international markets), access to finance, lack of information infrastructure, lack of physical infrastructures, macroeconomic instability, and ease of doing business. This book provides grounded hands-on and evidence-based solutions to these challenges with a view to use SMEs as effective vehicles for building resilient and sustainable economies in Africa.

References

Abisuga-Oyekunle, O. A., Patra, S. K., & Muchie, M. (2020). SMEs in Sustainable Development: Their Role in Poverty Reduction and Employment Generation in Sub-Saharan Africa. *African Journal of Science, Technology, Innovation and Development, 12*(4), 405–419. https://doi.org/10.1080/20421338.2019.1656428

Abor, J., & Quartey, P. (2010). Issues in SME Development in Ghana and South Africa. *International Research Journal of Finance and Economics, 39*, 218–228.

Akugri, M. S., Bagah, D. A., & Wulifan, J. K. (2015). The Contributions of Small and Medium Scale Enterprises to Economic Growth: A Cross-Sectional Study of Zebilla in the Bawku West District of Northern Ghana. *European Journal of Business and Management, 7*(9), 262–274.

Al-Haddad, L., Sial, S. M., Imdad Ali, I., Alam, R., Khuong, N. V., & Khanh, H. T. (2019). The Role of Small and Medium Enterprises (SMEs) in Employment Generation and Economic Growth: A Study of Marble Industry in Emerging Economy. *International Journal of Financial Research, 10*(6), 174–187.

Ayyagari, M., Beck, T., & Demirgüç-Kunt, A. (2007). Small and Medium Enterprises across the Globe. *Small Business Economics, 29*(4), 415–434.

Baduel, B., Geginat, C., & Pierre, G. (2019). *Private Sector Job Creation in MENA: Prioritizing the Reform Agenda Prepared.* IMF Working Paper WP/19/206, September 2019.

Beck, T., Demirgüç-Kunt, A., & Levine, R. (2005). SMEs, Growth, and Poverty: Cross-Country Evidence. *Journal of Economic Growth, 10*, 199–229.

Benzing, C., & Chu, H. M. (2009). A Comparison of the Motivations of Small Business Owners in Africa. *Journal of Small Business and Enterprise Development, 16*(1), 60–77.

Cant, M. (2012). Challenges Faced by SME's in South Africa: Are Marketing Skills Needed? *International Business and Economics Research Journal, 11*(10), 1107–1116.

Caprettini, B., & Voth, H. (2020). Rage Against the Machines: Labor-Saving Technology and Unrest In Industrializing England. *American Economic Review: Insights, 2*(3), 305–320. https://doi.org/10.1257/aeri.20190385

Dhanah, D. (2016). Small Businesses and Job Creation in South Africa. https://open.uct.ac.za/bitstream/handle/11427441/thesis_com_2017_dhanah_darlington.pdf?sequence=1.

Doole, I., & Lowe, R. (2008). *International Marketing Strategy: Analysis, Development and Implementation.* Cengage Learning EMEA.

Guili, H. E. (2018). Internationalization of African SMEs: Context, Trends and Challenges, Research Association for Interdisciplinary Studies, 144–152.

Human, J. H. (2021). African countries continue to have the highest poverty rates in the world. Development aid News Stream, February 25. https://www.developmentaid.org/#!/news-stream/post/84943/highest-poverty-rates-in-africa

International Finance Corporation. (2018). *SME finance and growth: evidence from RBL Bank.* World Bank.

International Labour Organisation (ILO). (2019). The Power of Small: Unlocking the Potential of SMES. Info Stories, October. https://www.ilo.org/infostories/en-GB/Stories/Employment/SMEs#intro

International Monetary Fund (IMF). (2018). *The future of work in Sub-Saharan Africa.* International Monetary Fund.

International Telecommunication Union (ITU). (2016). Trends in tech MSMEs and startup support. https://www.itu.int/dms_pub/itu-s/opb/gen/S-GEN-MSMES-2016-PDF-E.pdf

Jean-Paul, van B., & Mudavanhu, S. (2018). Digital Labor in Africa: A Status Report. Retrieved January 7, 2024, from https://diodeweb.les.wordpress.com/2018/01/digital-labor-in-africa-diode-paper.pdf

Kamunge, M. S., Njeru, A., & Tirimba, O. I. (2014). Factors affecting the performance of small and macro enterprises in Limuru town market of Kiambu

County. *International Journal of Scientific and Research Publications, 4*(12), 1–20.

Manzoor, F., Wei, L., Nurunnabi, M., & Abdul Subhan, Q. (2019). Role of SME in Poverty Alleviation in SAARC Region via Panel Data Analysis. *Sustainability, 11*(22), 6480. MDPI AG. https://doi.org/10.3390/su11226480

Matanda, M. (2012). Internationalization of established small manufacturers in a developing economy: A case study of Kenyan SMEs. *Thunderbird International Business Review, 54*(4), 509–519.

Mothobi, O. (2021). Digital Labor in Africa: Opportunities and Challenges. https://www.africaportal.org/documents/20971/Digital-labor-in-Africa-Jan-2021.pdf

Mugano, G. (2024a). Role of SMEs on Economic Development in Africa. In G. Mugano & N. Dorasamy (Eds.), *SMEs and Economic Development in Africa: Challenges and Policy Options.* Routledge.

Mugano, G. (2024b). SME Finance: Challenges and Options. In G. Mugano & N. Dorasamy (Eds.), *SMEs and Economic Development in Africa: Challenges and Policy Options.* Routledge.

Ocloo, C. E., Akaba, S., & Worwui-Brown, D. K. (2014). Globalization and Competitiveness: Challenges of Small and Medium Enterprises (SMEs) in Accra, Ghana. *International Journal of Business and Social Science, 5*(4).

Okubadejo, D. (2014). Financing for the Future: How Can Financial Services Best Support Inclusive Growth in Africa.

Organisation of Economic Cooperation and Development (OECD). (2004). *Promoting SMEs for Development.* Report of the 2nd OECD Conference of Ministers Responsible for Small and Medium-Sized Enterprises (SMEs Promoting Entrepreneurship and Innovative SMEs in a Global Economy: Towards a More Responsible and Inclusive Globalization. Istanbul, Turkey 3–5 June 2004.

Organisation of Economic Cooperation and Development (OECD). (2017a). *Enhancing the Contributions of SMEs in a Global and Digitalised Economy.* Meeting of the OECD Council at Ministerial Level Paris, 7–8 June 2017, OECD, Paris.

Organisation of Economic Cooperation and Development (OECD). (2017b). *Increasing Productivity in Small Traditional Enterprises: Programmes for Upgrading Management Skills and Practices.* OECD Working Party on SMEs and Entrepreneurship, CFE/SME(2016).

Organisation of Economic Cooperation and Development (OECD). (2017c). Enhancing the Contributions of SMEs in a Global and Digitalised Economy. https://www.oecd.org/industry/C-MIN-2017-8-EN.pdf

Oyekunle, O. A., & Sirayi, M. (2018). The Role of Creative Industries as a Driver for a Sustainable Economy: A Case of South Africa. *Creative Industries Journal, 11*(3), 225–244.

Panchal, K. (2020). The Poverty Capital of the World: NIGERIA. *Burgen Magazine*, August 28. https://www.borgenmagazine.com/the-poverty-capital-of-the-world-nigeria/

Rapanyane, M. B., & Sethole, F. R. (2020). The Rise of Artificial Intelligence and Robots in the 4th Industrial Revolution: Implications for Future South African Job Creation. *Contemporary Social Science, 15*(4), 489–501.

Runde, D. F., Savoy, C. M., & Staguhn, J. (2021). *Supporting Small and Medium Enterprises in Sub-Saharan Africa through Blended Finance.* Center for Strategic and International Studies.

Saleh, M. (2021). Extreme Poverty as Share of Global Population in Africa 2021, by Country. https://www.statista.com/statistics/1228553/extreme-poverty-as-share-of-global-population-in-africa-by-country/

Schreyer, P. (1996). *SMEs and Employment Creation: Overview of Selected Quantitative Studies in OECD Member Countries.* OECD Science, Technology and Industry Working Papers 1996/04. https://www.oecd-ilibrary.org/science-and-technology/smes-and-employment-creation_374052760815

Strydom, P. D. F. (2021). Digital Technologies, Employment and Labour-Market Polarisation in Africa. In W. Viviers, A. Parry, & S. J. Jansen van Rensburg (Eds.), *Africa's Digital Future: From Theory to Action (The Future of International Trade and Development Volume 1)* (pp. 101–127). AOSIS. https://doi.org/10.4102/aosis.2021.BK199.04

UNECE. (2022). *Small and Medium Enterprises in Economies in Transition: Challenges and Opportunities and UNECE Tools.* Informal Paper, UNECE, Geneva. https://dl.designresearchsociety.org/cgi/viewcontent.cgi?article=2911&context=drs-conference-papers.

United Nations Economic Commission for Africa (UNECA). (2021, March 2). 514 Million Africans Risk Falling Below the Extreme Poverty Line in 2021 Due to COVID. https://www.uneca.org/stories/514-million-africans-risk-falling-below-extreme-poverty-line-in-2021-due-to-covid-19

World Bank. (2023). *World Bank report Digital Africa: Technological Transformation for Jobs.* World Bank.

World Bank Group. (2018). Improving access to finance for SMES: Opportunities through Credit Reporting, Secured Lending and Insolvency Practices. https://www.doingbusiness.org/content/dam/doingBusiness/media/Special-Reports/improving-access-to-finance-for-SMEs.pdf.

World Bank Group. (2020). *Poverty and Shared Prosperity 2020: Reversals of Fortune.* International Bank for Reconstruction and Development / The World Bank.

Yoshino, N., & Taghizadeh-Hesary, F. (2016). *Major Challenges Facing Small and Medium-sized Enterprises in Asia and Solutions for Mitigating Them.* ADBI.

Correction to: SMEs Perspective in Africa

Gift Mugano and Nirmala Dorasamy

Correction to:

G. Mugano, N. Dorasamy, *SMEs Perspective in Africa*,
https://doi.org/10.1007/978-3-031-69103-4

The book was mistakenly published without listing "Sriram Divi" as the author of Chapter 5. Additionally, the co-author "Eustache Tanzala Kikasu" was not listed for Chapters 4 and 7. These names have now been included.

The updated versions of these chapters can be found at
https://doi.org/10.1007/978-3-031-69103-4_4
https://doi.org/10.1007/978-3-031-69103-4_5
https://doi.org/10.1007/978-3-031-69103-4_7

G. Mugano, N. Dorasamy, *SMEs Perspective in Africa*,
https://doi.org/10.1007/978-3-031-69103-4_11

Index

G. Mugano, N. Dorasamy, *SMEs Perspective in Africa*,
https://doi.org/10.1007/978-3-031-69103-4

The manufacturer's authorised representative in the EU is Springer Nature Customer Service Centre GmbH, Europaplatz 3, 69115 Heidelberg, Germany. If you have any concerns regarding our products, please contact ProductSafety@springernature.com

Printed and bound by CPI Group (UK) Ltd, Croydon, CR0 4YY
01/10/2026
02225953-0006